THE PRIVILEGES OF WEALTH

The American Dream is under assault. This threat results not from a lack of means, but from an unwillingness to share. Total household wealth increased by half in the past generation, but barely one fifth of American households captured this new wealth. For the rest, the dream of owning a home, gaining a secure retirement, and ensuring a college education for their kids is disappearing. Worse still, the widening wealth divide largely tracks our racial fault lines.

The Privileges of Wealth investigates the impact of the rising concentration of wealth. It describes how households accumulate wealth along three pathways: household saving, appreciation of assets, and family gifts and inheritances. In addition, federal wealth policies, in the form of assorted tax deductions and credits, act as a fourth pathway that favors wealthy households. For those with means, each pathway operates as a virtuous cycle enabling families to build wealth with increasing ease. For those without, these same pathways are experienced as vicious cycles.

The issue of wealth privilege is even more pronounced when examining the racial wealth gap. Typically, White households own ten times the wealth of Black or Latino families. This chasm results from the durability and transferability of wealth across generations and serves as a persistent legacy of our history of racial enslavement, expropriation, and exclusion. Current policies favoring the wealthy are simply cementing these wealth disparities.

This book explains how these sources of wealth privilege are systemic features of our economy and the basis of rising disparities. The arguments and evidence presented here offer a compelling case for how our current policies are undermining the American Dream for most Americans while fortifying a White plutocracy, with dire consequences for us all.

Robert B. Williams is Professor of Economics at Guilford College, USA.

ECONOMICS IN THE REAL WORLD

THE PRIVILEGES OF WEALTH

Rising inequality and the growing racial divide

Robert B. Williams

Routledge
Taylor & Francis Group

LONDON AND NEW YORK

First published 2017
by Routledge
2 Park Square, Milton Park, Abingdon, Oxon OX14 4RN

and by Routledge
711 Third Avenue, New York, NY 10017

Routledge is an imprint of the Taylor & Francis Group, an informa business

British Library Cataloguing in Publication Data
A catalogue record for this book is available from the British Library

Library of Congress Cataloging in Publication Data
Names: Williams, Bob (Robert B.), author.
Title: The privileges of wealth : rising inequality and the growing racial divide / Robert B. Williams.
Description: Abingdon, Oxon ; New York, NY : Routledge, 2017. | Includes bibliographical references and index.
Identifiers: LCCN 2016027622 | ISBN 9781138227491 (hardback) |
ISBN 9781138227507 (pbk.) | ISBN 9781315395586 (ebook)
Subjects: LCSH: Wealth--United States. | Income distribution--United States. | Social stratification--United States. | Equality--United States. | United States--Race relations. | United States--Economic conditions--21st century. | United States--Social conditions--21st century.
Classification: LCC HC110.W4 W55 2017 | DDC 339.2/20973--dc23
LC record available at https://lccn.loc.gov/2016027622

ISBN: 978-1-138-22749-1 (hbk)
ISBN: 978-1-138-22750-7 (pbk)
ISBN: 978-1-315-39558-6 (ebk)

Typeset in Bembo
by Integra Software Services Pvt. Ltd.

CONTENTS

FIGURES

TABLES

ACKNOWLEDGMENTS

Without the systematic efforts of the Federal Reserve Bank to investigate the composition and distribution of U.S. household wealth, I couldn't write this book. Aside from being huge, this debt is personal since my father, John B. Williams, worked his entire career at the Fed, ascending through the ranks to becoming Vice President of the 12th District. For the many lessons he taught me, I offer this book in his memory.

From the earliest drafts, I shared parts of the evolving manuscript with students taking my Research Methods and Poverty, Power, and Policy classes. You endured the rough writing and still emerging ideas and gave helpful feedback and several wonderful nuggets. No doubt, you enjoyed the role reversal as you wielded your red pens with gusto. Thank you.

Two very good colleagues and dear friends, Dr. Larry Morse and Bobby Wayne Clark, both suffered through as they edited an early draft as well. I owe each of you big time. Larry, you offered thoughtful comments and helpful guidance, especially on the technical analysis and the presentation of the evidence. Bobby, you encouraged me to prune my writing throughout. Although it may not appear to you that I was listening, I certainly tried. The remaining wordiness is simply a testimony to my stubbornness. Also, many thanks to my current colleague Dr. Natalya Shelkova. I appreciate your willingness to offer "second opinions" as needed on some of the technical analysis.

Throughout the review process, I gained immeasurably from the efforts of five different anonymous reviewers. In each case, you took your responsibilities seriously, as you offered well-considered comments. Not only did you identify key flaws in my arguments and analysis, you also offered specific remedies and helpful sources to redress the problems. Thanks to each of you, this manuscript has grown stronger, tighter, and clearer in its exposition. I greatly appreciate your kind words of support and found your criticisms a source of collegial collaboration. To the one reviewer who is likely disappointed to see this book in print, I hope you take a second look. Though I found some of your comments challenging to absorb, you made some essential suggestions that greatly improved this book. I want to thank each of you for making the review process function just as it should be. Obviously, you cannot be held accountable for the errors that remain.

I want to thank my editor at Routledge, Andy Humphries. From our first conversation, you've been an enthusiastic supporter of the project. You've managed the submission process with deft hands as you've identified excellent reviewers and ensured a quick turnaround on these reviews. You have that rare combination of understanding the big picture while giving careful attention to the essential details. Many thanks as well to your assistant editor, Elanor Best. I appreciate your help in managing all of the production issues and resolving problems as they arose.

Throughout the many years of writing, Virginia Ferguson of the Center for Principled Problem Solving has been an invaluable troubleshooter. Repeatedly, I came to you needing help on a variety of computer and layout problems. Each time you promptly and patiently helped me solve the crisis.

Expressing adequately my gratitude for the help I've received from my Wednesday afternoon group is a real challenge. Over the years, you've encouraged me to find my voice and to articulate it succinctly and clearly. Your unflagging support and withering criticisms provided the very push and pulls I needed. Thank you to each of you for your help on this journey.

Teaching at a private, liberal arts college is often more than a full-time affair, leaving precious little time for research and writing. I want to thank my employer, Guilford College, its study leave program and the Academic Dean's office for giving me the time and support to complete this project. Thankfully, I received two study leaves that gave me the time and space to conceptualize the book and eventually complete it.

Lastly, I want to thank my partner, Mary Beth Boone. Not only was I "away" spending countless hours on the computer as I worked on this book, even when I was with you, I was often away in my thoughts. Throughout you have been patient and forgiving of me.

Thank you so much.

1

CRACKS IN THE AMERICAN DREAM

That truly American dream

Deep within our national psyche lies the compelling allure of what we call the American Dream. It was manifest even at our country's founding. As the signers of the Declaration of Independence announced to the world: "We hold these truths to be self-evident, that all men are created equal, that they are endowed by their Creator with certain inalienable rights, that among these are Life, Liberty, and the pursuit of Happiness." From this and other pronouncements, the United States gained the reputation as the land of opportunity, serving as a magnet to millions of immigrants searching for a better life. While some among these voluntary immigrants[1] were fleeing religious or political oppression, most came with the desire for a fresh start and a fair chance to get ahead. Although many of us are separated by generations from our ancestors who first came to this land, the American Dream still frames our perceptions as we consider our future.

Our individual aspirations are unique to our personal circumstances and experiences. Yet, our dreams share common themes that comprise the larger American Dream. Given credit for coining the term, James Truslow Adams (1941) described it as "that dream of a land in which life should be better and richer and fuller for everyone with opportunity for each according to ability or achievement … regardless of fortuitous circumstances of birth or position" (p. 214–15). As suggested by Adams, the American Dream comprises two key points. Primarily, it is about the opportunity for upward mobility. If I work hard and play by the rules, my efforts will bear measurable fruit. For some, this might mean completing high school or college to gain a steady, well-paying job. For others, it entails owning a home or running a business. For most, it means achieving sufficient financial security to retire comfortably and to offer their children a better start to their lives. In addition, Adams said the American Dream is not available to a few, but afforded to all Americans. As each generation comes of age, all Americans should have the opportunity to attain measurable upward mobility.

The reality of general improvement from one generation to the next has sustained the American Dream to the present. The U.S. economy has served as a powerful engine for improving the material conditions of most Americans and affirming the prospect of upward mobility. Even among those who experienced little gain in their own lifetime, they watched their children grasp increased opportunities and claim greater rewards. Most of us can see material improvements in subsequent generations as we trace back our ancestry. Even among those excluded from this history, the Dream's pervasive appeal offers hope they can change their family's fortunes. To be sure, our laws and social norms have systematically excluded certain groups from living the dream. European immigrants removed or exterminated the native populations they encountered, enslaved Africans, and excluded Asians and Latinos from opportunity and property. For much of our history, the American Dream effectively had a "Whites Only" sign. In recent decades, the overtly racist laws and structures have been overturned, giving some hope we might finally realize the promise offered over two centuries ago.

Today, there is a new threat to the future of the American Dream. Numerous reports have documented rising income inequality as growing numbers of households have slipped from middle-class status. According to the U.S. Census Bureau (2015), real median family income fell from 2000 to 2010, the first decade to experience such a decline. Other reports cite the rising costs of health insurance, homeownership, and college tuition making it harder for households to attain or keep these symbols of Middle America. In a recent poll, respondents felt by a two to one margin that attaining the American Dream is harder than in past generations; by an even larger margin, they felt it would be harder still for the next generation (Bedard, 2011). In 2012, that bellwether of American culture, *Time* magazine, questioned its relevance as it ran a cover story titled "The history of the American Dream: Is it still real?"

Given the trauma of the Great Recession, it is unsurprising that many Americans are questioning whether the dream still exists. Numerous trends suggest the U.S. economy is experiencing rising inequality thereby jeopardizing its reality for many Americans. In any event, realizing the dream entails the acquisition of household wealth. Buying a home requires cash for a down payment. Gaining financial security demands ample savings to draw upon during times of duress. Building a retirement nest egg entails regular deposits into funds that yield rising asset values. Raising kids and offering them a head start in their lives requires more funds to access good schools, support extracurricular activities, and finance a college education. As Jim Cullen stated in his book *The American Dream: A Short History of an Idea that Shaped a Nation* (2004) attaining the dream requires that individuals have the means to direct their lives. He argued that "all notions of freedom rest on a sense of agency, the idea that individuals have control over the course of their lives. Agency, in turn, lies at the very core of the American Dream, the bedrock premise upon which all else depends" (p. 10). Clearly, achieving the American Dream requires the possession of sufficient wealth.

Historically, we have had limited opportunity to investigate the level and role of wealth in American society, despite its obvious importance. Though many forms of household wealth are visible, it is rarely the topic in public, or even private, conversation. Public policy has reflected these norms. The federal government knows much about our employment, salaries, and other forms of personal income; yet it has remained amazingly disinterested in understanding the wealth of American households. Despite this veil, economic historians have tried to understand the level and distribution of household wealth across society (Shammas, 1993). In most cases, they chose to examine the one instance where one's wealth becomes more public: at death. From their time-consuming investigations of probate court records, we have gained glimpses of the type, level, and spread of household wealth at different points in our history. However, these efforts have provided, at best, a dim and partial understanding of the accumulation and distribution of wealth.

Fifty years ago, researchers began to pierce this veil. In 1962, the Federal Reserve authorized the Survey of Financial Characteristics of Consumers in which they surveyed 3,600 American households about their net worth (Worth, 1964). It produced the first comprehensive snapshot of the allocation and distribution of wealth across households. After two more surveys in the mid-1980s, the Federal Reserve implemented an expanded survey in 1989 that became the basis of their regular triennial surveys. Other national surveys followed suit.[2] For the first time, we have the means to understand in detail the composition, extent, and distribution of household wealth across American society.

A picture of wealth

Even with the evidence in hand, conceptualizing the distribution of wealth is not easy. Most Americans recognize that the typical household has some wealth while a fortunate few have acquired a lot. Still, the disparities are striking and larger than most Americans believe (Norton and Ariely, 2011). As an illustration, I use the metaphor of a skyscraper in which each floor represents an increase in net worth.

Even the tallest building in the world, the Burj Khalifa with its 163 stories, cannot accommodate all American households without some mathematical sleight of hand.

Over the first 20 floors, each story signifies an increment of $50,000 in household net worth. For most households, this increment represents a significant improvement in their balance sheet, usually requiring years of discipline and patience to move up one floor. At this rate, occupants of the 20th floor have attained the celebrated status of becoming a millionaire. Yet, simply extending our metaphorical skyscraper up at this rate would require over 6,000 Burj Khalifas to accommodate the wealthiest Americans! Starting at the 20th floor, ascending to each additional story requires an additional $1 million. Continuing at this rate over the next 100 floors, residents must have at least $100 million to rise to the 119th floor. Even still, we need another change to include all Americans in our skyscraper. From this point up, it takes another $100 million to ascend each additional floor. One can find billionaires starting at the 128th floor. Yet again, we must increase the rate to accommodate virtually all Americans in our skyscraper. From this point to the top, ascending each floor requires an additional half billion. To gain access to the penthouse, one's net worth must be at least $36 billion. In 2015, only eight Americans were worth more than this amount as listed in the Forbes 400.

Entering this top floor, we would likely recognize many of its occupants, including Bill Gates, Warren Buffet, the Koch brothers, and Michael Bloomberg. As we descend through the floors below, we would notice several patterns. Many floors near the top would have no occupants while the remainder would have a handful, at best. Despite the amount of wealth needed to move from one floor to the next, the top of our skyscraper is sparsely populated. In surveying the occupants, one would certainly notice how many individuals are beyond middle age, how few women reside there in their own right, and how almost everyone is White. Our continued descent would yield only slight changes in the age, gender, and racial makeup of the residents, even as their numbers slowly increased.

Not until we arrive back at the 20th floor would we reach the confines where the bottom 90 percent of households reside. Even at this point, we are mingling with millionaires. To reach the "typical" American household, the one which has just as many wealthier as poorer neighbors, we need to descend to the seventh floor, 156 floors below the penthouse. Here, our residents form a much larger and more diverse crowd. Even still, we would notice relatively few Black and Latino households, particularly given their numbers in the population at large. As we resume our descent, the floors are more crowded while the occupants are noticeably younger, female, and less likely to be White.

Even as we reach the ground floor, we would not have seen every household. In 2013, nearly 12 percent of American households would reside below ground.[3] As these households experience debts that exceed their assets, they reside in the basement floors. Although they live in the same building as those observed in the penthouse, their view of the world could not be more different.

As we consider this skyscraper we may call American Wealth, several questions come to mind. As we consider the residents at each floor, how did they get there? Were they born on the floor they currently reside? Or are they temporary residents simply captured in the moment as they ascend or descend through the building over their lifetime? How is it that the vast majority of households headed by persons of color remain in the lower reaches of the building? Is this simply a legacy of our past or does it reflect current factors? Why is it that the top floors are so sparsely populated as compared with the lower floors? Fully half of the U.S. households reside in the bottom seven stories and basement while the remaining 156 stories are devoted to the affluent half.

Each of these questions considers the issue of wealth mobility, or the ability of households to rise or fall from one floor to the next. Indeed, they all suggest a further question: are the opportunities for the wealth mobility the same from top to bottom? Our hypothetical skyscraper suggests not. Rising one floor in the middle and upper reaches of this building requires a 20-fold, 2,000-fold, and even 20,000-fold increase in net worth over what it means near the bottom. Do these differences reflect different circumstances and opportunities? Quite likely, since the occupants of these floors hold wealth at 20, 2,000, and even 20,000 times the rate of the lower-level occupants. Consider a household whose net worth is $50 million. Earning the additional $1 million required to ascend to the next floor (a 2 percent increase) is easier than for a household with $500,000 who needs an additional $50,000 to rise one floor (a 10 percent increase). As our skyscraper suggests, the incremental rewards get larger as one ascends the building.

The opportunities for upward mobility vary in other ways as well. Like most modern buildings, our skyscraper has different means for moving between floors, including stairways, escalators, elevators, and express elevators. As I will show later in the book, only some building occupants have access to each of these conveniences. Most households in the bottom floors have only one means for upward wealth mobility: household saving. Only by not spending all of their current income can these households slowly increase their wealth. In most cases, this form of wealth acquisition feels like climbing long stairways, requiring continual exertion and self-discipline. As households accumulate wealth, they find that many forms of wealth can grow in value without much exertion. Interest-bearing accounts, stocks, and bonds are a few examples. These assets offer their owners the opportunity to simply stand in place, like on an escalator, and slowly rise to the next floor. Other assets, usually carrying more risk, can seem like an elevator as their sudden appreciation can lift their holders to new heights quite rapidly. Further, some fortunate individuals receive inheritances that can function like express elevators as the gifts boost them many floors higher overnight. Lastly, there are government wealth policies that assist the building occupants in their efforts to ascend to higher floors. As I will show, these policies work best in the upper reaches of the building, thereby supplementing the ample regular and express elevators already available. Though one might find these elevators in the building's bottom floors, their limited service restricts their availability to only the most talented or lucky occupants.

Not all movement within the skyscraper need be upward; misfortune and self-indulgence can generate a fall in wealth as well. Divorce, illness, and unemployment can strike virtually any household; throughout the American Wealth building, they pose hazardous holes through which unfortunate residents may fall to floors below. Yet, wealth offers help here. Arguably, the oldest motivation for wealth accumulation is its value as a safety net during times of distress. Today, wealth offers its owner the opportunity to purchase ample insurance to protect oneself from ruin. Through asset diversification, the wealthy can protect their nest egg from specific financial threats. As I will show in Chapter 7, wealthy householders experience much greater financial resilience in the face of financial collapse; they can suffer steeper declines in their wealth before they must make decisions that will limit future opportunities. Wealth serves as a safety net that protects its holders from many of the misfortunes that befall residents in the floors below them.

While pondering these issues, it is worth noting a further reality. Most tall buildings are rectangular or needle shaped. Good engineering practices generally assure that the bottom floors have the same or more space than the upper stories. Yet, our American Wealth building reflects a different truth. If we view floor space as a metaphor for access to resources, those at the top occupy floors that are many times larger than those below. The richest 1, 2, and 5 percent of households hold about 35, 47, and 63 percent of all household wealth. From a distance, our skyscraper might resemble a funnel with a long, narrow neck supporting a top fanning out. One wonders what keeps this structure standing.

The two equalities

Although the picture just provided clearly demonstrates we suffer from substantial wealth disparities, it does not prove that the American Dream is illusory. To clarify, we need to distinguish between two concepts of equality, the *equality of outcomes* and the *equality of opportunity*. Clearly, the current distribution of wealth violates any standard for equality of outcomes. The vast disparities, certainly in absolute terms, are unprecedented in our nation's experience. Yet, few Americans would advocate for a strict adherence to an equality of outcomes. Indeed, the American Dream argues for unequal outcomes since we expect individuals with varied merits to attain different degrees of upward mobility. Conversely, equality of opportunity is central to the American Dream. Rather than focus on where individuals end up, equality of opportunity considers where people started. Recognizing the difference is what researchers call *wealth mobility*.

As Stephen McNamee and Robert Miller explain in their book *The Meritocracy Myth*, there exists a strong connection between the American Dream and the promise of a functioning meritocracy. As they argue, meritocratic societies ideally reward individuals based on having the "right stuff," what they call a combination of talent, hard work, good attitude, and playing by the rules (2004, p. 197). Such a system requires some measure of equalized opportunity, but not equalized outcomes. In a meritocracy, individuals, regardless of birth or rank, have the opportunity to advance based on their personal merits. Most families would experience an increase in net worth over their (working) lifetime, also known as *wealth accumulation*. Assuming that individual skills, talents, and aptitudes are distributed unequally across the population, such a system could easily generate very unequal outcomes, not unlike what we see today. Nonetheless, during periods of economic growth and rising wealth, we would expect to see most households accumulating wealth at levels higher than their parents, thereby experiencing *absolute wealth mobility*. As Mark Robert Rank, Thomas Hirschl, and Kirk Foster argued in *Chasing the American Dream*, a "fundamental aspect of the American Dream has always been the expectation that the next generation should do better than the previous generation" (2014, p. 61).

However, there exists one important difference between a functioning meritocracy and the American Dream. In a meritocracy, we should find substantial *relative wealth mobility.* In other words, children raised in households with modest wealth will experience similar rates of wealth accumulation as their peers born into wealthier families. More problematically, relative wealth mobility requires both upward and downward mobility. For every household that achieves some measure of upward wealth mobility, another must suffer a relative decline. Of course, relative declines in wealth can accompany absolute increases in wealth as long as these increases are smaller than what others are experiencing. Consequently, a well-functioning meritocracy can manifest both widespread *absolute* as well as extensive *relative wealth mobility*, no matter the degree of unequal outcomes.

As we consider the dynamic consequences of such a system, a concern arises, one anticipated a half century ago by James Bryant Conant, president of Harvard University. According to McNamee and Miller (2004), Conant argued that a meritocratic system requires neither a "uniform distribution of the world's goods" nor a "radical equalization of wealth," but rather a "continuous process by which power and privilege may be automatically redistributed at the end of each generation" (Conant, 1940, p. 598, cited by McNamee and Miller, 2004). Otherwise, the unequal outcomes of one generation will limit the equality of opportunity of the next, creating what some have labeled the "intergenerational paradox" (Hochschild et al., 2003, p. 23). Given the chance, affluent parents will expand their children's opportunities to preclude any such downward mobility.

Alternatively, to use our building metaphor, what happens to the kids of families throughout the building? On what floor do they start their adult lives? Does their starting place unduly influence where they end up? The core concept of this book, *wealth privilege*, suggests "yes." Wealth privilege refers to the host of advantages that accrues to families with wealth as they attempt to accumulate additional wealth. Those who start out with more undoubtedly hold an advantage over their lifetime. To the extent that inequality among outcomes produces unequal opportunities for the next generation, the model of wealth privilege predicts a further escalation of unequal outcomes with each successive generation.

Are meritocracies stable systems, capable of regenerating themselves across generations? According to the Wealth Privilege model described in Chapter 3, meritocracies that produce modest wealth disparities likely are more stable than those that generate widely disparate results. Moderate wealth differences are less likely to bias the opportunities for future generations. Alternatively, by introducing some mechanism that mitigates the consequences of unequal outcomes on the equality of future opportunities, we can expect to extend the life expectancy of a meritocracy. Federal estate and gift taxes were created for just this purpose. Their proponents argued taxes were necessary to prevent *earned wealth* from one generation becoming *unearned wealth* for the next, a transfer that undermines the equality of opportunity. Without taxes or other safeguards, one would expect any meritocracy that generates widely disparate outcomes would eventually produce similarly unequal opportunities. Such a result would presage ever widening disparities, triggering a vicious cycle that would undermine the meritocracy over successive generations.

Worse still, those who most passionately embrace the American Dream usually behave in ways that undermine its persistence. Part of the American Dream, particularly for those who are parents, is to have the means to offer their children the opportunity for a better life. This entails providing whatever is necessary to promote their physical and emotional health as well as any educational, cultural, or social advantages. While Americans might believe strongly in the principle of equal opportunity, most parents behave in ways that undermine its reality, if they can. To protect their children from any reversal of fortune or downward wealth mobility, parents will assist them in every way possible. Most Americans likely support the principle of equal opportunity, except when it comes to their own children.

Whatever the cause, the potential for unequal outcomes to undermine the equality of opportunity produces *social stratification*. The ability of affluent parents to advantage their children using the array of benefits that household wealth affords creates a system in which birthright increasingly trumps individual merit. Under this system, relative wealth mobility will undoubtedly decline. Both the frequency and range of "rags to riches" occurrences will wane as each generation of young adults will find the "starting line" increasingly uneven. Moreover, the endowment given to the children of affluent parents increasingly will insulate them from a fall from "riches to rags." Relative wealth mobility will persist, but only within the relative strata in which individuals find themselves raised. In essence, an economic caste system, based on wealth, emerges, which I label a *plutocracy*.

Over time, one would expect a similar decline in absolute wealth mobility. Just as the prodigious American economy has preserved the allure of the American Dream for successive generations, so has its appeal fueled substantial economic growth. Lured by the prospects of a better life, each generation has offered its vigor and ingenuity, thereby stoking the fires of the American economy. However, a flourishing plutocracy likely would dampen future growth. Increasing the concentration of wealth into fewer hands would place more of the country's resources beyond the grasp of the next generation's potential entrepreneurs. As greater numbers of households confront ever bleaker prospects, the energy and resourcefulness that characterizes the American economy would wane. As economic realities decreasingly validate the dream, so will the dynamism that has fueled past economic growth and wealth creation. A decline in absolute wealth gains will follow suit. We can envision the concepts of meritocracy and plutocracy as defining a continuum as illustrated in Figure 1.1. This illustration includes the key attributes just discussed.

Determining the U.S. economy's current position is a contentious issue given its importance and complexity. Two recent studies offer some clarity. Dalton Conley and Rebecca Glauber (2008) compared the wealth rankings of households based on their parents' wealth status. They discovered that 41 percent of children raised in the bottom wealth quartile remained in that rank as adults. At the same time, almost 55 percent of children reared in the wealthiest quartile of homes retained this status as adults. More recently, the Pew Trust Economic Mobility Project found corroborating results. Despite using a different methodology, they

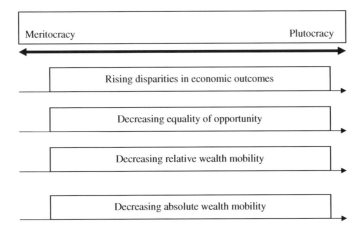

FIGURE 1.1 Meritocracy–plutocracy continuum

determined that 41 percent of children born in the bottom wealth quintile kept this rank as adults while the same percentage of those raised in the wealthiest homes kept their rank (Urahn et al., 2012). Both suggest that relative wealth mobility is limited, placing the United States some distance from the meritocracy side of the continuum. Without past evidence to make comparisons, we can only speculate whether these figures represent declines in wealth mobility, or simply a static, status quo.

Directly addressing this issue of relative wealth mobility is beyond the scope of this book. Instead, I examine the institutional circumstances and systemic influences that both advance and retard wealth accumulation. By investigating these broader factors, this book can address wealth mobility indirectly. For example, as wealth disparities widen, relative wealth mobility will likely decline, simply due to the increasing financial distance one must travel.[4] A parallel argument gained prominence recently when the White House dubbed it as the "Great Gatsby Curve." Corak (2013) concluded that the United States has the highest level of *income inequality* along with nearly the lowest measure of *income mobility* among 12 Organization of Economic Cooperation and Development countries. On the other hand, Chetty et al. (2014a) offered evidence that shows little change in *income mobility* over the past half century, taking some of the air out of this argument. As income and wealth are inextricably linked, one might expect similar findings concerning household wealth. However, very different circumstances influence the accumulation of wealth over a lifetime, causing it to be subject to far greater disparities across households. Further, wealth is much more durable and transferable across generations than is income, suggesting very different conditions affect intergenerational mobility.

In their remarkable book *Black Wealth/White Wealth*, Melvin Oliver and Thomas Shapiro argue persuasively that previous analyses of wealth by economists have largely ignored "the social context in which wealth generation occurs" (2006, p. 6). Instead, previous economic studies of wealth have simply examined the role of family transfers, household earnings, savings, and investment choices. This book attempts to redress that omission. The Wealth Privilege model discussed later argues that while the means of wealth accumulation may be open to all, the experiences of households vary substantially based on their race, family background, education, income, and wealth status. Moreover, the Wealth Privilege model documents how these differences translate into key advantages that explain both the current level of wealth disparities as well as the limited degree of relative wealth mobility. Further, the model predicts that the current wealth disparities will only continue to widen absent substantial changes in public policy.

Others have documented the rising concentration of wealth into fewer hands in recent decades (Bricker et al., 2014; Kennickell, 2009; Piketty and Goldhammer, 2014; Smith, 2001; Wolff, 1995). In this book, I offer corroborating evidence and introduce the Wealth Privilege model to explain the underlying sources of this trend. All indications suggest these principal causes will continue to widen the wealth disparities. Already, one can observe systemic shifts that will discourage wealth mobility in the future. Despite the vast increase in household wealth over the past generation, inheritance rates are declining while the size of these gifts is rising. This shift is contributing toward increasing inequality among young householders, those just starting out. Even worse, these same households are beginning their lives with less wealth today than did their peers a generation ago. Increasingly, young households able to attain a college degree find themselves mired in greater levels of debt, thereby deferring their capacity to accumulate wealth. These and other structural changes raise the alarm that the American economy is moving inexorably toward the plutocracy side of the continuum.

Some preliminary evidence

Over the past generation, the U.S. economy experienced two rather distinct periods. From 1989 to 2007, the American economy suffered only two rather mild recessions amidst long economic expansions that encouraged employment and business profit. Rising stock prices and housing values bolstered the wealth of many families. Indeed, as illustrated in Figure 1.2, the average wealth of American

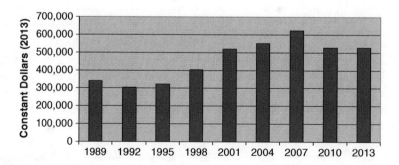

FIGURE 1.2 Average family wealth, 1989–2013
Source: SCF, 1989–2013

households nearly doubled over this period, even after adjusting for inflation. Not only did average family wealth nearly double from $300,000 in 1989 to over $600,000 in 2007, but the increase was steady and substantial through most of the period.[5] The relative prosperity of the time enabled American households the opportunity to build their financial nest eggs. Of course, the onset of the Great Recession brought a reversal of fortune. The financial crisis and the ensuing maelstrom eroded the gains of most families as stock values and real estate prices plummeted while unemployment and business failures skyrocketed. Even including this period of severe retrenchment, household wealth grew by 55 percent in real terms over the course of a generation. Yet, each of these two periods offers us a glimpse into the dynamics of wealth accumulation under very different circumstances.

According to conventional wisdom, periods of economic prosperity, like the early period, will act like "a rising tide that will lift all boats."[6] A growing economy should offer most households various opportunities to accumulate wealth and claim some portion of the American Dream. In good times, even households with modest means can save a part of their wages, bank these savings or even purchase a home, and then benefit as these assets appreciate. Although this is technically the case, the evidence illustrates a more complex picture.

One common way of depicting the distribution of wealth is by dividing households into five equal groups, or quintiles, based on their net worth. The top wealth quintile includes the richest 20 percent, while the remaining households are placed in descending order into the four remaining groups. Figure 1.3 illustrates the portion of all of the newly created wealth captured by each wealth quintile. The figure examines two periods to avoid giving undue influence to the events that accompanied the Great Recession. Over the prosperous shorter period, households across the wealth spectrum shared in gaining newly created wealth, though far from uniformly. The wealthiest households captured 87 percent, leaving the remainder to the middle three quintiles, which we might call our middle class. The poorest 20 percent of households actually lost ground during this period, at least relatively. These relative shares suggest that existing wealth disparities would only get larger.

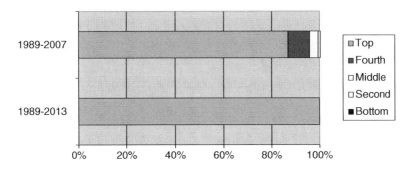

FIGURE 1.3 Shares of newly created wealth, 1989–2013
Source: Author's calculations from SCF, 1989, 2007, and 2013

When we consider the full period, including the Great Recession, the results are even more alarming. Only the wealthiest households experienced a perceptible improvement as a group.

By taking a different vantage, we can understand the implications of these trends more clearly. Figure 1.4 depicts the median wealth of households from each of the five wealth quintiles. As such, it illustrates how the circumstances of the past generation have affected wealth accumulation at different points along the wealth distribution. Up until 2007, the median levels for the four highest quintiles rose across the period.[7] However, the size of these gains varied tremendously. While the median wealth of the top wealth quintile rose from $600,000 to over $1 million, the comparable changes among the next three wealth quintiles were $125,000, $50,000, and $11,000, respectively.[8] Although this period of rapid wealth accumulation did bring relief to most households, it did so in a manner that exacerbated the existing wealth disparities. As the absolute differences in wealth among households increases, one must worry for its effect on wealth mobility.

The period after 2007 reveals a different picture as the median wealth of all five quintiles falls. By 2013, the median values for the three lower wealth quintiles had fallen below their levels in 1989. While the Great Recession damaged family nest eggs across the wealth spectrum, it did so disproportionately. In 2013, the absolute differences in wealth between the wealthiest families and the rest were the largest ever seen. As the evidence indicates, the American economy demonstrated its prodigious capacity to create wealth, though with singular stinginess.

Much of this book is devoted to explaining why the rising concentration of wealth is no anomaly. Initially, I introduce the Wealth Privilege model that describes the three pathways nominally available to all households as they strive to accumulate wealth: household saving, asset appreciation, and family support. As the evidence shows, households experience these pathways in quite different ways, largely depending on their wealth. Along each pathway, the acquisition of wealth confers increasing advantages, thereby expanding their capacity to accumulate wealth. For the most part, these privileges of wealth stem from rather mundane characteristics of a well-functioning market economy. The arguments offered

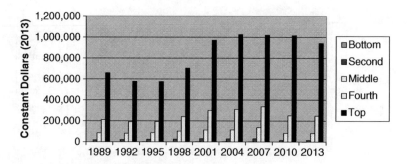

FIGURE 1.4 Median net worth by wealth quintiles, 1989–2013
Source: SCF, 1989–2013

certainly conjure the truism that "it takes money to make money." Later in the book, I summarize and identify the consequences of our federal wealth policies. Not only do these policies clearly favor the wealthy, recent policy shifts have tilted their favoritism even further. Together these arguments and the supporting evidence present a convincing case that explains the widening wealth gaps.

The trend toward increasing wealth inequality is not simply the result of advantages afforded the wealthy during times of prosperity or from favorable federal policies. In the six years since the onset of the Great Recession, the wealth gaps continued to widen, though for different reasons. Though the wealthy often lost more during the aftermath of the financial collapse due to falling asset values, their losses usually did not require structural sacrifices. In comparison, less affluent households experienced smaller losses, but these often led to asset liquidation, foreclosures, and bankruptcies. No longer owners of property, these households could not recoup their losses once the economy rebounded and property values followed suit. With their deeper pockets, richer households were able to maintain their asset ownership, keeping them well positioned as asset values resumed their climb. Understanding these disparate capacities offers further evidence of the advantages provided by wealth. Indeed, the dislocations suffered by many less affluent households may simply exacerbate the trends of widening wealth gaps once prosperity returns.

Perhaps nothing illustrates the consequences of these dislocations as does Figure 1.5, which depicts homeownership rates among the five wealth groups. The most dramatic changes occur for the bottom two wealth quintiles after 2007. The collapse of the housing market caused some homeowners to lose their homes, other would-be buyers to defer their plans, and persistent homeowners to watch their equity and net worth evaporate with the fall in home values. Indeed, the surprising discontinuities illustrated in Figure 1.5 demonstrate the limits of homeownership in providing a source of financial security as collapsing home values caused many homeowners to fall from the second to the bottom wealth quintile. Nonetheless, the vast differences revealed in Figure 1.5 along with the rising barriers to homeownership raise concern that future wealth gaps will grow even wider.

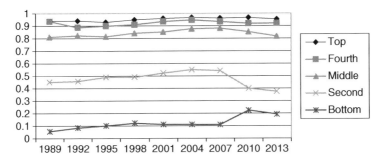

FIGURE 1.5 Homeownership by wealth quintiles, 1989–2013
Source: SCF, 1989–2013

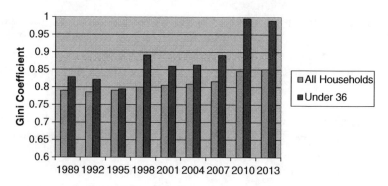

FIGURE 1.6 Trends in wealth disparities, 1989–2013

Even worse, there is evidence that the increased concentration of wealth is affecting the equality of opportunity as well. The most widely used measure of inequality, the Gini coefficient, illustrates this connection in Figure 1.6. To the unfamiliar, the Gini coefficient is a measure of inequality.[9] In the case of perfect equality, in which each household held the same amount of wealth, the Gini coefficient would equal zero. As actual wealth holdings become increasingly unequal, the coefficient becomes larger. Consistent with other estimates (Pfeffer et al., 2013), the Gini coefficient indicates only modest movement toward increased wealth concentration among all households, at least until 2007 and after. More alarming is the degree of wealth inequality among younger households. The Gini coefficient for this group has shown even wider wealth disparities, particularly in recent years.[10] Both the rising trend toward increased wealth concentration along with the widening differences between the two measures offer real concern that the inequality of outcomes may indeed be influencing the inequality of opportunity.

These widening disparities in both outcomes and future opportunities aggravate another critical challenge facing the U.S. Recall the changing racial makeup of residents in the hypothetical skyscraper as we descend the building. Virtually all of the occupants in the upper floors are White with a sprinkling of Asian Americans, while most Black and Latino households reside in the bottom floors. Recently, Oliver and Shapiro's *Black Wealth/White Wealth* as well as Dalton Conley's *Being Black, Living in the Red* brought attention to this racialized wealth gap; both books presented persuasive evidence linking the contemporary wealth gap to past racialized policies and practices.[11] Today, the relationship between household wealth and racial status remains both stark and complicated, as Figure 1.7 illustrates.

Several points from Figure 1.7 are worth mentioning. The typical or median household from all four groups experienced rising fortunes, particularly in the 15-year period from 1992 to 2007.[12] However, the absolute gap between White versus Black and Latino households grew substantially during this period, from about $100,000 to $150,000 per household. In 2010, the racial disparities had largely returned to where they were 21 years earlier, suggesting little, if any progress in reducing this gap. The experience of Asian or Other households was somewhat

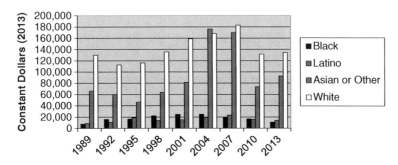

FIGURE 1.7 Median wealth by racialized group, 1989–2013
Source: SCF, 1989–2013

different.[13] Starting from a position midway between the other groups, they virtually eclipsed White households before falling back to resume their initial positions. It is likely that the 2004 and 2007 measures of Asian or Other wealth are anomalies. At this time, the housing bubble was expanding. Given the geographical concentration of Asian Americans in areas that witnessed strong gains in home prices, their fluctuating fortunes likely reflect the ebb and flow of home values.[14] Despite the different experiences of Asian or Other households, the figures in 2013 for all four groups show a remarkable resemblance to those in 1989. Despite the dramatic gains in wealth over the entire period, wealth disparities by race remain largely unchanged.

The racial wealth gap, so clearly illustrated in Figure 1.7, poses stark reminders of our nation's racial history. From our nation's very beginnings, government policies have encouraged the accumulation of wealth by White Americans at the expense of other Americans of color. Not only do these policies include enslavement and land expropriation, they also include such landmark laws as the Homestead Acts and the G.I. Bill.[15] Over generations, these and many more policies favored White Americans as they worked to improve their circumstances and attain the American Dream. With each generation, parents could offer their children better opportunities than they received, whether it was the family farm, increased education, or a union card. In contrast, countless local, state, and federal laws functioned to limit the opportunities of Americans of color. These policies of the past live today in the form of our contemporary racial wealth gap.

Yet, this racial wealth gap is not solely the result of our past. Throughout the book I show evidence of continuing discrimination experienced by Black and Latino households in particular. During the Great Recession, Black and Latino households suffered disproportionate losses as compared to White households. Black and Latino homeowners endured substantial declines in home values while Black-owned businesses experienced catastrophic losses. Even in good times, Black and Latino households bore a host of challenges not experienced by most White households. In many cases, these disparities result from their modest wealth holdings and their inability to attain many of the privileges of wealth. In this way, the many advantages given to wealth holders also function to sustain and even aggravate the racial wealth gap. Indeed, the very same forces that are encouraging the plutocracy are also supporting a new form of racial segregation, one based on household wealth.

Each of these trends should trigger alarm among all Americans. Although none specifically documents a decline in wealth mobility, each suggests conditions that are less hospitable to its persistence. Expanding wealth gaps between the rich and the poor increases the ground that mobile households need to cover. Rising disparities in asset ownership across our society will hobble those unable to afford the down payment for a home, start-up capital for a new business venture, or even regular deposits to their retirement fund. Conditions that increasingly favor some young householders at the expense of their peers and thereby tilt the supposed "level playing field" offered to subsequent generations will undermine their aspirations. Circumstances that limit wealth mobility can solidify our racial disparities, creating what Oliver and Shapiro (2006) labeled the "sedimentation of racial inequality" (p. 5). Each of these trends encourages the rise of an American plutocracy and renewed racial segregation as they threaten the realization of the American Dream.

Plan of the book

The next two chapters identify key forces that are driving the current trend toward wealth concentration. Chapter 2 discusses the crucial details of household wealth. It distinguishes wealth from income, two highly related but quite different concepts. In doing so, I argue why investigating wealth is even more significant than analyzing income. The chapter reviews the different forms of wealth as well as their specific attributes. In addition, it introduces the different types of debt and explains how debt is used to leverage further wealth. Lastly, I discuss the multiple ways that wealth can expand opportunities and thereby offer a source of power to its owners.

Chapter 3 introduces the core of the Wealth Privilege model. Economists have long argued that households typically accumulate wealth through household saving, family gifts and inheritances, as well as asset appreciation.[16] Though each of these offers a pathway to wealth accumulation, the model explains how households experience these pathways differently depending on their circumstances. For wealthy families, these pathways function like a virtuous cycle. For example, households capable of saving can purchase assets that generate added income. With this supplement, families can save even more, thereby accelerating the process. Further, employers and financial institutions can offer services that make saving easier for some. The ability to deposit portions of one's salary directly into a retirement or bank savings account limits the temptations that undermine saving. Many low-earning employees are not offered these opportunities. Not only must they actively save their earnings, frequently necessary expenses force them to *dissave*. This can entail rising credit card balances or other forms of debt. Escalating interest costs and higher debt payments squeeze their limited income even further, frequently requiring even greater debt levels. These households experience a savings pathway that operates as a vicious cycle instead. As all three pathways function similarly, I show how widening wealth disparities and growing wealth concentration are predictable consequences of a prosperous economy.

Chapter 4 takes a slight detour to consider the roots of the racialized wealth gap. Noting the durability and transferability of wealth across generations, I show how our current distribution of wealth is linked to past policies of racial enslavement, expropriation, and exclusion. I recall a host of public policies that benefited White households at the expense of various communities of color. For generations, these policies assisted White Americans in their quest to achieve the American Dream while systematically hindering Americans of color. This serves as an important reminder that there never were "the good ole days" when the American Dream was an inclusive reality.

In Chapter 5, I return to the present. Using detailed household data provided by the Survey of Consumer Finances (SCF), I document the various ways that wealth advantages affluent households as they seek to accumulate wealth. Not only do wealthy households earn higher incomes that foster increased saving, they also have greater access to credit and pay lower borrowing costs. Their increased access to health insurance offers better protection against unexpected health costs even as they report better health. In addition, they confirm higher rates of inheritance as well as larger gifts. At the same time, they experience less need to offer financial help to parents or other family members in distress. Lastly, their extensive holdings permit them to take greater risks as they invest in higher-yielding investments. Deeper pockets enable them to buy homes in select neighborhoods where houses appreciate faster. Given the racial wealth gap, these advantages largely privilege White households at the expense of households of color. Collectively, these sources of wealth privilege operate to reduce relative wealth mobility and perpetuate past inequalities.

The Wealth Privilege model predicts that households of different means experience quite different circumstances as they work to accumulate wealth. Chapter 6 examines that prediction as it investigates whether similar opportunities, decisions, and attitudes influence household wealth differently depending on their wealth status. Using quantile-regression analysis, I identify the key factors that affect wealth accumulation at different points along the wealth spectrum. The analysis offers a number of important insights. It indicates that asset ownership, much more so than household saving, offers the most effective means for wealth augmentation. Further, it corroborates key predictions of the Wealth Privilege model, including the real presence of both systemic obstacles and privileges, depending on one's wealth status. Interestingly, the analysis shows that attitudes toward credit, risk taking, and leaving a legacy have little impact on wealth outcomes.

Chapter 7 considers another source of wealth privilege: greater resilience during times of distress. The Great Recession offers an excellent case study. This chapter investigates how families fared over a two-year period while the economy was collapsing. By whatever measure, wealthier households suffered greater reversals in their net worth. Yet, their vast reserves protected them against structural reversals like bankruptcy, business liquidations, and distressed sales. While financially harmed, they remained well positioned for prosperity's return. These privileges did not inoculate Black and Latino families as they did White households. Despite the wealth gap, Black and Latino households suffered greater reversals proportionately than did White households. The chapter explores why.

Chapter 8 introduces the remaining facets of the Wealth Privilege model as it investigates our federal wealth policies. A collection of tax deductions, tax credits, and the estate and gift taxes, these policies directly affect households' capacity to accumulate and transfer wealth. Due to their design, most offer their greatest assistance to the wealthiest households, thereby operating in the same self-reinforcing manner as the wealth pathways described earlier. Since these policies favor the affluent, they also privilege mostly White households at the expense of their Black and Latino neighbors. Even worse, congressional changes to these programs over the past two decades have tilted their benefits toward the wealthy even further. At the same time, repeated revisions to our gift and estate taxes have stripped them of their effectiveness and relevance. These changes offer evidence of the remaining component of the Wealth Privilege model, the use of wealth to influence favorable, public policy.

The remaining chapter stitches together the different threads developed throughout the book. I argue that the Wealth Privilege model—operating through four virtuous cycles in the context of our racial wealth gap—is creating a White plutocracy. I document how the increasing concentration of wealth is upending the supposedly level playing field among young households. Not only are inheritance patterns shifting, but also the "starting line" is receding for most young householders, further tilting the playing field. This portends badly for the future of the American Dream. In response, I offer several policy prescriptions on how we might slow and even reverse these trends. These recommendations entail a full revamping of our federal wealth policies to shift the focus of wealth building from our most affluent neighbors to the least. Further, it calls for the enactment of an effective and substantial inheritance tax to restore the distinction between earned and unearned income.

Some initial caveats

For those of us studying American society, the concept of race offers nothing but conceptual problems. On the one hand, we know that race has no meaningful biological content. From a genetic standpoint, there are not different races, merely the human race. Instead, it is simply a social construction; our forebears created the idea to justify and defend their actions. At the same time, it remains a powerful concept that we cannot ignore. At the personal level, there is strong evidence that each of us experiences different physiological and cognitive responses to others, based on their race. No doubt, we all hope that we have learned to treat each individual fairly; yet, the evidence suggests it is not so simple.

Not long ago, I was preparing to take a trip to Africa. I was given a phone and charger that would work while there. Unable to figure out how the two worked, I took them to my local Radio Shack. Walking in the door, I saw a Black female working the counter rather than the usual White clerk. Immediately, I felt disappointment, thinking there was no way that I would get the help I needed. Nevertheless, I stepped up to the counter and within 30 seconds she had solved my problem, at least the electronic one. Later, I realized I held an implicit conclusion that White guys, especially those with glasses, were skilled at solving electronic problems. I held this view, even though I know one White guy, myself, who is not. Further, I had little faith that a woman, much less a Black woman, could demonstrate such expertise. Until I walked in that door, I was unaware of these perceptions.

Yet, the significance of race goes far beyond our interpersonal responses. By any measure of well-being one can consider, people of color lag far behind White people in the U.S. This is certainly the case with any measure of power and opportunity. As such, the concept of race still has enormous influence, even as it has no basis in reality. In recognition of this paradox, I prefer to use the term *racialized group* instead of *race*. The latter term suggests clear and immutable categories even as our history demonstrates that these are anything but static. *Racialized group* indicates it is a created concept, not a real one.

Even so, the concept of racialized group is also highly problematic. What exactly are the common traits shared by all who might consider themselves Latino that distinguish them from non-Latinos? In truth, it is difficult to square the life experiences of Cuban Americans with Puerto Rican Americans and Mexican Americans, to name just three groups. The circumstances of their immigration, the welcomes they received, and their integration into local communities have been substantially different; yet, they are lumped together into one group. Even worse is the Asian or Other category.[17] Within this group, we include Chinese and Japanese Americans, most of who emigrated generations ago, along with more recent émigrés from South Asia. Further, they are lumped together with Native American, Native Alaskan, Native Hawaiian, and Pacific Islander groups. Is there anything common to this category beyond their "Otherness"? Even White has an interesting wrinkle as it includes all persons of Middle Eastern and Arab descent. The upshot is that there is no sensible way of categorizing people by their racialized group, since it is such an arbitrary concept. Since we cannot ignore it, we must use caution when considering evidence based on racialized status.

Investigating wealth and its distribution across society offers other problems as well. To measure how shifts in wealth affect the typical household, researchers generally use median measures rather than mean measures, due to the concentration of wealth. Yet, this is not always suitable. From 1989 to 2013, real median wealth fell from nearly $85,000 to $81,000 suggesting a modest decline in household wealth. Though true for the typical household, mean real wealth rose from $341,000 to $528,000 over the same period, indicating a substantial rise in wealth. Both figures portray very different realities regarding what happened to household wealth over the period; simply relying on one measure can cause us to miss important insights.

Measuring wealth mobility generates other ambiguities. Take one household that increases its net worth from $10,000 to $20,000. On a percentage basis, this represents a 100 percent increase. Consider a second household that increases its net worth from $500,000 to $800,000. They experience a measly 60 percent increase. As mathematically inclined readers will note, this affluent household has cause for worry. If they continue to eke out 60 percent increases while the other household maintains 100 percent increases, they will lose their advantage—eventually. Yet, this math does not capture the true reality. By any stretch of the imagination, the wealthy household's gain of $300,000 is far greater than the $10,000 earned by the other household. Once again, each set of measures depicts a different insight. Even the celebrated Gini coefficient has challenges as I detail in Appendix A.

These problems aside, the purpose of this book is to investigate and understand the dynamics of wealth accumulation among American households. Returning to our skyscraper metaphor, this book examines why the distance between the top and basement floors is so vast and why this gap continues to widen. Although we will not trace the specific experiences of individual households, the analysis does offer insights regarding economic mobility throughout the building. The Wealth Privilege model, along with its three pathways, illustrates how circumstances change dramatically as one ascends the skyscraper. While some households have access to the express elevator, others are restricted to conventional elevators, escalators, and even simple staircases. This book also examines why most occupants of the upper floors are White while the bulk of Black and Latino households are found in the bottom and basement floors. Lastly, we will examine the various public policies created to help households build their net worth. Doing so will reveal that our government functions like a building manager who is more interested in meeting the needs of the penthouse residents than those at the bottom with their greater needs.

To investigate these issues carefully, I will rely heavily upon the Federal Reserve's triennial surveys of household wealth, now called the Survey of Consumer Finances (SCF). The SCF arguably offers the most detailed and representative picture of household wealth. The range and depth of its survey questions provide an unparalleled understanding of household assets and debt. To ensure a representative sample, the SCF randomly selects several thousand households to answer their questions. Since relatively few households hold vast amounts of wealth, simply using random sampling will likely cause the survey to miss these important respondents. Therefore, the SCF uses tax records to develop a second sample to ensure inclusion of the wealthiest households.[18] The Federal Reserve promises strict confidentiality to all responders to elicit voluntary participation. For these reasons, the SCF offers the most comprehensive understanding of contemporary household wealth, particularly at the top end.[19] Unfortunately, the survey does not follow households from one survey to the next; instead, it queries new households with each subsequent survey.[20] As such, it offers us momentary snapshots of what is actually a dynamic process unfolding over time. Without the means to follow specific households over time, our investigation of economic mobility must use indirect means. The analysis will identify the specific circumstances and systemic opportunities that households of different wealth status encounter.

Notes

1 It is important to acknowledge those Americans who are not descended from voluntary immigrants, but who descend from enslaved Africans, Native peoples already here, and former citizens of Mexico who found themselves in a new country due to shifting borders.
2 The Panel Study in Income Dynamics added questions about household wealth in 1984 while the National Longitudinal Study of Youth did the same in 1985. The Survey of Income and Program Participation followed suit in 1996.
3 Author's calculations using the 2013 Survey of Consumer Finances. Almost 13 percent of households had zero or negative net worth in 2013 as compared to 8 percent as reported in the 1962 Survey of Financial Characters of Consumers.
4 Increasing wealth disparities will increase the interquartile range, or the distance between the 25th and 75th percentile. Lengthening this range means one must experience greater increases or declines in wealth to move between the bottom two and upper two wealth quartiles.
5 The decline in average wealth from 1989 to 1992 reflects the aftermath of the 1990–1 recession.
6 President Kennedy is attributed with coining this phrase in a speech he gave in Heber Springs, Arkansas on October 3, 1963.
7 The initial dip from 1989 to 1992 is due to the aftermath of the 1990–1 recession.
8 By comparison, median wealth of the bottom wealth quintile grew from zero wealth to $56.
9 I encourage the unfamiliar reader to see the discussion on the Gini coefficient in Appendix A.
10 Some readers may be alarmed by the coefficient equaling 1.0 in 2010. Since net worth can easily be zero or negative, this means the Gini coefficient can exceed 1.0. I encourage the reader to visit Appendix A for a fuller discussion of these issues.
11 Due to data limitations, both emphasized the Black/White dichotomy at the expense of Latino as well as Asian or Other households.
12 This 15-year period represents an unusually prosperous time in the economy with just one mild recession in 2001.
13 I use this term reluctantly. Though the survey asks for details regarding the respondent's racial background, the public release includes all Native Americans as part of the "Other." Lumping them into this category effectively causes them to disappear statistically. Of course, I could argue that this is consistent with their treatment by Whites over the past 400 years.
14 As the smallest racial group, their size makes their figures more susceptible to fluctuations that result from the survey sampling process. I discuss their circumstances in greater detail in Appendix B.
15 I examine these policies in Chapter 4.
16 With Modigliani and Brumberg (1954), the life-cycle hypothesis has long dominated economists' understanding of household-wealth accumulation.
17 Respondents can select among the following categories: Asian, American Indian/Alaska Native, Native Hawaiian/Pacific Islander, or Other. For reasons of privacy, the SCF lumps all four categories in their public release. Though their motive is understandable, it has unfortunate consequences. One of the laments among the Indigenous peoples is their sense of being erased not only from history, but also from contemporary society and public policy. This step of aggregating them with Asians certainly does this.

18 The SCF provides sampling weights. Analysis that uses a weighted sample allows one to draw conclusions about the broader American society while using an unweighted sample does not.
19 Two other household surveys that are regularly used to examine household wealth are the Panel Study of Income Dynamics and the Survey of Income and Program Participation. Each has its own strengths and limitations, though as their names imply they are more focused on household income than wealth.
20 In 2009, the SCF made a notable exception to this protocol as it revisited households previously surveyed in 2007. These results form the basis of the analysis found in Chapter 7.

Bibliography

Adams, J. T. (1941). *The epic of America*. New York: Blue Ribbon.

Bedard, P. (2011). Fewer confident of reaching American Dream. US News and World Report, March. Retrieved from www.usnews.com/news/washington-whispers/articles/2011/03/30/fewer-confident-acheiving-american-dream.

Bricker, J., Dettling, L., Henriques, A., Hsu, J., Moore, K., Sabelhaus, J., Thompson, J., and Windle, R. (2014). Changes in U.S. family finances from 2010 to 2013: Evidence from the Survey of Consumer Finances. *Federal Reserve Bulletin* 100 (4): 1–41.

Chetty, R., Hendren, N., Kline, P., Saez, E., and Turner, N. (2014a). *Is the United States still a land of opportunity? Recent trends in intergenerational mobility* (No. w19844). Cambridge, MA: National Bureau of Economic Research.

Chetty, R., Hendren, N., Kline, P., and Saez, E. (2014b). *Where is the land of opportunity? The geography of intergenerational mobility in the United States* (No. w19843). Cambridge, MA: National Bureau of Economic Research.

Conant, J. B. (1940). Education for a classless society: The Jeffersonian tradition. *Atlantic* 165 (May): 593–602.

Conley, D. (1999). *Being Black, living in the red: Race, wealth, and social policy in America*. Berkeley: University of California Press.

Conley, D. and Glauber, R. (2008). *Wealth mobility and volatility in Black and White*. Washington, DC: Center for American Progress.

Corak, M. (2013). Income inequality, equality of opportunity, and intergenerational mobility. *Journal of Economic Perspectives* 27 (3): 79–102.

Cullen, J. (2004). *The American Dream: A short history of an idea that shaped a nation*. Oxford: Oxford University Press.

Hochschild, J. L. (1996). *Facing up to the American Dream: Race, class, and the soul of the nation*. Princeton, NJ: Princeton University Press.

Hochschild, J. L., Scovronick, N., and Scovronick, N. B. (2003). *The American Dream and the public schools*. Oxford: Oxford University Press.

Keister, L. A. (2000). *Wealth in America: Trends in wealth inequality*. Cambridge: Cambridge University Press.

Kennickell, A. B. (2009). *Ponds and streams: Wealth and income in the US, 1989 to 2007*. Washington, DC: Divisions of Research and Statistics and Monetary Affairs, Federal Reserve Board.

McNamee, S. J. and Miller, R. K., Jr. (2004). *The meritocracy myth*. Lanham, MD: Rowman and Littlefield.

Modigliani, F. and Brumberg, R. (1954). Utility analysis and the consumption function: An interpretation of cross-section data. *Franco Modigliani* 1.

Norton, M. I. and Ariely, D. (2011). Building a better America: One wealth quintile at a time. *Perspectives on Psychological Science* 6 (1): 9–12.

Oliver, M. L. and Shapiro, T. M. (2006). *Black wealth, White wealth: A new perspective on racial inequality*. New York: Taylor and Francis.

Pfeffer, F. T., Danziger, S., and Schoeni, R. F. (2013). Wealth disparities before and after the Great Recession. *ANNALS of the American Academy of Political and Social Science* 650 (1): 98–123.

Piketty, T. and Goldhammer, A. (2014). *Capital in the twenty-first century*. New York: Belknap Press.

Rank, M. R., Hirschl, T. A., and Foster, K. A. (2014). *Chasing the American Dream: Understanding what shapes our fortunes*. Oxford: Oxford University Press.

Shammas, C. (1993). A new look at long-term trends in wealth inequality in the United States. *American Historical Review* 98 (2): 412–31.

Smith, J. P. (2001). Why is wealth inequality rising? In *The causes and consequences of increasing inequality*, ed. F. Welch. Chicago: University of Chicago Press, 83–116.

U.S. Census Bureau. (2015). *Type of Family, All Races by Median and Mean Income* (Table F-7). Retrieved from www.census.gov/hhes/www/income/data/historical/families.

Urahn, S. K., Currier, E., Elliott, D., Wechsler, L., Wilson, D., and Colbert, D. (2012). Pursuing the American Dream: Economic mobility across generations. Retrieved from http://health-equity.pitt.edu/3942/.

Wolff, E. N. (1995). *Top heavy: A study of the increasing inequality of wealth in America*. New York: Twentieth Century Fund Press.

Worth, T. N. (1964). Survey of Financial Characteristics of Consumers. *Federal Reserve Bulletin*.

Yitzhaki, S. (1998). More than a dozen alternative ways of spelling Gini. In *The Gini methodology: A primer on a statistical methodology*, ed. S. Yitzhaki and E. Schechtman. New York: Springer, 11–32.

Yitzhaki, S. and Schechtman, E. (2012). *The Gini methodology: A primer on a statistical methodology*. New York: Springer.

2

A PRIMER ON HOUSEHOLD WEALTH

Distinguishing income and wealth

Most of us recognize the importance of wealth and income in improving a family's circumstances and expanding its opportunities. Fewer of us grasp the nuanced differences that distinguish these related concepts. Most discussions treat the two as interchangeable. Even among those who recognize their differences, the attention has usually focused on income at the expense of wealth. Yet, as Lisa Keister argues in *Getting Rich*:

> wealth may be an even more important indicator of well being because it provides both direct financial benefits and other advantages. The family home, for example, provides shelter and other current services to the owner. At the same time, home ownership can be one of the most beneficial investments a family can make.
>
> *(Keister, 2005, p. 6)*

Wealth provides a more enduring and multifaceted source of well-being than does income. As such, untangling and deciphering these two concepts is a necessary starting point for grasping the dynamics of wealth privilege.

Wealth and income are related concepts much like the chicken and the egg. Like the hen, most forms of wealth produce offspring or income. Savings accounts generate interest, residential and commercial real estate yields monthly rents, and business assets can produce profit income. Even wealth in the form of education and specialized training, what economists call *human capital*, generates added salary income. Just like the egg in a specially prepared omelet, consuming the generated income can bring much pleasure. Yet, if not devoured by current consumption, the egg can develop into another egg-laying hen. Similarly, any portion of my income I don't consume, called savings, can augment my wealth. I can deposit the savings into a bank account, purchase real property, pay for more education, or invest in a business venture. As my wealth expands, my income will normally rise as a result. Most forms of wealth generate income while any savings from this income can create more wealth. Together, they form a self-reinforcing feedback loop, or what we might call a virtuous cycle.

More technically, wealth represents a *stock* of goods that hold their value over time, while income is a *flow* of resources that, ideally, is regular and reliable. This stock-flow distinction is significant for several reasons. As a flow, income is well suited to meet our daily needs for food, clothing, and the other essentials of our lives. Because these needs are relentless, it is important that our income be regular and reliable as well. If these income flows occur in a dependable and recurring fashion, they can support a comparable stream of needs without concern. Unfortunately, many income flows are unreliable. Unemployment can occur without warning, rental properties go vacant, and businesses suffer unexpected losses and declines. Most forms of income are vulnerable to sudden, and sometimes wholesale, declines.

In contrast, wealth offers a more reliable and durable source of value. Even as my rental property lies vacant and yields no rent, it keeps its value as long as it retains its capacity to earn future rent. My business may not make its quarterly profit, but its value remains unaffected if it keeps its potential for future earnings. Of course, wealth can suffer sudden and immediate loss. Homes can burn down and banks can close without warning. However, different forms of insurance are readily available to limit these risks. Thanks to its increased durability, wealth has distinct advantages over income as a source of value.

Wealth serves as our primary financial cushion against unforeseen income losses. For those with no wealth to fall back on, even the simplest disruptions can escalate into overwhelming challenges. Lost days at work due to the weather or other disruptions can limit take-home pay. Bills go unpaid and collection costs rise. Delinquent rent payments may trigger an eviction that will create additional expenses and headaches. As McKernan et al. (2009) demonstrate, even modest amounts of wealth enable families to limit food insecurity and bill delinquency as they spend down their assets in response to life's misfortunes. Having wealth as a cushion can insulate households from small problems worsening into much larger ones. Serving as a buffer, even small amounts of wealth can offer households an important source of financial security. As households accumulate increased wealth, they gain greater protection against ever larger disruptions. Beyond having increased reserves to draw upon in times of crisis, they can take self-protective steps such as buying insurance to limit risk. Wealth offers households the resiliency to absorb and recover from the volatility of income flows. Much more than income, wealth provides financial security.

Wealth's durability does more than simply protect us from unforeseen disruptions. As life expectancies have increased, we must consider what happens when advancing age makes it increasingly difficult to work. While social security payments certainly help seniors offset the loss of employment income, rarely do these benefits provide a comfortable income. To overcome this gap between needs and means, households accumulate wealth because it holds its value. Gathering a financial nest egg can limit the fear of outliving one's resources and losing financial independence. As such, wealth offers another layer of financial security even as it funds a comfortable retirement.

Wealth provides more than simply financial benefits. Owning a car can expand one's employment opportunities. Buying a home can offer families both comfort and stability even as it serves as a family's most important investment. Wealth can finance needed education or training that can open career and occupational doors or it can serve as start-up capital to a new business venture. Wealth can advance one's political or social interests either in the form of political donations or charitable giving. Quite simply, wealth expands the choices, opportunities, and agency of its holder, causing it to be a concrete source of power. Alternatively, as Raymond Franklin provocatively argues: "Ownership carries with it domination; its absence leads to subordination" (1991, p. xviii).

Wealth's durability offers its holder some measure of immortality. Though I cannot directly bequeath my income, my education, or my occupational status to my children, I can transfer my wealth largely unimpeded. The options are many. As they are growing up, I can finance numerous activities and experiences that will nurture their talents and develop their skills. By purchasing a house in those neighborhoods that offer the strongest public schools, I can give them a head start. Alternatively, I can send them to the best private schools. Either way, they will gain substantial advantages as they look toward college. I can help them here as well. By underwriting their college education, I can expand their choice of schools and offer them the legacy of a college degree without debt. Further, I can pass my wealth along to a third generation as I help my kids buy a home in pricier neigh-borhoods with good schools. Labeled "transformative assets" by Thomas Shapiro (2004), these gifts have the capacity to expand the opportunities of their recipients. Finally, I can transfer my remaining wealth directly through in vivo gifts or wait until my death. Either way, my wealth can long outlive me as it potentially touches generation after generation. In this way, "wealth has the particular attribute of tending to reproduce itself in a multiplicative fashion from generation to genera-tion" (Conley, 1999, p. 25). In sum, living out the American Dream is much more about the acquisition of wealth than the attainment of income.

Wealth's capacity to hold its value over time produces one additional con-sequence worth noting. Its distribution across society resists dramatic shifts. While the distribution of income can fluctuate significantly in response to shifting circum-stances, the distribution of wealth is resistant to change. Recent shifts in social norms, public policies, and employment practices that have expanded opportunities for women and persons of color have generated improvements in educational attainment, professional status, and earnings among these groups. These same changes have affected the wealth gap only modestly. Wealth's durability means that any attempt to use public policies to alter the distribution of wealth will require sustained and concerted effort.

Composition of household wealth

Household wealth, or more properly household net worth, is simply the sum of all household assets minus all household debt.[1] A basic understanding of the major types of assets and debt is needed to grasp the dynamics of wealth accumulation. Not all assets generate value in the same fashion nor do different forms of credit carry the same cost. Starting on the asset side of the ledger, household assets fall into two categories, non-financial and financial assets. Non-financial or real assets, like cars, real estate, and business properties, are real objects that have value in themselves. They generate desired benefits or income, from which they derive their value. In contrast, financial assets like stock or bond certificates have little intrinsic worth. They gain their appeal through their contractual claims to future income.

Real assets

Vehicle assets

Following the format used by the SCF, real assets fall into five broad categories: vehicles, primary residences, other real estate, business assets, and an "all other" category. Cars and trucks comprise the bulk of the vehicles category, though it also includes planes, boats, and recreational vehicles. As physical assets subject to wear and tear, these vehicles generally lose their value over time, unlike many other assets.[2] New cars drop in value as they leave the showroom and continue to depreciate as they age. Only the few that achieve vintage status may reverse this decline as their continued operation defies their mounting age. While some purchase vehicles for their recreational value, the vast majority are bought to serve very functional needs. Buying a car or truck represents a major, and often first, investment for many households. Car ownership expands employment opportunities and reduces absenteeism caused by unreliable or inflexible public transportation. It comes as no surprise that vehicle ownership is more widespread than nearly all other forms of household assets.

Homes

While having a car is a virtual necessity, owning your own home is central to living out the American Dream. Whether a farm or ranch, townhouse or urban condominium, single detached structure or mobile home, homeownership represents an essential step in the pursuit of wealth. Like cars, these physical structures deteriorate; yet, their durability and longer life expectancy permits appreciation, if given the needed care and maintenance (U.S. Census Bureau, 2012).[3] This capacity to appreciate makes home ownership the single most important investment and source of retirement security for most households (Cho and Francis, 2011).[4] In addition to homeowner vigilance and maintenance, external circumstances influence the rate of appreciation. Similar houses in different neighborhoods appreciate at different rates depending on their proximity to specific amenities like parks or public transportation, their assignment to certain local schools, and even their demographic makeup. The selection of which house to buy can affect the homeowner's net worth.

This point deserves further illustration. Figure 2.1 tracks the value of a given house under different appreciation rates. It assumes a modest $100,000 home and compares the future value of that home if it annually appreciates at 2, 4, or 6 percent. The figure demonstrates the power of compound growth that many assets exhibit. In the early years, the absolute increases in home prices are modest, regardless of the rate. Over time, this changes, even dramatically. The 6 percent curve illustrates this clearly as it shows that patient ownership can pay generous dividends. Further, the differences in appreciation rates only become apparent with time. In the early years, the different rates produce only modest variations in house value. Over time, the differences become significant. After 40 years of homeownership, these modest differences in appreciation can produce house values that range from $200,000 to over $1 million, making a substantial impact on any household's fortunes. Lastly, Figure 2.1 illustrates the importance of acquiring assets at a young age.[5] Buying a home at age 25 can generate far greater rewards than waiting until age 35 or 45 as one can benefit more fully from the fruits of asset appreciation.

Of course, households rarely own a given home for more than 25 or 30 years. Americans are constantly on the move as we relocate to new towns and shift between larger and smaller homes. One estimate concluded that homeowners typically stayed at a given residence for about 12 years over the period 1985–2007 (Emrath, 2009). Our public policy accommodates our restlessness. Any asset, including homes, that rises in value creates a *capital gain* as measured by the increase itself. As long as you own the asset, the capital gain remains unrealized. Upon the sale of the asset, any capital gain is now realized and treated as income, subject to taxation. However, our tax policy has taken an unflinching stance toward capital gains realized from the sale of one's home. Homeowners under age 55 can protect any realized gain from taxation as long as they reinvest the earnings into a new home.[6] Even though we may not own the same home for 40 years, this exclusion allows restless homeowners to benefit fully from the reward of rising home values.

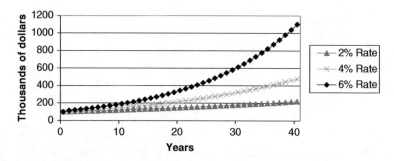

FIGURE 2.1 Home values under different appreciation rates
Source: Author's calculations

As many of us realized after 2007, housing prices do not rise every year, much less at some uniform rate. Instead, home prices have taken a roller coaster-like trajectory over the past decade. Many homeowners experienced several years of double-digit appreciation rates. With the housing collapse, many more watched their home values fall by 50 percent or more. This recent volatility aside, home-ownership has generally been an effective source of wealth creation. Housing prices have generally risen since the inception of the S&P/Case-Shiller Home Price Index in 1987. From 1987 to 2011, the 10-city composite index averaged 3.8 percent annual increases using a constant quality methodology (Federal Reserve Bank of St. Louis, 2016). In contrast, inflation averaged only 2.4 percent over the same period. Though home values have outpaced inflation, their trend is usually subject to cyclical fluctuations, though rarely on the scale witnessed recently. In addition, local circumstances influence housing prices causing some cities to experience much greater appreciation (Portland, OR) than others (Detroit, MI). Yet, for those who have held their home for an extended period, homeownership has served as an important source of new wealth in the manner suggested by Figure 2.1.

One last element of home buying deserves an explanation. Normally, home-buyers pay 10–20 percent down in cash and borrow the rest of the purchase price. This practice fosters homeownership since homebuyers need not wait years until they have fully saved the purchase price. Instead, they capture any appreciation while they are paying down the mortgage. This strategic use of debt is called *debt leverage* because it enables a homebuyer to capture all of the capital gain created by an asset whose value is many times larger than the modest down payment. It represents an essential tool used by households in accumulating wealth and a primary benefit of having access to credit.

At the same time, the size of the down payment along with accompanying closing costs creates a hurdle for many would-be homeowners. Frequently, the rent paid by tenants is comparable to the monthly payments on a house. Consequently, many renters have the income to become homeowners; they simply lack the means, or wealth, to produce a down payment. Unable to overcome this hurdle, many families are unable to access this important source of financial security and family well-being. Consequently, homeownership serves as an obvious example of how it takes money to make money.

Other real estate

Beyond their principal residence, households can own other properties, including vacation homes, timeshares, rental housing, and commercial buildings. Similar to homes, these properties generally appreciate if given care and maintenance. Different factors influence their likely rate of appreciation; for example, vacation homes and timeshares reflect the unique circumstances of their location. More generally, rising population, expanding wealth, and higher construction costs cause most properties to appreciate over time, just like principal residences. The value of rental properties reflects the future rents they might earn. Since cycles in business activity affect commercial vacancies more than residential, commercial properties experience greater price fluctuations. Comparing the Moody's/Real Capital Analytics' Commercial Property Price Index with the already mentioned S&P/Case Shiller Residential Price Index over the past decade, commercial properties nearly doubled in value during the bubble years similar to residential properties. Yet with the onset of the Great Recession, commercial prices fell even further than residential values, returning to levels found a decade earlier. Since 2010, commercial values have rebounded much more robustly as well (Real Capital Analytics, 2015).

Rental properties reward their owners beyond simple appreciation. Property owners can earn rental income that frequently exceeds all of their expenses. This opportunity to earn net income offers an immediate benefit even as they wait for more long-term appreciation. Leveraging with debt, they can earn substantial returns on rather modest down payments causing debt to act like steroids in pumping up their rates of return. As owners use the rental income to pay down their mortgage, they increase their stake in the property. As such, rental property offers three sources of increased wealth: a flow of net income from their rents, an increasing stake in the ownership of the asset as they pay down the debt, and full claims to any appreciation in the value of the property realized at the point of sale. Property ownership entails risks, but the rewards can be gratifying.

Business assets

For many Americans, running their own business captures their specific vision of the American Dream. Yet, few households actually realize what this means for accumulating wealth. Business ownership can include a sole proprietorship, partnership, subchapter S corporation, or some other corporate form. These businesses serve a wide range of markets, engage in varied industries, and differ in size and complexity. Nonetheless, they all aspire to generate net profit for their owners. Most businesses fail to meet this standard reliably, or even ever. Not many survive long. The few that generate net profit can experience volatile earnings that reflect shifting conditions largely beyond their control. Though these challenges make business ventures quite risky, the potential rewards are large. Likely, most of the residents on the upper floors of our skyscraper gained their entrance through this avenue.

The value of any business reflects its expected flow of future profit. Shifting conditions can elevate a business's expected net earnings thereby substantially inflating its worth, often overnight. Circumstances that double or triple earnings will proportionately increase the business's value. As predictions inevitably have a subjective element, business values can skyrocket beyond the increase in earnings. Business owners generally use debt to leverage even greater returns. By attracting outside investors willing to lend them money, they can finance expansions that will swell their revenues and stock values. In this way, business ownership can generate meteoric rises in net worth that offer their owners an express lane to substantial wealth. The recent experience of Facebook and its impact on the fortunes of Mark Zuckerberg and other principal owners is but one example.

Although the potential rewards to owning one's business are high, so are the risks. Shifting circumstances raise and lower the value of business assets, often without warning. External conditions can revalue a business's assets to zero, even as their physical conditions remain unharmed. For many small business owners, the clear separation between one's personal assets and business assets does not exist. Those whose ventures fail can lose their home as business creditors demand compensation from the owner's personal assets. While a corporate business structure prevents such exposure, business owners can still lose their entire stake in the business.

Although the risks are high, the opportunities for profit are equally expansive, particularly in an economy buffeted by technological, global, and policy shifts. Frequently, these forces create what economists call *monopoly rents*. These rents offer businesses the opportunity to extract unusual levels of net income; sometimes these opportunities are temporary, while others are more enduring. For a time, Microsoft gained a virtual monopoly over the operating systems of desktop computers, even as many argued that Apple provided a superior product. I might still prefer Microsoft's product since having the same system as my neighbor meant I could go to them for help and advice. Other firms benefited from early entry into China as they shifted manufacturing toward a vastly cheaper labor force while keeping their product prices high. Still other firms benefited from public policies that limited competition ranging from defense procurement to the use of the public airways; each offered the beneficiary extraordinary terms. In most of these cases, professional contacts and social networks influenced which business happened to be "in the right place at the right time."

Other real assets

The last remaining category of real assets is a catchall group called miscellaneous non-financial assets. These include cash, gold, jewelry, and furs as well as a multitude of collectibles including art, (rare) books, coins, fine furniture, and antique cars, to name but a few. Although many owners collect these items for their enjoyment, they can serve as investments as well. Each is subject to appreciation as advancing time both ages these assets and makes them scarcer. They are equally vulnerable to price declines as fashions and tastes shift. Despite the breadth of this category, these assets represent a small and relatively unimportant facet in the accumulation of wealth.

Financial assets

Unlike real assets, financial assets have little intrinsic value other than the contractual claim that the specific asset holds. Bank statements offer no value other than documenting your claim to cash withdrawals equal to the balance. Stock certificates that demonstrate ownership in a company have no inherent value other than their legal declaration. Nonetheless, financial assets offer households varied opportunities to store and increase their wealth. Their capacity to increase in value reflects the level of risk and liquidity they carry. Assets susceptible to volatile fluctuations in value yield higher returns as a necessary lure to attract investors. Asset liquidity refers to the ease with which one may exchange the asset into cash. While I can immediately withdraw my money from my checking account, I will pay a penalty to withdraw funds from my certificate of deposit (CD). Lowered liquidity subjects the asset holder to more risk since unexpected emergencies may require instant cash.

Liquid accounts and CDs

Checking, savings, money market, and call accounts offer households the greatest liquidity other than cash itself. With some exceptions, these accounts offer depositors interest income based on their fund balance. The offered interest is modest since depositors can withdraw their funds with negligible delay or cost. Further, federal deposit guarantees secure most of these fund balances limiting the risk of loss. These accounts offer safety and convenience more than avenues for wealth accumulation. More importantly, they provide an effective cushion against adverse events. When unexpected bills or unemployment spells wreck a family's budget, funds deposited in these accounts can protect them from dire consequences.

CDs give households higher interest rates without requiring much added risk. They do so by limiting how quickly you can withdraw your funds. CDs carry a minimum waiting period in which the funds must remain untouched; those with longer maturity periods offer higher interest rates. Early withdrawals incur a significant penalty. As these accounts are federally insured, they remain reasonably secure investments.

Bonds and bond funds

Households interested in earning more from their assets can purchase U.S. savings bonds, other government bonds, or corporate bonds. Somewhat like CDs, these bonds pay their holder a specific amount on a given date. Investors can purchase these bonds at a lower price today, knowing what amount the bond will pay on its maturity date. The difference between the purchase price and its value at maturity determines the bond yield, or rate of return. As no government agency insures payment of these bonds, they carry a higher risk of default or non-payment. Bonds judged to have a higher default risk will require a higher yield or interest rate to attract investors; for this reason, bonds with a more distant maturity date generally will offer higher yields as well. Bondholders can retain their investment until its maturity date for a certain return or sell the bond to another investor at a price that reflects current conditions. In addition, investors can purchase individual shares in bond funds that buy a variety of bonds rather than simply acquire specific ones. As these funds increase in value, these increases are passed on to the investors minus some fee for operating expenses.

Stocks and stock funds

Even bonds may not generate sufficient returns to satisfy some households; in their search for increased earnings, these households may buy stocks or equity shares. Stock shares offer their owner a claim on business profit, often in the form of declared dividends. As the profit expectations of the business rise and fall, so does the share price. This price volatility is one reason that stocks carry more risk. Even worse, companies that experience financial default will see their stocks become worthless.[7] Although bondholders can suffer a similar fate, they are less vulnerable as they have a prior claim over any remaining corporate assets. To lure investors to ignore these risks, stocks yield returns that are more generous. Over its 60-year life, the S&P 500 stock index has generated average annual returns of 7.4 percent. Over the same period, inflation has averaged 3.4 percent annually, meaning that stocks have yielded a healthy 4 percent return above inflation. Within this long-term average, individual stocks as well as the broader index have experienced extended periods of decline as well as growth. As with bonds, households wary of picking individual stocks can buy shares of funds that invest in a broad range of stocks and pass along their earnings.

Whole life insurance

Life insurance policies offer households protection against unexpected loss as well as another means to increase their wealth. These policies come in varied forms. Term-life insurance policies simply compensate the beneficiary upon the death of the insured. These policies require regular payments and offer no cash until the insured dies; they merely safeguard the future without offering any liquidity. In contrast, whole-life insurance policies provide liquidity. Making regular payments to the insurer swells the cash balance the policy will pay upon death of the insured. The cash balance reflects not only past payments, but also any earnings on the accumulated funds. Many whole-life policies offer a cash-out policy, in which the insured can withdraw funds prior to death. Usually, this option triggers some penalty. As a rule, life-insurance policies are more effective in providing financial security in the event of the death or disability of a primary wage earner; nonetheless, they offer further, if modest, opportunities to increase one's wealth.

Managed accounts

Managed trust accounts and annuities refer to two specially tailored assets. Managed trust accounts are simply financial accounts created to benefit a designated individual, often with specific provisions on how and when the money can be used. Affluent parents use these accounts to offer targeted assistance to their children or grandchildren. If carefully designed, these trusts can limit any tax liability from estate and gift taxes. Annuities are accounts that make regular payments, often monthly, to a designated beneficiary. Just like the trust accounts, the fund balances of these annuities earn income. Although they can appreciate, these fund balances usually decline over time depending on the pace and size of the withdrawals. They are designed not so much to increase one's wealth, but rather to limit tax liabilities and provide a reliable source of income to a chosen beneficiary.

Retirement accounts

Retirement accounts, including various pensions as well as individual retirement (IRA) and Keogh accounts, offer households longer-term investment vehicles. Funds deposited into these accounts are invested in a variety of areas, including bonds, stocks, and real estate, making them subject to the same risks and rewards already described. What distinguishes these accounts is their preferential treatment under the U.S. tax code. Depending on the account type, deposits may be tax deductible, thereby exempting them from current income taxes. Fund earnings are similarly exempt from taxation until the funds are withdrawn. As many households will experience a lower tax bracket in retirement, the delay in tax liability offers a secondary benefit. For other approved retirement funds like the Roth IRA, fund deposits are not tax exempt. However, all fund earnings are sheltered from income taxes, even when withdrawn. For those households with high-income tax brackets, this exemption can offer substantial savings. To enjoy such preferential treatment, these funds must remain untouched as early withdrawal triggers a sizeable penalty.

Miscellaneous financial assets

The last group of financial assets is the catchall category of assets that includes loans to individuals, royalties, income from oil, gas, and mineral leases, any deferred compensation, and future proceeds from lawsuits. Taken together, this collection of assets accounts for a small part of the household net worth and in most cases simply provides an income stream.

It is instructive to examine the relative importance of each type of asset as illustrated in Table 2.1. In 2007, about two thirds of all household assets were real or non-financial assets with the balance comprised of financial assets.[8] Among individual categories, only primary residences, other real estate, business, and retirement assets constituted more than 10 percent of the total. Together, these four categories accounted for over three quarters of all household assets. When we examine the dispersion of these assets across households, we find a different picture. Virtually all households possess some form of both financial and real assets. Yet, a majority of U.S. households held assets in only the following categories: bank accounts and CDs, vehicles, homes, and retirement accounts. Of these four, liquid bank accounts and vehicles offer households extremely limited opportunities for wealth appreciation. For the bulk of American households, homes and retirement funds represent the primary source of wealth appreciation and retirement security. Relatively few households hold any of the remaining assets that offer substantial opportunity for wealth accumulation.

TABLE 2.1 Household asset categories by percentage, 2007

Asset category	Percentage of assets	Percentage of households
Real assets	66	92
Vehicle assets	3	87
Homes	32	69
Other real estate	11	19
Business assets	20	14
Other real assets	1	7
Financial assets	34	94
Liquid and CDs	5	92
Bonds and bond funds	3	19
Stocks and stock funds	10	24
Whole-life insurance	1	23
Retirement accounts	12	53
Managed accounts	2	6
Miscellaneous accounts	1	10

Source: SCF, 2007

Household debt

Any measure of wealth or net worth also includes debt. Since debt reduces net worth, we often view it negatively and try to avoid it. As we have seen, however, debt serves as a strategic tool in the purchase of new assets as households accumulate wealth. Debt leverage enables households to purchase assets beyond their current means and capture any resulting income stream or asset appreciation. As households pay down their outstanding debt, they can use their rising equity stake as collateral for new debt that permits additional asset purchases, income streams, and asset appreciation. In this way, debt leverage functions like steroids in the wealth-accumulation process. Further, preferential tax policies offer additional encouragement for debt leveraging.

Like any tool, debt leverage is subject to abuse and misuse. Despite earning substantial incomes, some households find it difficult to live within their means. To finance their current lifestyles, they employ increasing debt to make ends meet. Rising debt leads to increased interest charges that further strains household finances. Even when used more prudently, debt leverage offers added risks for households. Households routinely use credit to purchase a home or car. Since neither of these purchases yields income, households repay these debts using some other dedicated income stream, usually their employment income. This makes them more vulnerable to unemployment spells. The loss of income may require them to sell either the car or home at a steep discount. Using debt to purchase income-generating property also yields higher risks. Unexpected tenant vacancies can generate losses, and even foreclosure, if the owner is unable to meet debt payments.

Lastly, some households assume debt as they have few, if any, options. For households without a financial cushion, unemployment and even reduced hours may require greater dependence on debt to make ends meet. Injury, death, or divorce may trigger income losses that require increased debt to meet essential payments. Unexpected medical costs can force some households to desperate levels of debt. Natural catastrophes can devastate households with limited insurance coverage. In many of these cases, increased debt may offer households their only option.

Household debt largely falls into one of two categories: secured and unsecured debt. Secured debt is linked to a specific asset that is subject to repossession in the event of a default; two obvious examples are home mortgages and home-equity loans. The value of the secured property limits how much the lender will loan. As a protection, the lender will restrict the loan amount to some percentage beneath the appraised value of the property. This gives lenders greater security in retrieving their funds if the loan defaults and they must sell the property. Unsecured debt includes loans not specifically tied to any assets; instead, the loan is linked more ambiguously to the household's credit worthiness and financial means. Since unsecured loans offer the lender less security in the face of borrower default, these loans carry higher interest rates to offset the higher risk.

Secured debt

Three types of assets usually back secured debt: residential real estate, vehicle assets, or other assets. Debt secured by residential real estate retains a favored position within the tax code, since mortgage interest remains tax deductible while other forms of household debt lost this advantage in 1986. This tax benefit effectively reduces the after-tax costs of this debt for most property owners anywhere from 10 to 40 percent depending on one's taxable income and state income tax provisions. For high-income households, these generous tax provisions make this form of debt leveraging very attractive. Although car loans lost their privileged position in the tax code, their secured status means they carry lower interest rates than unsecured loans. Similarly, loans secured by other real estate, life-insurance balances, pension assets, and stock shares carry lower interest rates than other forms of credit.

Unsecured debt

Unsecured debt includes education loans, installment loans, credit card balances, and other unsecured lines of credit. While these sources of debt are more widely available to all households, they do come at a price, namely higher interest rates. Since they are unconnected to any particular asset, they are more vulnerable to abuse as there is no obvious limit to what the borrower can handle. For example, generous credit card limits may lead to borrowers running up credit balances that far exceed their capacity to repay.

As depicted in Table 2.2, over three quarters of U.S. households hold some form of debt. For the reasons previously explained, mortgage debt serves as the most

TABLE 2.2 Debt holding by category, 2007

Types of household debt	Percentage of debt	Percentage of households
All	100	77
Mortgage	75	49
Other residential	10	6
Vehicle	5	35
Educational	3	15
Other installment	2	10
Credit card balances	3	46
Other	1	7

Source: SCF, 2007

popular form of debt and accounts for the lion's share of household debt. Of course, it is only available to those households capable of owning a home. Debt on second homes and rental housing as well as on vehicles adds another 15 percent of the total debt. Secured debt constitutes fully 90 percent of all household debt. In terms of popularity, only credit card debt and vehicle debt rival mortgage debt as the source of credit chosen by households.

Other sources of wealth

Human capital

The real and financial forms of wealth just described constitute the bulk of household wealth; however, other sources of wealth require mentioning. The most important among these is what economists call "human capital." Human capital results from a wide variety of household expenditure that enables beneficiaries to command higher salaries as they offer employers increased productivity and value. Foremost among these expenditures is a college education. Extensive evidence demonstrates how college graduates earn substantially higher salaries, suffer fewer and shorter spells of unemployment, receive more expansive health insurance, and collect increased pension benefits. Specialized training in highly sought-after technical fields offers a source of additional worth. Even on-the-job experience produces value as veteran employees gain organizational knowledge and skills to work effectively with others. Like real assets, many forms of human capital are subject to depreciation if the skills remain unused or become obsolete.

Investment in human capital requires up-front expenditure that some households cannot afford. A college education is perhaps the most lucrative investment that a person can make. Yet, the rising cost of a college education place it out of reach of many otherwise qualified students and their families. In 2007, the average net price for tuition, fees, room and board for public universities exceeded $10,000 per year, making a four-year college education a $40,000 investment (College Board, 2012,

p. 19). Though college loans are available, research shows that student debt substantially reduces the financial rewards of college (Elliott and Nam, 2013). While other human-capital expenditures rarely match this price tag, their intangible nature makes it unlikely that households can obtain secured credit to finance their investment. Few lenders will offer their best rates to households seeking help as they invest in specialized training or move across the country to locations that are more lucrative. Households have few options other than self-financing to make these investments.

Social capital

Social capital serves as another form of wealth; it refers to the value or benefits that result from social networks. The truism "it is not what you know, but who you know" captures the essence of social capital. Our social networks offer each of us role models who provide guidance on how we might live our lives. Whether these role models are viewed affirmatively or disdainfully by society, they provide a context for who we might realistically become. Further, our social networks frame our opportunities. As McNamee and Miller (2004) explain in *The Meritocracy Myth*, an extensive literature demonstrates the role of social capital in raising both educational attainment and financial success. Parental encouragement promotes academic aspiration among adolescents, reduces dropout rates, and extends educational attainment. Beyond college, social capital "affects employment opportunities, mobility through occupational ladders, promotions, earnings, and entrepreneurial success" (McNamee and Miller, 2004, p. 73). Parents can share their social network with their children as they make their way in the world, but cannot fully bequeath it after death. Though important, this form of wealth defies easy measurement.

Cultural capital

Lastly, cultural capital represents the knowledge, skills, values, and experiences that enable individuals to function successfully within specific groups. According to Marcia Millman (1991) in her book *Warm Hearts and Cold Cash*, cultural capital has been the primary legacy that most parents share with their children, since the vast majority has no financial wealth to give. Yet, as McNamee and Miller (2004) argue, transmitting cultural capital from one person to another requires a considerable investment of time and effort. Knowing how to dress, act, and talk during a business lunch or outings at the country club is information not widely dispersed nor easily taught. Affluent parents can offer their children the necessary life experiences that prepare them for these settings. Having this knowledge enables one to function effectively in higher-status situations, thereby opening doors and opportunities. Even more than social capital, measuring this form of wealth raises substantial challenges. Along with the other forms of capital, cultural capital offers significant ways by which households can expand their net worth and share their good fortune with their children.

Wealth, opportunity, and power

Whatever form it takes, possessing wealth expands opportunities. Earning a college diploma opens various occupational and professional doors. Access to a wide and resourceful social network increases prospects. Knowing how to act in rarefied social situations brings acceptance and credibility. Yet as McKernan and her colleagues aptly remind us: "Wealth is not just for the wealthy" (2009, p. 1). Even a modest financial cushion offers households the opportunity to make better choices—such as buying in bulk or purchasing the best-value appliance or car rather than the cheapest brand. It offers the means by which families can get ahead and extricate themselves from poverty. During times of natural calamity or financial distress, ample savings help households weather these periods and avoid damaging consequences like foreclosure or eviction. By providing some measure of financial security, wealth offers households the prospect for better health as they experience less stress and anxiety. Even modest reserves help allay the haunting worries over how they will pay their looming expenses or next unexpected emergency. Freed from such worry, households can consider their future more fully.

Wealth offers households the means to expand future opportunities as well. There are few investments, certainly none as widely available, which offer the same rate of return as a college education. Yet, many qualified students do not apply for lack of funds even as they recognize the future opportunities lost. Most other forms of wealth appreciate over time providing their holders with increased opportunities in the future. Yet, this expansion can function on multiple levels. Buying a home in an exclusive neighborhood can serve as a smart investment. At the same time, moving into this affluent neighborhood can enlarge one's social network and open new possibilities. This purchase can provide one's children with the experiences needed to move comfortably in high-status situations. Lastly, it can provide admission to the best public schools available locally. As the different forms of wealth expand synergistically, so follows an expansion of opportunity.

The wealthy have greater opportunities to express their social values and political views. Through philanthropy, wealthy households can fund organizations that promote values and services that reflect their interests. Larger donors may receive local, regional, and even national recognition of their generosity and specific interests. Through political contributions, the affluent can get access to candidates and elected officials. In the post- *Citizens United* v. *FEC* era,[9] they also can finance without limit advertising campaigns that promote their personal views. They can fund political action committees that support candidates favorable to their economic and political interests. Through either charitable or political funding, the wealthy can promote their specific interests and influence the cultural, social, and political sphere.

Lastly, the different forms of wealth offer myriad ways that parents can increase the opportunities of their children. They can share the full resources of their social network with their kids. Affluent parents can expose their children to varied enrichment experiences that will prepare them for future professional and social expectations. By purchasing a home within the district boundaries of academically superior public schools, parents can offer their children an educational advantage. Affluent parents have the means to pay for tutors or other services that might address their children's educational needs. By underwriting the cost of college, parents can widen their children's options as they consider private as well as public universities. Financial support can leave their kids college educated and debt free. They can help with a down payment on a starter home as well as serve as a safety net during challenging periods. These represent but a small number of ways that wealthy parents can augment their children's opportunities. In most of these cases, the beneficiaries of this support may not view this help as an inheritance, but simply part of their family experience.

All of this discussion about expanding opportunities simply suggests how wealth provides power. Achieving financial security and insulating oneself from life's uncertainties certainly is one form of power. Having access to a wider range of prospects along with the means to act on these opportunities conveys the very meaning of power. Indeed, the capacity of wealth to expand power appears to have no limits.

Conclusion

Much more than income, wealth serves as the primary means by which American households can attain some measure of the American Dream. The acquisition of wealth offers households a financial cushion to absorb unexpected reversals and fund a comfortable retirement. It provides them with the means to assist, and even assure, the financial prospects of their own children. The possession of wealth expands the range of choices, whether households are considering different career options or home purchases. The durability of wealth, even across generations, makes it a reliable source of power. Furthermore, the capacity of different forms of wealth to appreciate makes it a particularly appealing source of power; its potential to enhance opportunities appears to have no limit. No wonder there exists such strong motivation for its accumulation long after any real concerns of financial insecurity vanish.

This basic understanding of the different forms of household wealth anticipates the arguments and insights of the Wealth Privilege model. Simply explaining the different types of household wealth as well as strategies like debt leverage makes it clear how wealth begets more wealth under favoring conditions. In the next chapter, I discuss how the pathways to wealth accumulation create tailwinds for the affluent and headwinds for those lagging behind. The discussion of these forms of wealth also raises substantial concerns regarding the two inequalities. Given the varied forms that wealth may take, it is clear that households benefiting from the inequality of outcomes have the means to produce a comparable inequality of opportunity for subsequent generations. Not only can affluent households leave their estate to their children, they can offer them substantial advantages in cultural, social, and human capital. Their desire and power to make their portion of the American Dream a reality can undermine a key facet of what makes this dream uniquely American.

Notes

1 For stylistic reasons, I tend to use the terms "wealth" and "net worth" interchangeably although some may question whether wealth can be negative. Net worth certainly can be negative.
2 Other household assets like furniture, appliances, and clothes suffer a similar fate of declining value. However, the SCF ignores these assets due to the difficulties in measuring their value as well as their limited liquidity.
3 According to the U.S. Census of Housing, the real median price of single-family homes has appreciated every decade from 1940 to 2000. Not all of this increase is simply appreciation; some is attributable to increased home size and greater amenities.
4 Because building construction is so labor intensive and somewhat unresponsive to productivity-enhancing technology, prices of new construction tend to rise even faster than inflation. The rising price of new homes, a key rival to existing homes, allows the appreciation of existing homes.
5 I make this point much more graphically in Figure 3.1.
6 For those older than 55, the tax treatment becomes even more generous as they are exempt from paying taxes on any realized gains from their home, up to $1 million.
7 Owners of once mighty General Motors stock experienced this shock in 2009 in the midst of the Great Recession.
8 I use evidence from 2007 for a reason. Recall from Chapter 1 that it represented a peak year for wealth and wealth ownership.
9 In 2010, the U.S. Supreme Court ruled (5–4) that freedom of speech rights trumped the government's restrictions on independent political expenditures, largely eliminating any limits on political contributions.

Bibliography

Cho, S. W. S. and Francis, J. L. (2011). Tax treatment of owner occupied housing and wealth inequality. *Journal of Macroeconomics* 33 (1): 42–60.

College Board (2012). *Trends in college pricing, 2012*. Retrieved from http://trend.scollegeboard.org/sites/default/files/college-pricing-2012-full-report_0.pdf.

Conley, D. (1999). *Being Black, living in the red: Race, wealth, and social policy in America*. Berkeley: University of California Press.

Elliott, W. and Nam, I. (2013). Is student debt jeopardizing the short-term financial health of US households? *Federal Reserve Bank of St. Louis Review* 95 (September/October).

Emrath, P. (2009). *How long buyers remain in their homes: Economics and housing policy*. Washington, DC: National Association of Home Builders.

Federal Reserve Bank of St. Louis (2016). *S&P/Case-Shiller 10-City Composite Home Price Index*, April 29. Retrieved from https://research.stlouisfed.org/fred2/series/SPCS10RSA.

Franklin, R. S. (1991). *Shadows of race and class*. Minneapolis: University of Minnesota Press.

Keister, L. A. (2005). *Getting rich: America's new rich and how they got that way*. Cambridge: Cambridge University Press.

McKernan, S. M., Ratcliffe, C., and Vinopal, K. (2009). *Do assets help families cope with adverse events?* Washington, DC: Urban Institute.

McNamee, S. J. and Miller, R. K., Jr. (2004). *The meritocracy myth*. New York: Rowman and Littlefield.

Millman, M. (1991). *Warm hearts and cold cash: The intimate dynamics of families and money*. New York: Free Press.

Real Capital Analytics (2015). *Commercial property price indices*. Retrieved from www.rcanalytics.com/Public/rca_cppi.aspx.

Shapiro, T. M. (2004). *The hidden cost of being African American: How wealth perpetuates inequality*. Oxford: Oxford University Press.

Standard and Poor Dow Jones Indices (2016). *S&P/Case-Shiller 20-City Composite Home Price Index*, April 26. Retrieved from www.standardandpoors.com/indices/sp-case-shiller-home-price-indices/en/us/?indexId=spusa-cashpidff-p-us———.

U.S. Census Bureau (2012). *Median home values 1940–2000*, June 6. Retrieved from www.census.gov/hhes/www/housing//historical/values.

3

PATHWAYS TO WEALTH ACCUMULATION

In a field one summer's day a grasshopper was hopping about, chirping, and singing to its heart's content. A group of ants walked by, grunting as they struggled to carry plump kernels of corn.

"Where are you going with those heavy things?" asked the grasshopper.

Without stopping, the first ant replied, "To our ant hill. This is the third kernel I've delivered today."

"Why not come and sing with me," teased the grasshopper, "instead of working so hard?"

"We are helping to store food for the winter," said the ant, "and think you should do the same."

"Winter is far away and it is a glorious day to play," sang the grasshopper.

But the ants went on their way and continued their hard work.

The weather soon turned cold. All the food lying in the field was covered with a thick white blanket of snow that even the grasshopper could not dig through. Soon the grasshopper found itself dying of hunger. He staggered to the ants' hill and saw them handing out corn from the stores they had collected in the summer. He begged them for something to eat.

"What!" cried the ants in surprise, "haven't you stored anything away for the winter? What in the world were you doing all last summer?"

"I didn't have time to store any food," complained the grasshopper; "I was so busy playing music that before I knew it the summer was gone."

The ants shook their heads in disgust, turned their backs on the grasshopper, and went on with their work.[1]

A version of Aesop's Fable

We are all familiar with Aesop's fable of the ant and the grasshopper. That this fable has survived thousands of years bears witness to our need to explain differences in wealth. Clearly, its moral insight still resonates today. Through diligence and self-discipline, the ants are ready for winter. They have worked and saved all summer to create a sufficient stock of food to carry them through the winter. Among economists, our current understanding of wealth accumulation stems largely from this view. Equally familiar is the concluding interaction between the grass-hopper and the ants; the ants hold all of the power. They can decide whether to help the poor grasshopper or not. Even the disgust and self-righteousness that the ants express toward the grasshopper is familiar to us. Many contemporary "haves" convey similar feelings toward the "have nots." As old as this fable is, it still speaks to us today.

A modern theory of wealth accumulation

Today, economists offer the Life Cycle Hypothesis (LCH) to explain household saving and wealth accumulation. Introduced a half century ago (Modigliani and Brumberg, 1954), this hypothesis provides a perfect guide for ant behavior. According to the theory, households save some portion of their income during their employment years (or "summer") in anticipation of their retirement years (or "winter"). The hypothesis assumes that households want to maximize their con-sumption at a level they can maintain throughout their lifetime. To continue this level of spending during retirement, households must save enough during their peak earning years to accumulate a financial nest egg. According to the theory, household wealth should rise as the household head ages and then experience a significant decline during retirement. Indeed, to achieve the goal of maximum constant spending, households ideally would exhaust their wealth just as death occurs. Certainly, differences in family inheritance, in earnings, and in asset appreciation will all affect the magnitude of household wealth, but saving behavior is the key.

Despite its apparent reasonableness, the LCH has resisted clear vindication. In its defense, there is substantial evidence corroborating the link between household age and net worth. Older households nearing retirement age do command greater wealth. However, other evidence (Dynan et al., 2004) suggests that wealthy households in retirement spend their nest egg far less quickly than the theory predicts. Several explanations rescue the model from this anomaly. As the time of death is neither predictable nor encouraged, it makes sense that households would overstate their remaining life expectancy and unduly preserve their wealth. Similarly, uncertainty regarding one's health later in life and the rising cost of health care may also encourage affluent households to hoard their nest egg. Who among us wants to ask our kids for help if we outlive our means? In this case, end-of-life bequests may be unintentional as death occurs sooner than expected. Alternatively, some parents may possess a bequest motive in which they desire leaving some legacy to their kids, even if they have offered help previously (De Nardi, 2004). Any of these motives can explain why households deplete their net worth more slowly than the basic theory suggests.

Two other observations pose greater challenges to the Life Cycle Hypothesis. The theory predicts that, among households of a given age, the distribution of wealth will reflect the distribution of household income; thus, wealth inequality among households should mirror income inequality. Yet, the evidence clearly shows wealth disparities far exceed income differences. Even more damning, rich households accumulate wealth far beyond what their higher income would suggest (Cagetti and De Nardi, 2008). To address these inconsistencies, some wonder whether wealth-poor households save less due to having decreased patience, risk aversion, or desires to leave a bequest (Heer, 2001; Hendricks, 2004). We might call this the "culture of poverty" argument. Others argue that households engage in precautionary saving. Uncertain about their future earnings, households may save more today as a precaution against future reversals (Huggett, 1996). The wealthy are far more likely to start a business venture. In recognition of the risks inherent in this step, they may build up added net worth as a precaution. Yet, less affluent households also face many risks, including increased unemployment. Arguably, these households face greater perils than the wealthy, who can mitigate their risks by diversifying their assets as needed. Even with the precautionary saving motive, the LCH does not offer a convincing explanation for why wealth remains so concentrated in the hands of so few households (Cagetti and De Nardi, 2008). Given the discussion in the last chapter, it is interesting to note that the conventional LCH neglects the possibility that wealth holds any intrinsic value of its own.[2]

Not only does the LCH fail to explain the current disparities in wealth, its portrayal of household behavior seems to fit only some households and their use of certain forms of wealth. Among White, college-educated, and urban households, Wolff (1981) finds evidence corroborating the LCH. Even in this case however, the model explains only a small portion of the differences. The corroborating results disappear when he examines households of color as well as rural and less educated households. In addition, the model poorly explains the behavior of the wealthy. Wolff did find more support for the LCH when he examined differences in "life-cycle wealth" only. This type of wealth includes checking deposits, durable goods, and home equity; it represents wealth that households accumulate for later liquidation. Conversely, the model did not accurately explain differences in "capital wealth," the other forms of wealth largely the province of the wealthy, including stocks and bonds, investment real estate, and business equity. In summary, Wolff suggests the LCH is realistic for some households and some categories of wealth. However, he concludes it poorly explains the circumstances and behaviors of households at both ends of the wealth spectrum. His results suggest that these three groups face very different realities when it comes to wealth accumulation.

Wolff's evidence that the LCH offers an incomplete explanation for wealth accumulation is not particularly surprising. At a minimum, the theory assumes that households anticipate both a "summer" and a "winter" in their lives. What would happen to the ants' strategy if they had no period of prosperity in which to prepare for winter? Or how would the ants behave if their "summer" was unpredictably interrupted by bouts of unemployment or health problems? How could they prepare for winter with such interruptions? Households operating under these conditions may share similar concerns about their retirement years, but not have the opportunity to do much in anticipation.

Conversely, what happens to those who anticipate suffering no winter at all? Unlike most of us, the very wealthy earn much of their income from sources other than direct employment. These sources of income will likely continue even after retirement from work. Further, the very rich can experience incomes that defy dissaving. As an example, Carroll (2000) argues, "recent press accounts have estimated Bill Gates's net worth at $40 billion. Assuming a ten percent annual rate of return, Gates would have to spend $4 billion a year, or over $10 million a day, on non-durable goods and services simply to avoid further accumulation" (pp. 476–7). Spending that much cannot be easy. Although the purchases of fine art, jewelry, and additional vacation homes could easily meet this threshold, these expenditures would count as assets that might add to his wealth over time.

Asking why the rich save as much as they do, Carroll (2000) argues that neither the LCH nor a bequest motive adequately explain their behavior. Instead, he offers a motive he labels the "capitalist spirit." Simply stated, he argues that affluent households pursue wealth for its own sake rather than the extra consumption it might provide. Wealthy households may pursue additional wealth out of simple greed, for reasons of philanthropy, or the pursuit of power and social status. To be sure, Carroll offers only anecdotal evidence to support his contention. However, given the multiple benefits of wealth detailed in the prior chapter, his argument is persuasive. Less affluent households similarly value the financial security and increased independence that wealth brings, in addition to the power it conveys.

Due to its elegant simplicity, the Life Cycle Hypothesis has demonstrated its usefulness in examining a diverse set of economic topics and issues. Yet, even with this important infusion of the "capitalist spirit," the LCH is limited by its singular focus on individual household saving as the source of wealth accumulation. True, such saving must occur for households to increase their wealth; it is a tautological requirement given the definitions of wealth and income. Nonetheless, its exclusive focus on household saving out of current income causes it to neglect other factors, including how intergenerational transfers and investment opportunities can influence saving. Affluent households with children likely will pay for private education, outside tutoring, extracurricular activities, and enrichment experiences that will benefit their kids. Parents capable of financing their children's college education will offer their children a legacy of higher income, increased fringe benefits, reduced spells of unemployment, and better prospects for promotion. All of these "investments" in their kids will appear as expenditures that reduce their household saving. Nonetheless, these expenses likely will raise the expected income their children can anticipate and thereby increase their capacity for saving and the accumulation of wealth. Alternatively, other households may use some of their modest income to support aging parents or other family members in need. These transfers will likely appear as expenses as they divert potential savings into family help. While the LCH treats all households as if they are operating on a level playing field, the ground is anything but even.

The LCH focuses solely on individual household decisions as the determinants of household wealth. In doing so, it ignores two important facets. Given the capacity of wealth to expand opportunities, the model ignores the very different circumstances that different wealth groups face. Quite simply, the acquisition of wealth brings opportunities for even greater amounts of wealth. In his book *The Hidden Cost of Being African American*, Thomas Shapiro argues that different "opportunity structures" can explain the accumulation and distribution of household wealth, particularly along racial lines (2004, p. 2). The wealthy do not simply have more wealth; their greater holdings offer broader opportunities to grow their wealth further. Consequently, the racial wealth gap discussed in Chapter 1 produces a racial opportunity gap as well. Further, latent racial bias in labor markets, credit markets, and housing markets simply exacerbates these disparities even further.

In addition, the LCH ignores the important role that public policy plays in encouraging wealth accumulation, both past and current. Federal land policies in the nineteenth century as well as the GI Bill benefits in the last century transformed household wealth in ways still in evidence today. These programs reflected the racial norms of their day as they offered their benefits invidiously. Today, we have a vast web of tax-code exemptions and deductions that favor some households at the expense of others. The LCH overlooks all of these policies as well as their impact on wealth accumulation.

Extending the Capitalist Spirit model

Like the Capitalist Spirit model, the Wealth Privilege model argues multiple motivations drive wealth accumulation. No doubt, households seek wealth to buffer their selected spending level from life's instabilities. In addition, the acquisition of wealth is a prerequisite for any interpretation of the American Dream. Buying a home requires a cash down payment to obtain a conventional mortgage. Running your own business demands a substantial financial stake before others will offer their treasure. Securing a comfortable retirement requires the accumulation of sufficient assets. In addition, preparing your children for their future can range from paying for their college education so they graduate debt free to helping them buy a home in a neighborhood with access to superior schools. Achieving each of these elements of the American Dream requires wealth in one form or another.

The acquisition of wealth does more than simply enable families to realize their version of the American Dream. Even modest accumulations free households from the anxiety of financial insecurity. Access to wealth offers households an expanded horizon of opportunities as they consider better employment prospects, increased education and training, or relocations to more promising locations. Wealth can open additional doors of opportunity as it can leverage offers of credit to fund a variety of investment. As households accumulate substantial sums, wealth can bring increased social status as well as influence. Organizations of all stripes are eager to include affluent individuals on their board of directors. Participation on these boards provides an opportunity to influence their mission and direction. More broadly, wealth can fuel philanthropic desires for undertaking good works and gaining recognition. In the political realm, large sums of wealth can yield substantial influence and power, particularly in a world unrestrained by the *Citizens United* ruling. In many cases, household wealth can generate these benefits simultaneously. Equity in one's home not only provides comfortable housing, but also serves as a source of retirement needs and offers stability and peace of mind. For all of these reasons, wealth offers households a variety of benefits that demonstrate its value in its own right and explains its unabated pursuit by some.

The Wealth Privilege model extends the Capitalist Spirit model as it considers the different circumstances that households experience as they strive to accumulate wealth. In particular, this model examines the primary pathways of wealth accumulation: not only household saving, but also asset appreciation, and family gifts and inheritances. Further, the Wealth Privilege model examines how the conditions along each of these pathways changes, particularly in their support of wealth accumulation. In considering each of these avenues of wealth accumulation, we can see how both racialized and wealth status can affect the wealth-building process and thereby explain the shifting patterns of wealth in this country.

Three pathways to wealth accumulation

Recognizing the many benefits of household wealth explains the motive for its accumulation, but not the means by which households do so. Essentially, households amass wealth in three ways.[3] First, as already discussed, households can save some portion of their current income to supplement their pool of savings and purchase assets like cars, homes, and stock shares. For many households, particularly younger ones, this path often represents its primary means of wealth accumulation, at least initially. Second, once households acquire some assets, they usually experience increased accumulation simply by managing these (mostly appreciating) assets responsibly. As discussed in the last chapter, many forms of wealth appreciate in value largely on their own. Of course, households can accelerate this process by their asset-portfolio choices and their willingness to assume increased investment risks. In some cases, talented and driven entrepreneurs like Bill Gates, Mark Zuckerberg, and others can accumulate vast fortunes as they guide small business startups into commercial empires.[4] Third, intergenerational transfers within families will supplement (or detract from) what wealth households are able to accumulate through saving and asset appreciation. These family transfers include not only financial gifts and inheritances, but also the provision of human capital (education), social capital (professional contacts), and cultural capital (comfort with power). While we normally view these transfers as one way (from older to younger generations), that is not always the case as many children find themselves supporting parents who outlive their wealth.

These three wealth pathways share a common trait. Each offers households a self-reinforcing feedback loop, or virtuous cycle, in which repeating the cycle becomes easier and easier. In the Household Saving pathway, households able to save some portion of their current income can invest those savings into income-generating assets, from savings accounts to rental properties. These new investments supplement their existing sources of income. Earning greater income makes further saving even easier, thereby permitting the acquisition of new income-generating assets. Given the strong link between household income and saving, it is clear how each can increase the other without limit.

The Asset Appreciation pathway functions in a similar manner. As households accumulate assets like homes and stocks, they benefit from any price appreciation these assets provide. In some cases, substantial patience is required before any appreciation appears while in other cases patience alone can produce substantial rewards. Rising asset values strengthen credit worthiness, permitting the owners to purchase additional assets on credit. Over time, these newly purchased assets appreciate thereby raising household net worth, thus offering further investment opportunities. Although always subject to market risks, this cycle can persist unabated, with an added twist. As their investment portfolio increases in value, households can assume more risk since they have greater opportunities to diversify their investments. Able to take more risks, they invest in higher risk assets and often experience higher rates of return.[5] In this way, larger investment portfolios generate disproportionately higher rates of return and fuel even faster appreciation.

Lastly, the Family Support pathway functions in a comparable way across generations. Affluent parents have numerous ways they can offer their children a head start in life. With the gifts of a superior education, cultural experiences, and social contacts, their children can parlay this help into higher salaries and increased saving. Wealthy parents can provide further help by offering in vivo gifts at such milestone events like college, weddings, starter homes, and the schooling of grandchildren (Oliver and Shapiro, 2006, p. 156). According to one study (Mayer and Engelhardt, 1996), one fifth of first-time homebuyers received help from family with their down payment. In attaining homeownership at an earlier age, these families can gain more fully the benefits of asset appreciation. Further, research (Chiteji and Stafford, 2000) shows that parents can transmit their financial knowledge to their children, giving them more exposure and comfort with different investment opportunities. The most visible form of family transfer is the gift of wealth at one's death. Each of these gifts certainly functions additively as they help their recipients move further along the Household Saving and Asset Appreciation pathways. Affluent parents free their children of the worry or need to divert their own savings to help financially distressed family members. In most cases, parents offer these gifts with the only expectation that their kids do the same for the next generation. With all of these advantages, most can accumulate enough wealth to do the same or more for their own children, thereby perpetuating the process.

Of course, these three pathways complement and reinforce each other. Graduating from college debt free not only provides the possibility for a substantial income, but also for immediate wealth accumulation. Without the burden of student debt, households can save immediately for the down payment on a "starter home." Getting family help with the down payment only sweetens the experience. Households fortunate enough to access the Asset Appreciation pathway at an earlier age simply gain more years to profit from its fecundity. As rising asset values swell household income, saving becomes even easier. Each of these contributes to greater wealth accumulation, offering families greater opportunities to assist their children. The synergies are substantial.

In contrast, asset-poor households experience these wealth-building pathways quite differently. Households unable to earn adequate income due to unemployment, divorce, disability, or death of a breadwinner encounter a vicious, not virtuous, cycle. To supplement their insufficient earnings, they may liquidate saved assets. In doing so, they are sacrificing future income as they consume their wealth to meet current expenses. Without this income source, their inadequate earnings decline further. Unless their prospects improve, they will continue to liquidate assets. Dire circumstances may force households to sell their homes, cars, and even their tools in order to pay their current bills. Alternatively, they can draw upon credit to meet their current needs. As their credit balances mount and their interest charges escalate, escape from this debt spiral becomes increasingly difficult. The very same forces that favor the affluent show disfavor to families forced to draw down their wealth to make ends meet.

The Family Support pathway operates in a similar fashion. While we generally view family transfers as simply going from older to younger generations, the reality is more complex. In many families, parents or siblings may suffer extensive health problems that generate unpaid medical bills. Other families have relatives unable to support themselves. Lastly, parents and grandparents simply outlive whatever savings they were able to accumulate. Under these circumstances, younger households must often respond to requests for help from older family members. Providing such assistance diverts the critical savings required to build their own retirement fund. Their generosity today may require them to make a similar request of their children later. Not only does the wealth of one generation reach into the next, but the lack of wealth of one generation can inhibit the next as well. In this way, households from less affluent families not only start out with less, but they experience greater likelihood of diverting precious savings from their own needs to help their kin.

In a similar, though less dramatic fashion, the Asset Appreciation pathway functions poorly for households of modest means. For most households, the purchase of a car or truck acts as their initial, major investment. Often, these vehicles are essential in generating family income. As jobs have left the central cities, having a reliable car is critical to finding and retaining employment. As a commute vehicle, a car gives the individual a wider scope to accept better-paying jobs. However, cars lose their value over time, along with other household assets like furniture and home appliances. Since most wealth-poor families have the bulk of their assets tied up in these three categories, their experience of asset ownership is quite different. As these assets depreciate over their limited lifetimes, their declining value undermines household wealth even as they require eventual replacement, often on credit.

Households who achieve homeownership through the purchase of mobile homes likely experience similar depreciation since two thirds of these homeowners rent the land their home sits on (Collins and Dylla, 2001). Unlike affluent households, asset ownership does not offer the wealth poor an easy source of wealth accumulation.

Each of these pathways can discourage wealth building not only separately, but also in tandem. Research shows that middle-class families with family members suffering from economic hardship have greater difficulties accessing the Asset Appreciation pathway. In one study, Colleen Heflin and Mary Pattillo (2002) showed that households related to siblings in poverty have lower rates of bank-account ownership as well as homeownership. Similarly, Ngina Chiteji and Darrick Hamilton (2005) demonstrated that middle-class families with parents in poverty have reduced rates of bank-account ownership, stock ownership, and net worth. Having family members in financial distress does appear to limit one's ability to access the Asset Appreciation pathway. Further, Chiteji and Hamilton (2002) concluded in subsequent research that nearly 12 percent of the racial wealth gap between White and Black families is attributable to family members in need. Just as affluent family networks can favor households in multiple ways, so can families in need limit the opportunities of their kin.

Undoubtedly, some will see the three pathways as simply three versions of household saving. In the abstract, they are correct since any increase in wealth requires some form of saving. Economic orthodoxy conflates different forms of saving as it assumes rational decision makers are calculating constantly among various choices to spend or save. Yet, recent research suggests context and form is important. This has shown companies that use "opt out" rather than "opt in" mechanisms for their employee-retirement plans witness increased participation rates (Choi et al., 2005; Madrian and Shea, 2001). Simply presuming different forms of saving are identical causes us to ignore important distinctions. Resolving to save some portion of one's salary income is clearly different from deciding to leave untouched any capital gains in their stock fund or home. Likely, households treat a family gift or inheritance differently than a raise in salary, though both are income when received. Economists recognize these differences as they distinguish *active saving* from *passive saving*. The former refers to not spending some portion of one's income while the latter refers to leaving any capital gains unspent. Most of us would admit that the former takes much more discipline and persistence than the latter.

Returning to the concept of wealth privilege

The mechanisms and circumstances just described provide the infrastructure that gives rise to the concept of wealth privilege. As mentioned in Chapter 1, wealth privilege results from a confluence of institutions, policies, and personal behaviors that favor the wealthy as all households strive to better their circumstances. Several points are worth mentioning. Many of the systemic circumstances and institutional forces that encourage wealth privilege appear largely natural, even inevitable. It seems inescapable that higher-income households will find it easier to save a larger portion of their income, thereby disproportionately adding to their stock of wealth. With their larger and more diverse portfolio, would we not expect wealthier households to take greater risks and thereby earn higher returns? Regardless of their resources, parents will assist their children as best they can in assuring them a head start in their lives and careers; wealthier parents simply have greater means to do so. Each of these sources of privilege results from predictable and largely unavoidable behaviors.

Some sources of wealth privilege not only appear inevitable, but also stem from benign, even beneficial, decisions. It may strike us as unfair that wealthier households pay lower interest rates when they borrow funds; yet, all borrowers benefit when lenders make perceptive judgments regarding the credit worthiness and loan-repayment risks of their applicants.[6] Their offer of lower interest rates to selected borrowers reflects their judgment that these borrowers carry a lower risk of loan default. Similarly, given our preference to avoid undue risks, it is understandable that riskier investments entail higher rewards to attract investors. As many of these high-risk investments will fail, society is better off if their investors have the means to survive these losses rather than face financial ruin. Lastly, it is understandable why individuals with more schooling and specialized training can command higher salaries, even though the costs of these educational programs exclude many talented individuals. While each of these realities makes sense, they each contribute to the larger system that advantages the wealthy.

Not all sources of wealth are inevitable consequences of a functioning market economy. Sendhill Mullainathan and Eldar Shafir (2009) argued that low-income households face challenges to their saving not only from their low incomes, but also their greater likelihood to remain "unbanked." While affluent households get their paychecks deposited directly into their bank accounts, low-income households often are paid by check or even cash. Without a banking relationship, they must rely on check-cashing services and their service fees to get access to their earnings. As cash, their potential savings are vulnerable to theft, impulse buying, and pilferage by family members. As the authors note, differential access to banking services is not haphazard, but reflects

> a built-in asymmetry in banks' incentives between credit and savings for the poor and the rich. Regarding poorer clients, banks have a greater incentive to promote debt (which can be lucrative, delayed, and compounded) rather than savings (which are bound to be modest), as opposed to the treatment of the wealthy, whose debt is likely to be repaid with little penalty and whose savings promise to be large and valuable.
>
> (Mullainathan and Shafir, 2009, p. 134)

While banks work hard to meet the savings needs of the affluent, their high minimum balances and substantial fees thwart the efforts of modest savers. Similarly, bill-payment reminders and automatic billing protect the affluent from inadvertent fees and interest charges, demonstrating another way that the financial services industry functions effectively for some customers.

Other institutional practices favor saving among the affluent over the poor. While renters and homeowners may make similar monthly payments, only the homeowner will get credit for saving. That portion of their monthly mortgage payment that reduces their outstanding loan balance represents an important, though non-discretionary form of saving. Individual retirement accounts and 401(k) savings accounts are tailored to the savings needs of the affluent and they receive generous tax exemptions. While the wealthy can focus on long-term savings, low-income households need to save for rainy-day funds they can use as circumstances dictate. Substantial penalties for "early" withdrawal from these retirement plans make them quite unappealing to modest savers. Like the financial services industries, these tax-exempt savings plans serve the needs of the affluent, but not those striving for affluence.

Other sources of wealth privilege are more disturbing. Extensive evidence shows that persons of color—even accounting for similar education levels—suffer lower salaries, higher unemployment, and fewer promotions than do White employees. African Americans continue to pay higher interest rates on car loans, home mortgages, and education loans (Chiteji, 2010). Even today, many neighborhoods remain racially segregated; this permits, if not causes, White homeowners to experience higher rates of appreciation in their homes (Flippen, 2004). This residential segregation leads to different educational experiences for our kids and contributes to the racialized disparities in test scores and high-school graduation rates prevalent in our communities. These educational disparities, along with the differences in wealth among the White, Black, and Latino communities, produce similar differences in college attainment rates, employment prospects, and household incomes. While these disparities have their roots in the overt discrimination of our past, they remain largely in place given current practices and policies.

All three pathways contain a threshold that delineates whether the cyclical forces either retard or propel households in their pursuit of increased wealth. Below this threshold, families face headwinds that frequently create vicious cycles. Often ignored by banks, low-income households struggle to make ends meet, frequently triggering some form of dissaving. Any liquidation of household assets or rising debt balances simply encourages additional dissaving and reinforces the cycle. Wealth-poor households experience asset depreciation, not appreciation, as their primary asset, their car, loses value over time. Among families of limited means, financial reversals may be felt across the entire extended family. The dire needs of one family member can severely drain the modest resources of others, whose desire to help can increase their own vulnerability when trouble strikes them directly. Beyond each threshold, circumstances change dramatically. Household saving becomes easier with rising income. Asset appreciation rises with increased wealth and greater diversification. Family support to children becomes more generous as each generation of parents strives to offer increased help to their children. Although the actual position of each threshold is unclear, they do determine whether households experience headwinds or tailwinds in their efforts to accumulate wealth.

As discussed, earlier versions of the LCH model have been at a loss to explain the yawning gap in household wealth explained in Chapter 1. According to the conventional LCH model, wealth disparities should reflect differences in household income. Incomes have become more unequal over the past generation, but not enough to account for the vast disparities in wealth. While the Capitalist Spirit model can explain the high concentration of wealth among the very rich (Francis, 2009), the Wealth Privilege model offers opportunity as well as motive. Each of the three pathways illuminates the old truism that "the rich get richer." That these pathways function in ways that complement each other only strengthens the argument. Further, unlike the LCH, there are few limits on how much wealth the affluent might accumulate. As the possession of wealth offers direct benefits like security, status, and power, there is no reason to think that allure of greater wealth would ever disappear. Sure, some very affluent individuals likely do decide that further wealth is no longer worthy of their time and effort. Yet, their wealth and its value have little to do with continued effort on their part. Their investments in rare art, real estate, stock holdings, and vast business interests rise and fall in value for reasons largely beyond their control. According to the Wealth Privilege model, the sky is the limit on how much wealth the rich might hold.

Despite the intuitive appeal of this argument, some caution is called for. Family gifts and inheritances have been long viewed as an important source of wealth concentration. Since such wealth transfers may contribute nearly 40 percent of total net worth, yet only benefit a third of households, it certainly makes sense. However, with detailed evidence in hand, Edward Wolff and Maury Gittleman conclude, "somewhat surprisingly, that inheritances and other wealth transfers tend to be equalizing in terms of the distribution of household wealth" (2011, p. 22). No matter that wealthy households benefit in much greater numbers from larger gifts, the authors argue that the inheritances are proportionately more important to wealth-poor households than to the wealthy. Their conclusions suggest a more nuanced and complex world.

However, their analysis suffers from a significant problem. Ideally, one would compare household wealth before and after each gift to assess the impact of family transfers on wealth distribution. Due to data limitations, Wolff and Gittleman (2011) examined only the post-gift wealth. To estimate the full effect of a given inheritance, they assumed that households avoid consuming the gift, instead investing it at a reasonable rate of return from the time of its receipt to the present.[7] Using these elevated figures, they compared the value of any inheritances to current net worth to assess the importance these transfers play in family finances. They found these inheritances comprise a much smaller share of the current holdings of the wealthy, thereby arguing they play an equalizing role on wealth.

According to the LCH, it makes sense to assume households experience comparable rates of return. However, under the Wealth Privilege model, this assumption is problematic. Affluent households have much greater leeway in investing their gifts in higher-yielding assets while asset-poor households invest theirs in safer, liquid assets. If one assumes different rates of asset appreciation, then wealthy households could easily benefit disproportionately from inheritances, yet appear less dependent on them years later. Nonetheless, their conclusions should caution any embrace of the Wealth Privilege model without clear supporting evidence, an issue I return to in later chapters.

Does the Wealth Privilege model predict "the poor will get poorer"? Here the issue is more complicated. What is clear is that households of modest means and background face several key challenges. While the affluent can expect help from at least two of the wealth pathways, wealth-poor households frequently have only the Household Saving pathway as an initial avenue to increased wealth. Understandably, fewer options mean higher risks. Their household income will determine to what extent these households can use this pathway to their advantage. Those fortunate to have a college education might command an ample salary that permits sufficient savings to purchase a home and other appreciating assets. To the extent they can benefit from the Asset Appreciation pathway, they may enjoy a significant increase in household wealth over their lifetime. Of course, this projection presumes neither the existence of student loans nor calls from family members in financial distress, either of which would divert limited savings. In either case, family heritage can impede their progress. Further, these households are particularly vulnerable to any circumstances that might disrupt their saving behavior. Unexpected bouts of unemployment or periods of illness can quickly eliminate their savings and interrupt their financial ascent.

As households get beyond the pathway thresholds, they can experience modest financial mobility. Even households with moderate incomes may save some portion, although the resultant trickle of savings requires patience and continual good fortune to build a sizeable nest egg. Financial prudence will guide these households to invest their savings in safe, but low-yielding assets that will require further discipline and patience. Only as these households attain home ownership will they experience appreciable gains in net worth; even these increases will require further forbearance. Their progress likely will be modest despite their patience and discipline. Given the self-reinforcing nature of these pathways, the larger gains will result only as households move further along the various pathways.

Lastly, households with limited net worth are particularly susceptible to the full variety of setbacks that may visit any family. Unemployment, illness, business failure, or natural disaster can be a devastating experience for any household, although they pose greater threat to the wealth poor. Not only can these circumstances wipe out any savings and erase any assets, they can push these households back beyond the thresholds on each pathway. Income loss or new expenses can upset the family budget causing a forced curtailment of household saving. Any required liquidation of hard-earned assets can reverse gains made along the Asset Appreciation pathway. Financial distress can spiral and generate calls for help from other family members. Widespread calamities can undermine whole families that once were financially stable. Under the best of circumstances, these episodic events may take years for households to recover, if they ever do.

As an extension to the LCH, the Wealth Privilege model offers a compelling explanation for the growing disparities in household wealth. The model predicts that affluent households will experience substantial upward mobility over their working lives. Due to their good fortune, they have access to two, if not all three of the wealth accumulation pathways. As they travel the Asset Appreciation pathway, they find their wealth appreciates without much effort. The self-reinforcing nature of each pathway means their efforts reap larger and larger increments in newly acquired wealth. The intrinsic benefits that come with additional wealth expand without limit, suggesting there is little restraint on the growth of their fortunes.

The Wealth Privilege model predicts that upward wealth mobility is less certain and more muted at the bottom end of the wealth spectrum. For the majority of households that start their adult lives with few assets other than their human capital, only the Household Saving pathway offers an avenue to increased wealth. Their household income will govern how much they can benefit from this avenue. Despite their limited opportunities, some extraordinary households will emerge and experience substantial wealth accumulation. For those without a college education or high income, the stingy assistance offered by the three pathways will limit their financial ascent. What limited wealth they are able to accumulate will likely go toward buying a car and perhaps a mobile home, neither of which will increase in value. While they may persist in saving some portion of their income, setbacks like bouts of unemployment or periods of illness can wipe out those savings quite rapidly. Having access only to the savings pathway, their financial progress is vulnerable to any circumstances that might disrupt their solitary avenue to increased wealth. For these households, their prospects for much, if any, upward mobility are limited indeed.

The Wealth Privilege model also suggests the rising inequality of outcomes will generate similar disparities in opportunities. The model describes how parents have the motivation and sometimes the means to offer their children an advantaged start in life. Not only can parents pass along their financial wealth, but also they can provide their children with various forms of social, cultural, and human capital that will shape their future. While it is impossible to measure fully the value of these gifts, we can gain some understanding of their impact by examining Figure 3.1. It illustrates three scenarios by which parents are able to help their children. In the Full case, parents help their 25-year-old child complete college without any debt and provide the down payment for their first house. In the Moderate scenario, the parents help their child complete college debt free but are unable to help with a down payment. This delays the home purchase until age 35, when the individual has saved enough for their down payment. Under the Limited scenario, the parents help fund their child's college education, but not without taking on some debt. It takes this person ten years to pay off their college debt and another ten years to save enough to buy a home at age 45. Figure 3.1 tracks what happens as the different individuals buy a modest starter home priced at $100,000. While the difference in family help may be as little as $20,000, the difference in outcomes is much larger. By age 80, the accumulated value of each of these homes may differ by hundreds of thousands of dollars. While inflation may reduce these disparities, taxes will not, as I explain later in the book. Given how the Asset Appreciation pathway functions, rather small differences in family help can produce large changes in outcomes. Unless there are limits placed on how much parents can help their children, the

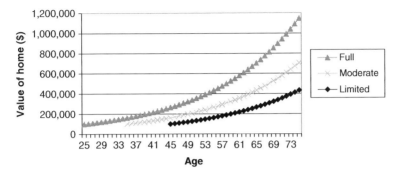

FIGURE 3.1 Consequences of family help
Source: Author's calculations

disparities in outcomes of one generation certainly will cause widening disparities in opportunities of the next. As subsequent cohorts of young adults experience widening disparities in their starting positions, these differences will add further cause to the growing concentration of household wealth. In addition, this change will undermine whatever meritocratic elements remain and further diminish the American Dream.

Perhaps most importantly, the Wealth Privilege model offers an improved framework for examining the racial wealth gap. While much of the past literature on this gap (at least by economists) has used the LCH, it is clear that the standard model offers a poor vantage since it largely ignores the different circumstances that racialized status can bring. By assuming most households simply attempt to equalize their lifetime spending, the LCH model neglects the considerable evidence of racial discrimination in employment and credit markets still present today (Bertrand and Mullainathan, 2003; Munnell et al., 1996). Similarly, the LCH largely ignores the limited presence of property owners and entrepreneurs of color in many residential neighborhoods and business districts. These remaining racial barriers preclude households of color from accumulating wealth at the same rate that comparable White households experience. Indeed, while there is substantial disagreement within the literature of what best explains the racial wealth gap, there is a strong consensus that White households accumulate wealth much easier than Black households do (Scholz and Levine, 2004). In contrast, the Wealth Privilege model can easily incorporate these remaining racial barriers as part of its analysis.

Conclusion

The Wealth Privilege model provides a persuasive explanation for the rising disparities in household wealth. Each pathway to greater wealth functions as a self-reinforcing system that aids the affluent at the expense of the wealth poor. This assistance to the wealthy has no limits. No caps exist that restrict how much income households may earn and save for the future. There are no limits to how much risk households might assume in their quest of asset appreciation. There are few barriers on how much parents can bequeath their heirs to assure their financial security. Each of these features of wealth privilege complements the others, thereby illuminating why the gaps in household wealth are widening.

As significant as these three systems of privilege are, they do not give us the full story. If so, we should expect rising wealth concentration as an inescapable consequence of our American brand of market capitalism. As the sources of wealth privilege just discussed are largely endemic to our economy, we would presume that our history would reflect ever increasing wealth concentration. Though the historic evidence is spotty, it does suggest that we have experienced periods of declining as well as rising wealth inequality.

It is unclear whether the three systems already discussed could adequately explain such an ebb and flow. The full answer may lie in another source of wealth privilege not addressed here. Since our nation's inception, the federal government has designed policies supporting households in their quest to accumulate wealth and achieve economic security. As these policies have changed over time, they could account for the ebb and flow of wealth disparities over our history. Though a complete accounting of these laws is beyond the scope of this book, I discuss two elements of these policies. In the next chapter, I review past federal wealth policies that produced the glaring racialized wealth gap evident today. I explain how the design of these policies helped White households gain their current predominance in the ownership of U.S. wealth. In a later chapter, I examine contemporary federal wealth policies and demonstrate how they have served as an additional source of wealth privilege. Indeed, they may offer the most compelling argument for the substantial increase in wealth concentration over the past generation. Rather than helping those with the greatest needs, these policies have simply assisted those with the greatest affluence in their quest for increased wealth. Like the three systems discussed here, this fourth system functions as a virtuous cycle for those with increasing wealth and does so without limit.

Notes

1 My appreciation to Hurst (2003) for a reminder of this fable and its connection to the issues at hand.
2 Carroll's Capitalist Spirit addendum is an exception that I discuss shortly.
3 Since wealth accumulation along any of the three pathways requires some form of saving, one might question whether there are three pathways, or only one. However, "saving" along each of these pathways usually entails a different set of decisions, as will be discussed.
4 Others, like lottery winners, may realize substantial gains through luck and continual "investments."
5 This point is supported by the survey data, which I share with the reader in Chapter 5.
6 Part of the interest that all borrowers pay goes toward the repayment of bad loans. When loan defaults rise, lenders will raise interest rates to cover their higher level of expected losses.
7 They use a 3 percent real rate of return that reflects the return earned by high-grade, long-term corporate bonds.

Bibliography

Bertrand, M. and Mullainathan, S. (2003). *Are Emily and Greg more employable than Lakisha and Jamal? A field experiment on labor market discrimination* (No. w9873). Washington, DC: National Bureau of Economic Research.

Cagetti, M. and De Nardi, M. (2008). Wealth inequality: Data and models. *Macroeconomic Dynamics* 12 (S2): 285–313.

Carroll, C. (2000). Why do the rich save so much? In *Does Atlas shrug? The economic consequences of taxing the rich*, ed. J. B. Slemrod. Cambridge, MA: Harvard University Press.

Chiteji, N. S. (2010). The racial wealth gap and the borrower's dilemma. *Journal of Black Studies* 41 (2): 351–66.

Chiteji, N. S. and Hamilton, D. (2002). Family connections and the Black-White wealth gap among middle-class families. *Review of Black Political Economy* 30 (1): 9–28.

Chiteji, N. S. and Hamilton, D. (2005). Family matters: Kin networks and asset accumulation. In *Inclusion in the American Dream: Assets, poverty, and public policy*, ed. M. Sheraden. Oxford: Oxford University Press, 87–111.

Chiteji, N. S. and Stafford, F. P. (2000). *Asset ownership across generations*. Ann Arbor, MI: Population Studies Center.

Choi, J. J., Laibson, D., Madrian, B. C., and Metrick, A. (2005). *Saving for retirement on the path of least resistance*. Philadelphia, PA: Rodney L. White Center for Financial Research.

Collins, M. and Dylla, D. (2001). *Mind the gap: Issues in overcoming the information, income, wealth, and supply gaps facing potential buyers of affordable homes*. Washington, DC: Neighborhood Reinvestment Corporation and LISC Center for Homeownership.

De Nardi, M. (2004). Wealth inequality and intergenerational links. *Review of Economic Studies* 71 (3): 743–68.

De Nardi, M., French, E., and Jones, J. B. (2009). *Why do the elderly save? The role of medical expenses*. Washington, DC: National Bureau of Economic Research.

Dynan, K. E., Skinner, J., and Zeldes, S. P. (2004). Do the rich save more? *Journal of Political Economy* 112 (2): 397–444.

Flippen, C. (2004). Unequal returns to housing investments? A study of real housing appreciation among Black, White, and Hispanic households. *Social Forces* 82 (4): 1523–51.

Francis, J. L. (2009). Wealth and the capitalist spirit. *Journal of Macroeconomics* 31 (3): 394–408.

Heer, B. (2001). Wealth distribution and optimal inheritance taxation in life-cycle economies with intergenerational transfers. *Scandinavian Journal of Economics* 103 (3): 445–65.

Heflin, C. M. and Pattillo, M. (2002). Kin effects on Black-White account and home ownership. *Sociological Inquiry* 72 (2): 220–39.

Hendricks, L. (2004). How important is preference heterogeneity for wealth inequality? Retrieved from http://papers.ssrn.com/sol3/papers.cfm?abstract_id=555902.

Holme, J. J. (2002). Buying homes, buying schools: School choice and the social construction of school quality. *Harvard Educational Review* 72 (2): 177–206.

Hubbard, R. G., Skinner, J., and Zeldes, S. P. (1994). The importance of precautionary motives in explaining individual and aggregate saving. *Carnegie-Rochester Conference Series on Public Policy* 40 (June): 59–125.

Huggett, M. (1996). Wealth distribution in life-cycle economies. *Journal of Monetary Economics* 38 (3): 469–94.

Hurst, E. (2003). *Grasshoppers, ants, and pre-retirement wealth: A test of permanent income*. Washington, DC: National Bureau of Economic Research.

Johnson, H. B. (2006). *The American Dream and the power of wealth: Choosing schools and inheriting inequality in the land of opportunity*. New York: Taylor and Francis.

Juster, F. T., Smith, J. P., and Stafford, F. (1999). The measurement and structure of household wealth. *Labour Economics* 6 (2): 253–75.

Madrian, B. C. and Shea, D. F. (2001). The power of suggestion: Inertia in 401 (k) participation and savings behavior. *Quarterly Journal of Economics* CXVI (4): 1149–87.

Mayer, C. J. and Engelhardt, G. V. (1996). Gifts, down payments, and housing affordability. *Journal of Housing Research* 7: 59–78.

Modigliani, F. and Brumberg, R. (1954). Utility analysis and the consumption function: An interpretation of cross-section data. *Franco Modigliani* 1.

Mullainathan, S. and Shafir, E. (2009). Savings policy and decision-making in low-income households. In *Insufficient funds: Savings, assets, credit, and banking among low-income households*, ed. R. M. Blank and M. S. Barr. London: Russell Sage Foundation, 121–45.

Munnell, A. H., Tootell, G. M., Browne, L. E., and McEneaney, J. (1996). Mortgage lending in Boston: Interpreting HMDA data. *American Economic Review* 86 (1): 25–53.

Oliver, M. L. and Shapiro, T. M. (2006). *Black wealth, White wealth: A new perspective on racial inequality*. New York: Taylor and Francis.

Orfield, G. and McArdle, N. (2006). *The vicious cycle: Segregated housing, schools and inter-generational inequality*. Cambridge, MA: Joint Center for Housing Studies, Harvard University.

Ross, S. L. and Yinger, J. (2002). *The color of credit: Mortgage discrimination, research methodology, and fair-lending enforcement*. Cambridge, MA: MIT Press.

Scholz, J. K. and Levine, K. (2004). US Black-White wealth inequality. In *Social inequality*, ed. K. Neckerman. London: Russell Sage Foundation, 895–929.

Shapiro, T. M. (2004). *The hidden cost of being African American: How wealth perpetuates inequality*. Oxford: Oxford University Press.

Wolff, E. N. (1981). The accumulation of household wealth over the life-cycle: A microdata analysis. *Review of Income and Wealth* 27 (1): 75–96.

Wolff, E. N. and Gittleman, M. (2011). Inheritances and the distribution of wealth or whatever happened to the great inheritance boom? *Journal of Economic Inequality* 1300: 1–30.

4

RECOGNIZING OUR PAST

To this point, I have discussed wealth's proficiency in leveraging future opportunities. To understand the current disparities in household wealth, we must look back as well.

Wealth's durability and transferability across generations means that its current disposition reflects past circumstances and opportunities. Whatever our current wealth status, most of us can look backward at our family tree and view a progression of improving prospects. In each generation, parents struggled to expand the opportunities of their children. They usually did so. With each generation, then, children attained more education that in turn brought more employment options. Each generation usually earned higher incomes, offering them greater opportunities to save and help their own kids even more generously. In this way, our current wealth is deeply rooted in our individual family histories. However, the current disparities in wealth result from more than the assorted pluck and luck of our ancestors. As we consider the current patterns in household wealth, particularly across racialized groups, we must recall our history of racialized attitudes, policies, and institutions that selectively favored some over others. Although we have rescinded these laws and practices, their consequences remain plainly in view.

To understand our nation's history regarding wealth and race, we must revisit our foundational document, the U.S. Constitution. This document enshrines two contrary impulses that inform our federal wealth policies. The U.S. Constitution reflects a bold experiment in creating a government whose charge is to provide an expansive set of individual rights broadly shared. The document references these rights in the Preamble as it argues that the role of government is "to promote the general Welfare, and secure the Blessings of Liberty to ourselves and our Posterity." It enumerates the blessings of liberty throughout the original document as well as in the quickly adopted Bill of Rights. While most of these rights are political, some refer to economic rights, including the Fifth Amendment which prohibits the taking of "property, without due process." Here, the constitution cements the most important right regarding property, the right of the individual owner to retain their valued item. To offer further protection, the U.S. Constitution forbids the imposition of "direct" taxes on individual property, whether real or personal.[1] In this way, the U.S. Constitution enshrined essential rights that encouraged the pursuit and accumulation of private wealth, as well as protected that wealth from taxation.

Although the U.S. Constitution enumerated a broad set of individual rights, it did so for a relatively narrow group of persons, namely White males. The constitutional guarantees against the taking of property without due process and just compensation did not cover the vast tracts of land still possessed by Native Americans in 1790. Over the following century, one tribe after another would lose its traditional land, often without any compensation. As the authors argue in *The Color of Wealth*, "federal policies toward the American Indian have methodically removed wealth from Native populations" (Lui et al., 2006, p. 36). For persons of African descent, these constitutional guarantees did not enforce their most basic economic right, the right to keep the fruits of one's labor. Indeed, the property claims of slaveholders trumped this right. According to the constitution, individuals were bound to return to the legal owner any person who had escaped from slavery, even if their local state laws prohibited it. Only a select few received the broad set of rights enshrined in the constitution.

Curiously, while the constitution clearly enumerates its protection of specific individual rights, its restrictions on who benefits are stated opaquely. Rather than speak of slavery or enslaved persons explicitly, the constitution refers to "persons held to Service or Labor" and "all other persons." Indeed, the document identified three key groups: free persons including those temporarily in indentured contracts, "Indians not taxed" or those living on native lands, and "all other persons" which refers to those enslaved. Given the social norms of the time, persons refer to males only. Recognizing these coded words is important, since all subsequent legislation that limits participation by persons of color follows this precedent. Rare is the federal policy that clearly states "for Whites only," even though many were designed and applied in this manner.

Expropriation of "Colored" wealth

For most of our nation's history, people created wealth by harvesting the richness of the land. Whether it was capturing coveted pelts and furs, lumbering the vast forests, tilling the rich soils, or extracting precious metals or valued minerals to fashion iron and steel, the wealth of America stemmed largely from the bounty of nature. Even those employed in shipping, banking, and insurance owed their prosperity to the transport and sale of these products around the world. To capture this bounty, one needed access to or, better yet, ownership of the land that yielded these rewards. More than any other single factor, land ownership provided the means to capture its riches. Consequently, as one considers what happened to land claims over the expanse of our nation's history, one cannot help but recognize its impact on wealth today.

Native peoples' land losses

At the time of ratification of the U.S. Constitution, Native Americans occupied virtually all of what would become the United States except for the narrow strip east of the Appalachian Mountains. By 1894, the various Indian tribes had lost 90 percent of their land held a century earlier. Over the next 40 years, they would lose over half of the remainder. Figure 4.1 offers a stark reminder of this startling transformation. The remaining tribal lands of peoples whose ancestors occupied the entire continent just centuries ago have been relegated to mostly small parcels in the largely arid and unforgiving West.

Such losses occurred for reasons as varied as the land itself. In some cases, the diseases carried by Europeans wrought such devastation on Indian communities that the few survivors moved west to avoid further contact. In other cases, White immigrants hungry for land ignored Indian claims and settled as they saw fit. As tensions among the wary neighbors boiled over into violence, Whites triumphed due to their ever expanding numbers and superior weaponry. Throughout much of the nineteenth century, the federal government was at war with one tribe or another that chose to resist the expansion of White settlers.[2] The federal government signed hundreds of treaties

FIGURE 4.1 Remaining Native American lands
Source: U.S. Geologic Survey, U.S. Department of the Interior, Indian Lands (map), "The National Map Small Scale." Last updated December 15, 2014. Accessed at http://nationalmap.gov/small_scale/printable/fedlands.html#list.

with various Indian nations; some were negotiated with willing participants, while most were simply imposed. Lastly, certain treaties required the remaining tribal lands to be divided into private allotments to those tribal members who could demonstrate their Indian ancestry. Despite their different circumstances, each of these methods transferred land from Native to largely White hands.

This wholesale transfer of a continent from Native residency to White ownership occurred under the umbrella of federal policy. The first Congress adopted the Indian Trade and Intercourse Act of 1790 setting the parameters of federal policy toward lands occupied by native peoples. Under this and subsequent laws, Congress retained its constitutional authority in overseeing all trade and interactions with the Indian nations. This law prohibited any land sales to individuals or states outside of federal treaties. Though some states ignored this federal authority and made separate deals with specific tribes, the vast majority of land transfers occurred under federal treaties.

Faced with waves of European immigrants hungry for land, the federal government executed over 350 treaties with different Indian nations in a hundred-year span (Kappler, 1904). The aim of these treaties was formalized in the Indian Removal Act of 1830. As its name implies, this treaty sought to remove all Native peoples from lands east of the Mississippi and to offer them lands further west as compensation. This treaty itself led to the forcible removal and resettlement of the Cherokee, Choctaw, Chickasaw, and Seminole nations along the horrendous "Trail of Tears." As Figure 4.1 corroborates, this policy was implemented with stark efficiency as almost all vestiges of Native American occupancy in the eastern United States has been eliminated, except for local names. In anticipation of these removals, the Indian Intercourse Act of 1834 selected a large swath of land on the Great Plains as the permanent home of the resettled Eastern Nations.[3] That this offered land already had occupants did not seem to concern those in Washington. At the time, this land was beyond the migration of most White settlers and viewed without interest. However, as ever larger waves of White immigrants pushed west, these lands gained value. Subsequent treaties reduced this "Indian Territory" to the eastern half of the current state of Oklahoma. Later laws shrunk this parcel further.

Virtually all of these land seizures occurred after the adoption of constitutional guarantees against the taking of private property. As the constitution viewed Native peoples not as American citizens, but rather as peoples of separate nations, the constitutional promises did not apply. Although separate nations, the Indian nations were not viewed as sovereign countries. In several key rulings, the U.S. Supreme Court spelled out the limited rights of these nations. In *Johnson* v. *M'Intosh* (1823) the court ruled that Indian tribes held "Indian title" or occupancy rights to their land, but did not have the right to dispose of the land as they saw fit. Instead, under the "doctrine of discovery," the court ruled that the federal government held ultimate title to the land, meaning it would revert to federal control once Indian occupancy ended. With this legal judgment, native peoples could never fully profit from the wealth of their lands; at best, they could earn the income that the land generated only as long as they maintained occupancy. Lastly, the judgment meant they could sell their occupancy rights to only one buyer, the federal government.

Seeing what was happening to neighboring tribes, the Cherokee decided to retain their lands through a process of assimilation. Restructuring their society to resemble their colonial neighbors, they shifted to individual farming, light manufacturing, and the development of small towns. They adopted a written alphabet to encourage writing, the creation of newspapers, and even a constitution to formalize their political independence. Rather than mollify their White neighbors, these changes fueled further envy and resentment. The Georgia legislature began passing laws that extended state jurisdiction over tribal lands, in clear violation of federal law. It then began a land lottery system in which the state of Georgia would distribute parcels of Cherokee land without any compensation to the current occupants. Under a provision of the constitution that directs the Supreme Court to hear cases between foreign powers and individual states, the Cherokee took their case directly to the court. The Supreme Court argued the Cherokee had no standing to sue since the Cherokee were neither U.S. citizens nor a sovereign nation, but rather a "domestic, dependent nation" whose relationship to the U.S. resembled "that of a ward to his guardian" (*Cherokee Nation* v. *Georgia*, 1830). With this argument, they refused to hear the case. Unable to defend against encroachment by the state of Georgia, Cherokee resistance was largely broken. Most submitted to the rising pressures and migrated west along the infamous "Trail of Tears."

Latino land losses

Native peoples were not the only group that held property desired by White settlers. After a brief war with Mexico ended with the capture of Mexico City in the fall of 1847, the U.S. government imposed the Treaty of Guadalupe Hidalgo that inflicted severe penalties. Under the treaty, Mexico lost more than half of its national territory; the ceded lands became the basis of ten southwestern states, from Texas to California. Overnight, tens of thousands of Mexican citizens lost their country as the border moved south to the Rio Grande. Under Article X of the treaty, the U.S. government promised to honor all property claims of current residents. However, Article X was absent from the version ratified by the U.S. Senate. Instead, Congress created land commissions to verify pre-existing property claims and adjudicate any conflicts.

In California, the commission operated under the California Land Act of 1851. Under this law, property owners had two years to submit their claims with all supporting documentation. The three-member commission, none of whom could read Spanish, examined these claims to determine whether they met all Mexican and American legal standards. The burden of proof rested on the claimants, not the government. Although most claimants spoke only Spanish, the proceedings were conducted in English, using American jurisprudence. These unfamiliar procedures forced the landowners to bear heavy litigation costs, including the hiring of rapacious lawyers, some of whom required a contingency fee equal to one quarter of the land under judgment (Clay and Troesken, 2005). They endured substantial travel costs as the hearings were held in either San Francisco or Washington, DC. Once the commission confirmed the claim, the property owners were still required to pay for a legal survey of their land, which often reduced their holdings further. Even then, claims could be appealed to district courts and eventually to the Supreme Court; most claims were not settled for 15 years (Jelinek, 1998). Waves of White immigrants lured to California by the false hopes of the Gold Rush squatted on these lands. Many clear-cut the timber and exhausted the soils as they refused to permit the "defeated Mexicans" from retaining control over millions of acres (Jelinek, 1998, p. 235).

Ultimately, 80 percent of the Californian claims were confirmed.[4] Still, 3 million acres became part of the public domain. Even this figure overstates how well the rancheros fared. Due to pressures of squatters and substantial litigation costs, many sold land to pay mounting bills. Indeed, across the territory taken from Mexico, land ownership among Latinos declined significantly. Whereas over 60 percent of the Mexican households owned land in 1850, the figure had fallen to 29 percent by 1860 (Amott and Matthaei, 1991, p. 73). In California, wealthy White immigrants assumed control over the sprawling Mexican ranches, causing a monopoly of land unprecedented in any other state (Jelinek, 1998, p. 237).

Japanese property losses

More recently, federal policy led to further confiscation of property and businesses. Amidst the hysteria generated by the Japanese attack on Pearl Harbor, President Roosevelt invoked Executive Order 9066. Over the next six months, authorities relocated over 110,000 persons of Japanese or Korean descent into internment camps for the duration of World War II.[5] Over 60 percent were U.S. citizens. With no information on whether or when they might return to their lives, they had as little as one week to settle their affairs. These circumstances forced business owners to sell their businesses and any equipment unless they knew able and trustworthy non-Japanese colleagues to manage their affairs (Taylor, 1983). Homeowners who could not find suitable tenants or friends to look after their homes had to do the same. Even tenant farmers lost their crops and their valued leases to well-tended land. Households that owned cars and other larger personal items needed to sell them or risk losing track of them while behind barbed wire. Both the short notice and the competition among families selling the same items forced them to sell their valued possessions at pennies on the dollar. Even those who trusted government assurances to keep their personal possessions in safe storage found them stolen, lost, or destroyed upon their return (Taylor, 1983). Lastly, many who saved at Japanese-owned banks found their accounts frozen as financial authorities acted on fears that these banks would finance anti-American activities.

Proponents of these relocations often cited national security concerns, yet there is little evidence to support this. Even at the time, the FBI argued that mass incarcerations were unnecessary. What caused this massive dislocation and economic loss for the Japanese community? Along the West Coast, there existed a deep envy among the White community regarding their Japanese neighbors.

Austin Anson, managing secretary of the Salinas Valley Grower-Shipper Vegetable Association, sums up this view:

> We're charged with wanting to get rid of the Japs for selfish reasons. We might as well be honest. We do. It's a question of whether the white man lives on the Pacific Coast or the brown men. They came to this valley to work, and they stayed to take over. They offer higher land prices and rents than the white man can pay for the land. They undersell the white man in the markets. They can do this because they raise their own labor. They work their women and children while the white farmer has to pay wages for this help. If all of the Japs were removed tomorrow, we'd never miss them in two weeks, because the white farmers can take over and produce everything the Jap grows. And we don't want them back when the war ends, either.
>
> *(Krebs, 1995, p. 49)*

At the time of the relocation, Japanese growers dominated the fresh produce market. In the Los Angeles area, they contributed virtually all of the local production of peppers, tomatoes, broccoli, celery, radishes, snap peas, and spinach (Krebs, 1995, p. 48).

There is no definitive estimate of the losses suffered by the detainees. While many sources refer to a Federal Reserve Bank estimate of $400 million, its origins are unclear. What is clear is that these liquidation sales generated a massive transfer of wealth from households of Japanese descent to their mostly White neighbors. In addition, the three years spent in the concentration camps generated additional losses. Not only did they lose the opportunity to earn income during this period, but they also lost the chance to gain valuable work experience and further education. To estimate these impacts, Aimee Chin (2005) compared the subsequent earnings of men of Japanese descent who lived in the Hawaiian Islands and therefore avoided mass incarceration with those who lived on the West Coast. Controlling for a number of factors, she concluded that those men who suffered this experience witnessed a 9–13 percent decline in annual earnings 25 years later (Chin, 2005). Although the government awarded compensation to some internees immediately after the war and later in 1988, these amounts were too little to compensate fully the victims for their losses.

Enslavement of African labor

Slavery produced a more personal and profound form of expropriation than even the examples of dispossession of land and property cited above. The enslavement of another person eliminates the most basic economic right, the right to one's labor and talents. As slaveholders could earn far more from the work produced by their enslaved workers than was required to meet their daily requirements, the system enriched one at the expense of the other. The mostly White slaveholders could purchase additional land and more enslaved persons to work the added acres. With growing profit, they could build mills to grind the locally produced grains. They could invest in local banks, insurance firms, and shipping companies that supported the transportation and merchandising of cotton exports around the world. Parents could send their sons off to the best schools to prepare them for professional careers that might extend beyond the plantation. Deprived of their own labor, the enslaved parent could offer little to his sons and daughters. Many states outlawed the education of those enslaved. The permanence of the slave system meant that enslaved households had little real hope for something better in the future.

Strictly speaking, much of the slave system predates the establishment of the U.S. Constitution and thus is not the result of federal policy, per se. Slavery existed in all 13 colonies, though it was expiring in a number of northern states by 1789.[6] Yet, the constitution was not simply a neutral arbiter that left slavery as an issue of "states' rights." At several key points, it strengthened slavery as an institution and it assisted its expansion over much of the continent. Most importantly, by treating enslaved persons as chattel property, the constitution placed the full weight of federal power in the defense of slaveholding. With the adoption of the Bill of Rights, the constitution prohibited the federal government from depriving persons of their "life, liberty, or property without due process; nor shall private property be taken for public use without just compensation." This provision did not apply to slavery's impact on the enslaved's lack of liberty; instead, it defended slavery from any encroachments. Further, the stringent amendment process meant the slave-holding states could effectively block the abolition of slavery by political means. Only the voluntary secession of the 11 Confederate states permitted the remaining states to pass a constitutional amendment abolishing slavery during their absence from the Union.

The U.S. Constitution did more than serve as a bulwark for slavery; it facilitated its expansion beyond the original colonies. The three-fifths compromise gave slave-holding states greater influence in electing presidents and controlling the House of Representatives.[7] One issue that bedeviled the federal government during the antebellum period was whether slavery could expand to the "territories." Early in this period, the anti-slavery forces seemed to have the upper hand. The Northwest Ordinance of 1787 prohibited the extension of slavery into the upper Midwest, while the Missouri Compromise of 1820 excluded slavery in the "western territories" north of the 36° 30° parallel. After 1820, Congress refused any further limits on the expansion of slavery until the Civil War and even undermined its earlier stance (Finkelman, 2011, p. 71). During this period, annexations of both Florida and Texas led to new slaveholding states, while the Compromise of 1850 permitted the expansion of slavery into the newly acquired New Mexico and Utah territories. Lastly, the Nebraska-Kansas Act of 1854 effectively repealed the 1820 compromise by allowing popular sovereignty to determine the existence of slavery in any new territories. Rather than simply limit slavery where it existed in 1789, the U.S. Constitution facilitated its expansion through lands west of the original 13 states.

Further, the constitution defended slavery even in areas that had abolished it. One provision explicitly required that escaping enslaved persons be returned to their owner upon legal claim. The Fugitive Slave Act of 1793 implemented this constitutional provision, as it required the federal government to assist in the return of persons fleeing slavery. Under this act, slaveholders could seize persons in Free states and, with proof before a judge, compel their return. The act created penalties for any who assisted those fleeing slavery. In essence, the property laws of slaveholding states trumped local state laws that abolished slavery. Several Free states responded with "personal liberty" laws that prohibited local officials from executing their duties or providing local jails for detaining alleged fugitives (Morris, 1974). In response, Congress passed the Fugitive Slave Act of 1850 that lowered the burden of proof and imposed even harsher penalties on those who assisted runaways or did not enforce their return. These laws, along with underlying racial attitudes, encouraged the kidnapping of free Blacks off northern streets and their forcible return south to slavery (Wilson, 2015).

Each of these examples of wealth expropriation shares two important traits. First, constitutional protections against the loss of property without due process did not apply to persons of color. In each of these cases, the legal system failed to protect persons of color from the loss of their land, property, and even livelihood. In some cases, the U.S. Supreme Court led the charge.

Second, the policies and decisions that took these forms of wealth overwhelmingly benefited White Americans. Virtually all slaveholders during the Antebellum South were White Europeans.[8] So were nearly all of the bankers, shippers, and merchants who benefited from the trade of cotton and enslaved persons. Mostly White neighbors purchased the possessions, homes, and businesses of the Japanese forced to settle their affairs under duress. The flood of European immigrants claimed most of the land made available by the forced removal of Native peoples and disputed land titles of the former citizens of Mexico.

These massive transfers of wealth formed the foundation of our current wealth disparities. This does not mean that all White Americans living at the time of these events benefited. Mostly, only those Whites who already had wealth or connections could benefit much. Even at the height of slavery, most historians believe, only about one fourth of southern households were slaveholders; for most, the cost of purchasing an enslaved person was beyond their means. To purchase the homes or businesses of desperate Japanese, the buyers needed some source of cash. Until homesteading laws lowered the price of land and eased the cash requirements, only settlers with means could purchase large tracts of land. These policies mostly offered wealthier White Americans exceptional opportunities to expand their holdings.

Advantaging White wealth

Homesteading laws

Federal homesteading laws augured a new form of federal wealth policy, one that resembles our contemporary policies. Under the constitution, the federal government took responsibility for all lands acquired from foreign governments and taken from the Indian nations. In need of revenue to finance public expenditure and pay wartime debt, the federal government chose to sell relatively large lots (640 acres) to the highest bidders. This policy gave wealthier individuals the opportunity to claim prime land while excluding the vast majority of immigrants who had little cash. Undeterred, many immigrants simply moved further west, squatted on unclaimed land, and built farms without formal title. Recognizing this reality, Congress passed the Preemption Act of 1841 that allowed squatters to purchase their land for $1.25 an acre. Even at this price, many homesteaders could not afford to gain title to their claims. Some simply moved further west.

The Homestead Act of 1862 expanded the opportunity of land ownership. It offered 160 acres of unclaimed land to persons who would take residence within six months, make improvements, and stay for five years. Meeting all of these stipulations, the homesteader could gain title to the land for a nominal fee. Individuals able to make their way west could earn a livelihood and gain some measure of economic independence. In five years, the claimant could build a modest home, raise crops or animals, and own a sizeable parcel of land. As their children grew up, the extended family could make claims on adjacent lands. The Homestead Act not only brought an amount of economic security to its beneficiaries, it offered an important and valuable ladder to upward mobility (Shanks, 2005). Owning property conferred social status and key political rights, including the right to vote and hold public office. As areas developed, towns emerged that brought added educational and commercial opportunities for their sons and daughters. For many households, the Homestead Act served as the catalyst for greater prosperity and wealth over subsequent generations.

Over the next 70 years, the Homestead Act offered land to almost 1.5 million households and gave title to over 246 million acres of land, an amount that is equivalent to the states of Texas and New Mexico combined (Shanks, 2005, p. 25). According to one estimate, this federal largesse may have benefited fully 46 million Americans living today whose ancestors were actual homesteaders (Shanks, 2005, p. 29). Virtually all of this land went into the hands of White landowners.

Several reasons explain why the Homestead Act largely benefited Whites. It specified only citizens or those eligible for citizenship could apply. Although this language sounds reasonable, in 1862 only Whites met these criteria.[9] Under the Naturalization Act of 1790, only "free white persons ... of good character" were eligible to become naturalized citizens. This effectively excluded any non-White immigrants, including those Latinos whose national boundary had moved southward. This precluded even Native people born on a reservation. While the Naturalization Act of 1870 changed this status for those of "African descent," it did not do so for other groups, including immigrants arriving from Asia. The Homestead Act intentionally favored White immigrants, and subsequent laws largely continued this practice.

While non-White immigrants could not apply for homestead claims, their children, if born in the United States, were eligible. However, during the period that homestead claims were highest, federal policies were restricting further immigration from Asia. The Chinese Exclusion Act of 1882 prohibited further immigrants from China, while the Gentlemen's Agreement with Japan stemmed the flow of Japanese nationals. Only later in the twentieth century did the flow of immigration shift from Europe to Asia and Latin America; by this time, the homesteading movement had exhausted the better land.

Further, simply staking a claim did not always lead to prosperity. Though the land itself required no cash, homesteaders needed some money to stake a successful claim. At minimum, they required cash to travel to the local land office to stake a claim, buy seeds and tools to plant a crop, and purchase necessities prior to harvest. According to one estimate, this required $600–$1,000, an amount beyond the reach of most emancipated Blacks (Deverell, 1988). Without some stake to fall back on, homesteaders could lose their claim if they suffered an adverse harvest in their first couple of years. Certainly, the White authorities who ran the local offices would have given little encouragement to potential Black homesteaders. Given the prevailing racial attitudes, their claims for land would have generated indifference, if not outright hostility and evasion. Most freedmen resided in the former Confederate states, while the land offered by the Homestead Act was in the upper Midwest; this placed the added obstacles of gaining information and traveling to the new land. Despite these barriers, thousands of freedmen and their families did migrate west, particularly to Kansas, Nebraska, and Oklahoma (Painter, 1992). Like their White counterparts, many of these Black homesteaders found the climate more forbidding and the challenges more unyielding than promised. Nonetheless, a small proportion of the 1.5 million households that patented their claims were Black.

The Southern Homestead Act of 1866 offered freedmen a more local option as well. This law targeted 46 million acres of public land in five states—Alabama, Arkansas, Florida, Louisiana, and Mississippi—for similar dispersal. For the first six months, only loyal Whites and newly emancipated Blacks could apply. However, these states had already undergone substantial development. Their remaining public lands were largely pine forests and bottom swampland; either required significant effort and capital to make the necessary improvements. This offer of free land lasted only ten years as the end of Reconstruction brought the law's repeal. In that time, 28,000 households completed their land claims for roughly 3 million acres, about 6 percent of the total (Lanza, 1999, p. 41). Estimates suggest between 4,000 and 5,500 Black households gained property through this law (Shanks, 2005, p. 30). Even in this case, Black households were unable to take advantage of the opportunity at rates their share of the local population would dictate. Yet, the law did offer these few households an important step in establishing their economic independence.

The G.I. Bill

In the twentieth century, the Servicemen's Readjustment Act, better known as the G.I. Bill, represents the most celebrated public policy to promote widespread upward mobility. Worried by the prospect of veterans returning to an economy with limited opportunities and high unemployment, the bill offered a bevy of benefits, including a year of unemployment benefits, low-cost loans to start a business or farm, cash payments for tuition and living expenses, and low-interest mortgages. These benefits expanded the opportunities of returning soldiers as they stimulated new businesses, catapulted college graduation and homeownership rates, swelled household wealth, and enlarged the postwar middle class. Altogether, the G.I. Bill assisted 7.8 million veterans in gaining additional education, with 2.2 million of those attending colleges and universities (Olson, 1973, p. 602). According to a congressional study, those who completed vocational training or college earned $10,000 to $15,000 more annually than those who had not (Herbold, 1994, p. 104). With the help of low-cost mortgages, another 2.4 million veterans bought homes over the seven-year period after World War II (U.S. Department of Veterans Affairs, n.d.). For them and their families, homeownership transformed their prospects, as they could now benefit from the postwar housing boom and rising home values. However, the program's generosity did not extend to all veterans nor help all communities. Though the G.I. Bill is written in race-neutral terms, its implementation did not meet this standard.

The uneven treatment received by Black servicemen and other veterans of color largely resulted from a society still segregated and overtly racist in attitudes, practices, and policies. Only after meeting with a delegation of Black leaders in 1940 did President Roosevelt endorse the full inclusion of Black soldiers in the military, though in strictly segregated units. Not until 1948 did his successor, President Truman, desegregate the military against serious resistance. In higher education, circumstances were even worse. White veterans could use their education benefits at any college or university that deemed them academically qualified; Black veterans received a list of 100 colleges as suggested by the Office of Education's publication entitled "Colleges for Negroes" (Turner and Bound, 2003, p. 151). In the south, all education was highly segregated. Black veterans interested in using their G.I. benefits to attend college could enroll in only the historically Black colleges and universities (HBCUs). Much smaller and underfunded as compared to their White counterparts, the HBCUs could not meet the deluge. Though these colleges nearly doubled their enrollments and stretched their facilities to breaking point, they still turned away over half of their applicants in both 1946 and 1947 (Olson, 1973, p. 74).

In the north, Black applicants faced different barriers. Some traditionally White institutions enrolled Black students, though always in small numbers. In 1946, the University of Pennsylvania counted only 46 Blacks among its 9,000 students (Herbold, 1994, p. 107). At nearby Princeton University, the student newspaper conducted a survey to gauge student attitudes toward Black matriculation. The results showed that over 60 percent of the student responses were opposed to Black attendance while those who supported it did so only under strictly enforced quotas and bans on where they might live (Herbold, 1994, p. 107). In either the north or south, Black veterans found strict limits on the use of their G.I. Bill education benefits.

Other barriers limited Black opportunities in vocational education. The G.I. Bill created regional counseling centers to assist all returning soldiers utilize available Veterans Administration benefits and training opportunities. In the segregated south, the norms of Jim Crow dictated separate forms of assistance. Even then, many counseling centers lacked Black counselors to serve veterans of color. Only a dozen Black counselors served in Georgia and Alabama while none served in Mississippi (Onkst, 1998).

Other systemic factors limited overall Black participation in the G.I. Bill and its benefits. For several reasons, Black participation in the military was lower than for Whites. Early on, the military could not accommodate the mass of Black volunteers given the requirement of segregated units, quarters, and functions. More Black volunteers were disqualified for service due to poor literacy and educational levels. The separate education systems in which White schools received better funding and support generated lower levels of educational attainment among Blacks. Not only did this preclude many from serving in the military and being eligible for G.I. benefits, fewer Black veterans were academically ready for college and other vocational training programs. Lower household incomes and fewer resources in the Black community meant that even those veterans who aspired to higher education could not support their families on the stipend provided. One potential explanation for the unequal treatment can be ruled out. Shortly after the bill's passage, a survey of enlisted men showed that 43 percent of Black G.I.s expressed an interest in some postwar education versus only 25 percent of White G.I.s (Turner and Bound, 2003, p. 151). Despite this interest, the overwhelming barriers caused Black veterans to experience much lower rates of college attainment than did their White soldiers at arms.

Federal Housing Association/Department of Veterans Affairs programs

Owning land, whether farm or ranch, served as a significant source of wealth in our agrarian past. With the dawn of the twentieth century, the country was leaving its rural roots. As Americans moved from family farm into towns and cities, home-ownership remained beyond the means of most families. Back then, most lenders required homebuyers to put up 50 percent or more in cash. Even then, lenders offered only five- to ten-year mortgages and expected the remaining balance on that date (Green and Wachter, 2005). Circumstances permitting, lenders would refinance this outstanding balance with another loan. Given these strict requirements, homeownership usually required years of saving for the purchase. This offered most homeowners little time to profit from any appreciation in their home. These high financial hurdles limited demand for homes when owners needed to sell, placing further restrictions on any capital gains homeowners might expect. During this time, homeownership did not serve as the bastion of financial security or wealth accumulation that it does today.

Even with this risk-averse system of home mortgages, the Great Depression played havoc with the housing market in ways remarkably similar to those of the

Great Recession. Under the cumulative weight of sagging stock portfolios, business failures, and skyrocketing unemployment, property values fell precipitously. As mortgages came due for refinancing, lenders were wary of making new loans. Homeowners forced to sell in a depressed market caused prices to plummet further in a self-reinforcing cycle. Foreclosures rose as borrowers could neither sell their homes nor gain new financing. As the crisis deepened, fully 10 percent of all homes went into foreclosure (Green and Wachter, 2005, p. 90). To restore financial stability to the housing market, Congress created the Federal Housing Administration (FHA).

To stabilize the home mortgage market, the FHA created an insurance program to guarantee home mortgages. Banks could now lend to new homebuyers knowing the federal government would guarantee the loans if they went into default. Yet, the FHA went far beyond simply insuring the market and restoring lender confidence. Working with state and federal authorities, the FHA secured waivers from the different state-wide "safety and soundness" regulations that fragmented the home mortgage market. These regulations limited the length of mortgages and their loan to value ratios to reduce the risks of default. Getting quick waiver of these regulations, the FHA created a national standard for home mortgages that permitted smaller down payments and longer terms. Over the next generation, mortgage loans increased initially to 20 years and eventually to 30 years in length, while down payments fell to 20 percent and eventually to 5 percent (Green and Wachter, 2005, p. 96). These changes profoundly transformed homeownership. Many more households could purchase homes while still relatively young. The longer terms and fixed interest rates meant homeowners could predict their monthly mortgage payments, giving an additional source of financial stability. The self-amortizing loans enabled households to reap any increase in value even as they slowly paid down their balances. In the postwar period of rising incomes and low unemployment, large segments of American society could cross the threshold of homeownership. Growing demand generated rising values for current owners and cause for new construction. Though the homeownership rate had languished around 45 percent from 1900 to 1940, it jumped to over 60 percent by 1960.

The FHA mortgage insurance program ultimately committed the full might of the U.S. Treasury as guarantor of these loans. To limit exposure, the agency designed the mortgage program as self-financing with borrowers charged an extra 0.5 percent to pay for loan defaults.[10] Still, the agency worried about the risks it was assuming. To limit these risks, it required strict appraisal guidelines established by the Home Owners' Loan Corporation. These appraisal guidelines incorporated neighborhood characteristics to supplement information collected on borrower credit worthiness and the property's condition. Knowledge of neighborhood circumstances could screen out those loans most likely to go into default over a 15- or 20-year period if home values in a particular neighborhood fell due to deteriorating conditions.

To achieve this end, the federal government developed residential security maps for all neighborhoods. After an assessment, each neighborhood received a letter and color coding. Top-graded areas obtained an "A" designation and were colored green. Viewed as the most desirable, these neighborhoods were "homogeneous" in population, experienced high demand in good times and bad, and had room for growth (Hillier, 2005, p. 216). Neighborhoods still highly desired, but with limited room for future expansion, were graded "B" and colored blue. Below these neighborhoods stood those colored yellow and graded "C." "C" neighborhoods had older, often poorly maintained housing, and were deemed vulnerable to an "infiltration of lower grade population" (Hillier, 2005, p. 217). The bottom neighborhoods received a "D" grade and were colored red.[11] Already, "D" neighborhoods suffered from low homeownership rates, poorly maintained housing, and an "undesirable population or an infiltration of it" (Hillier, 2005, p. 217). Homebuyers looking at properties in "A" and "B" neighborhoods could get an FHA-approved loan, but not so for those looking at properties in "C" and "D" neighborhoods. Lending authorities deemed these latter mortgages too risky.

These residential security maps reflected prevailing beliefs that shifting residential patterns among residents of different racialized groups would undermine property values. The FHA's own *Underwriting Manual* makes this point explicitly: "If a neighborhood is to retain stability, it is necessary that properties shall continue to be occupied by the same social and racial classes" (Gordon, 2005, p. 207). In the name of maintaining property values and stabilizing the mortgage market, these maps determined where mortgage lending would occur and thereby reinforced the existing rigidities of residential segregation. Further, they would generate disparate opportunities. Those selling properties in the desirable neighborhoods could expect many buyers, while those owning properties in other neighborhoods would watch them languish in value. Regardless of the intent, this policy favored White property owners at the expense of most property owners of color.

Such disparate treatment extended even further. After the war, the G.I. Bill offered veterans even more generous mortgage terms. Qualifying veterans could purchase a home with no down payment and still qualify for mortgage insurance at a cheaper rate using a combination Department of Veterans Affairs (VA)/FHA loan.[12] Unfortunately, this VA loan program adopted the appraisal guidelines used by the FHA. Due to imprecise records, it is unclear how many veterans of color were able to acquire these loans. Yet, some evidence does exist. In a study of the New York/New Jersey metropolitan area in 1950, about 500,000 mortgage records documented the borrower's racialized status. Of these, almost 16 percent were VA loans, with all but 0.1 percent of these held by White borrowers. In the same year nationwide, almost 98 percent of the FHA-insured loans went to White borrowers (Gordon, 2005, p. 209).

Many factors caused these disparities. During this period, racially restrictive covenants on property were widespread and legal. Not until its ruling in *Shelley* v. *Kraemer* (1948) did the Supreme Court strike these covenants down as unconstitutional. Even so, the FHA recommended such covenants in its Underwriting Manual until 1950 (Collins and Margo, 1999, p. 21). The appraisal maps not only favored White neighborhoods, but also encouraged new construction in the expanding suburbs. Understanding the guidelines, developers made sure to keep these properties exclusively for Whites only. Realtors and lenders supported these efforts by steering potential buyers into targeted neighborhoods and approving only those loans that would meet FHA guidelines. Prominent textbooks on real estate warned their readers about the influx of "undesirable" groups triggering price declines (Jackson, 1985, p. 198). Lastly, courageous households of color that disobeyed the social boundaries of White-only neighborhoods often encountered White violence as their neighborhood "welcome." All of these factors skewed the generous federal benefits toward White households.

Still, it is a mistake to think that these systemic advantages offered to White homebuyers precluded rising homeownership among households of color. Borrowers of color could still obtain mortgages without federally funded mortgage insurance. But, these borrowers were subject to loans with higher down payments, shorter terms, and higher interest rates. Over time, private mortgage insurers were able to narrow the gap and offer terms similar to those provided by FHA/VA loans. From 1940 to 1960, homeownership among Black households rose from 20 percent to nearly 40 percent (Jackson, 1985, p. 37). Although the racial gap in homeownership grew during this period, largely due to the selective generosity of federal programs, many Black households used this period of expanding employment and rising incomes to attain homeownership.

Limiting opportunities

Federal policies created other obstacles to impede the efforts of our ancestors of color to participate in the American Dream. Though the 14th Amendment extended citizenship rights to all born on U.S. soil, the Naturalization Act of 1870 limited naturalized citizenship to Whites and "aliens of African nativity and to persons of African descent." In a land of immigrants, that left newcomers of Asian and Latin American descent, as well as Native Americans born on reservations, outside the pale. This policy created a tiered system that encouraged discrimination of those ineligible for citizenship rights. In particular, this form of discrimination largely penalized Asian immigrants as their surging numbers in the last half of the 19th century threatened newly arrived Whites all along the West Coast.

Efforts to restrict Latino and Asian immigrants started even earlier. The discovery of gold in California lured tens of thousands of seekers from not only the east, but from around the world. Given their proximity, thousands of Mexicans and other Latinos flocked to the gold fields. Unhappy with the sight of these foreigners finding "their" gold, White Californian authorities passed the Foreign Miners Tax that imposed a monthly tax of $20 on all *foreign* miners.[13] This tax represented a confiscatory sum: about two weeks' pay (Gendzel, 2009, p. 77). Its selective enforcement on Latino claims, including some *Californios* who were citizens, generated a period of resistance and violence, after which many simply left the state disgusted. While White residents assumed many of the abandoned claims, so did a number of the newly arriving Chinese. They became the new threat and the target of a revised law called the Foreign Miners Tax of 1852. This time, the law assessed a monthly tax of only $3 per month. Instead of driving out the Chinese miners, the tax served the state as an important source of revenue, comprising somewhere between one quarter and one half of the total state budget during this period. A later amendment to this law in 1862, entitled *An Act to Protect the Free White Labor against Competition with Chinese Coolie Labor, and to Discourage the Immigration of the Chinese into the State of California*, leaves little doubt what goals these laws had.

Employment restrictions on Asian immigrants did not stop at mining gold. California, along with other western states with sizeable Asian populations, passed a series of laws restricting employment opportunities. Federal courts struck down some of these laws, including those that prohibited Chinese laundries, limited the number of aliens a business could hire, and excluded aliens from fishing coastal waters (Kim and Kim, 1976, 384–5). The courts left standing those state laws that required citizenship for licenses to practice medicine or law. Given state powers to license a variety of skilled professions, these rulings allowed states to restrict entry into a variety of occupations, including teachers, funeral directors, barbers and hairdressers, as well as veterinarians and pharmacists (Kim and Kim, 1976, p. 386). A number of states required citizenship among those vying for public employment. In 1896, the federal government joined the effort when it enacted the rule that only citizens could sit for the civil service exams (Kim and Kim, 1976, p. 386). These professional and employment restrictions on primarily Asian and Latino immigrants limited their economic opportunities and imposed financial hardships.

Limits placed on immigrant participation in the economy did not end there. Once again, California led the nation in passing legislation that prevented immigrant ownership of land. In prior decades, Japanese newcomers settled in rural areas and quickly showed their skill in raising crops. In response to White growers, the state passed the Alien Land Law of 1913 that prohibited land ownership for agricultural purposes by those "ineligible for citizenship." Many Japanese responded by deeding their land to their children (who had citizenship by birthright) or forming corporations and signing 99-year leases to the land (Gendzel, 2009, p. 79). Not to be deterred, the state passed another law seven years later that effectively closed these loopholes. As a result, many Japanese reluctantly left farming, only to compete with Whites in the remaining occupations still open to them.

At least a dozen other states followed suit and passed laws restricting land ownership by immigrants ineligible for citizenship. Along with the employment restrictions, these prohibitions placed severe limits on how much wealth these households could possibly build. Going a step further, Kansas passed a law in 1933 that prevented Asian immigrants from inheriting property as well (Associated Press, 2002). As they are based on citizenship status, these restrictions could only last a generation or two, depending on the birthplace of the children. Yet, their impact is still perceptible today. Many of these affected individuals are the parents and grandparents of those alive today.

Even with citizenship, Americans of color could not expect equal treatment. Two Supreme Court decisions gave federal permission to states interested in imposing racial discrimination. In the infamous *Plessy* v. *Ferguson* decision, the court majority argued they saw "no annoyance or oppression" suffered by Homer Plessy or any person of African descent forced to ride in separate rail cars (*Plessy* v. *Ferguson*, 1896). By this decision, the Supreme Court claimed that *separate but equal* treatment did not violate constitutional rights. Just three years later, the court heard a related case. In *Cumming* v. *Richmond County Board of Education*, three Black citizens sued the local school board for its decision to support a Whites-only high school with no provision for the secondary education of Black children in the county. The school board pleaded it could not afford to educate all children, only the less numerous White kids. In this case, the Supreme Court majority sided with the school officials. Declining to intervene, the majority argued

> the education of the people in schools maintained by state taxation is a matter belonging to the respective states, and any interference on the part of Federal authority with the management of such schools cannot be justified except in the case of a clear and unmistakable disregard of the rights secured by the supreme law of the land.
> (*Cumming* v. Richmond County Board of Education, *1899*)

The court majority clarified that any disregard of rights might be apparent if it "appeared that the board's refusal to maintain such a school was in fact an abuse of its discretion and in hostility to the colored population because of their race" (*Cumming* v. *Richmond County*). In this opinion, the court clarified its principle of *separate but equal* by signifying that separate trumps equal. Further, their decision argued there are no violations of equal protection as long as economic, as opposed to racial, reasons are given for the disparate treatment.

These two decisions gave federal imprimatur to the Jim Crow system of segregation that emerged at this time. Under Jim Crow, state and local laws as well as social customs dictated which educational, occupational, employment, and business opportunities were open to individuals based on their racialized group. The contrasting opportunities open to different racialized groups certainly affected the incomes earned and the wealth generated during this period. The vestiges of this complex system remain today as one investigates measures of educational attainment, professional participation, unemployment spells, and business ownership by racialized group.

While Jim Crow has long been associated with the South, comparable systems of racialized stratification operated outside the South, as well. In 1906, the San Francisco Board of Education segregated its county schools to prevent the education of White students in proximity with Latino, Asian, or Native American children. Throughout Northern cities, the use of residential covenants, zoning laws, and local practices by realtors and lenders cemented a rigid pattern of housing segregation. Across the country, one can find historical examples of laws, practices, or customs that advantaged White residents at the expense of other groups. Though the means differ from location to location and the disadvantaged group may change from one place to another, the one constant was their privileging of Whites over other groups.

Conclusion

Given the durability and inheritability of property and wealth, it is clear how past policies can explain our contemporary disparities in household wealth. Past actions that stripped the land and property from Native, Latino, and Japanese ancestors have clear repercussions today, as each generation had much less to offer their children. Most freedmen from slavery had little to show for the generations of work they and their families endured. Signature federal programs like the Homestead Act and the G.I. Bill helped millions of households achieve portions of the American Dream, but prevailing racial attitudes caused these programs to lavish their generosity on White households. For over a century, legal discrimination restricted the economic opportunities of different groups of color, along with immigrants from Asia and Latin America. While our racial attitudes have changed, their consequences are evident today in the racial wealth gap.

All of these past policies advantaged White households. In helping White households obtain a tract of land, a college education, and a home, these policies boosted their efforts to accumulate some measure of wealth. Parents could offer their children more education and greater opportunities. Each generation could build on what they had received and offer their children an even better start. Just because these past policies uniformly privileged White Americans does not mean that they helped all Whites. Nonetheless, these past policies do explain why a disproportionate number of wealthy Americans are White, while a similar disproportion of the impoverished is not.

In some cases, the racial prejudice underlying these policies was overtly stated, as evidenced by the bluntly named *Indian Removal Act* of 1830. More often, these policies of racial discrimination signaled their intentions more subtly, relying on coded terms. While racial animus certainly drove all of the policies, the causes of disparate treatment frequently extended beyond the scope of the offensive laws. The G.I. Bill assisted far fewer Black than White veterans, in part due to the VA's unwillingness to provide adequate staffing at the local counseling centers. Yet, the sources of unequal treatment extended far beyond. Many Black veterans did not obtain a college education due to the limited number of college seats open to African Americans. Many others never qualified for college due to the poor educational opportunities permitted under *Cumming* v. *Richmond County Board of Education*. Even if the VA had implemented the benefits without racial bias, broader systemic obstacles still would have precluded truly equal treatment.

This brief history also illustrates the regenerating power of race privilege in our history. Initially, these policies operated to expropriate much of the wealth held by persons of color. Native Americans and Mexican citizens lost much of their birthright land, enslaved Africans lost their liberty and their labor, and Japanese Americans sold much of their property under duress. Later discriminatory policies were less confiscatory. Jim Crow segregation and the alien land laws largely focused on restricting the opportunities of persons of color, not taking their wealth away.[14] More recently, the G.I. Bill offered returning veterans generous access to middle-class wealth.

Though the bill itself contained race–neutral language, its implementation amidst a racially segregated society skewed its distribution of benefits. Even when the design of policies is not overtly preferential, they still can privilege Whites at the expense of persons of color. Though the policies adapt and mutate over time, they persist in generating the same impact. Indeed, the court ruling in *Cumming* v. *Richmond County Board of Education* may herald the future in arguing that equal protection is not violated when economic, as opposed to racial, reasons are given as the cause of disparate treatment.

Contemporary concerns regarding the persistence of the American Dream naturally generate a lament for times past. However, as this chapter demonstrates, there was no golden age when the American Dream reigned supreme, at least not without a "Whites Only" sign.

Notes

1 This prohibition restricted taxes on income or wealth, as they are direct taxes on property. The 16th Amendment largely ended this limit on congressional powers in 1913.
2 It is instructive that rarely are the "Indian Wars" counted as part of the wars fought in our history.
3 This original designation of "Indian Territory" included most or all of the following states: Oklahoma, Kansas, Nebraska, Iowa, Minnesota, North and South Dakotas, Wyoming, and Montana, along with a good portion of Colorado.
4 In New Mexico, only 24 percent of claims were confirmed. However, a controversial GAO report (Sawtelle et al., 2004) concludes that this figure is closer to 70 percent.
5 Since Korea was under Japanese control, persons of Korean descent were considered threats as well.
6 In 1780, Pennsylvania initiated a gradual abolition of slavery. Within the decade, New Hampshire, Connecticut, and Rhode Island followed suit, while Massachusetts abolished slavery immediately. By 1804, both New York and New Jersey enacted gradual abolition measures.
7 This compromise increased the slaveholding state shares of the Electoral College and the House of Representatives as it counted enslaved persons as part of each state's population.
8 There were isolated cases of free Blacks enslaving other Blacks, as well as some Cherokee slaveholders.
9 At this time, freedom for Black Americans did not equate to citizenship.
10 For a long time, this added charge meant little. The FHA guarantee meant private lenders could offer much lower interest rates to potential borrowers, more than offsetting this FHA premium.
11 This is where the practice of "redlining" gets its name.
12 The VA offered a mortgage guarantee of 50 percent up to $2,000. The borrower would pay the 0.5 percent interest premium on the remainder of the loan balance covered by the FHA guarantee.
13 Just a few years earlier, California was part of Mexico.
14 Individual acts of violence as well as more organized "race riots" maintained the threat of violence and expropriation throughout this period.

Bibliography

Amott, T. and Matthaei, J. A. (1991). *Race, gender, and work: A multicultural economic history of women in the United States*. Montreal: Black Rose Books.

Associated Press (2002). Many states pushed to eliminate racist anti-Asian laws, May 28. Retrieved from www.asianam.org/law_against_asian-american.html.

Cherokee Nation v. *Georgia* (1830). 30 U.S. 1.

Chin, A. (2005). Long-run labor market effects of Japanese American internment during World War II on working-age male internees. *Journal of Labor Economics* 23 (3): 491–525.

Clay, K. B. (1999). Property rights and institutions: Congress and the California Land Act 1851. *Journal of Economic History* 59 (1): 122–42.

Clay, K. and Troesken, W. (2005). Ranchos and the politics of land claims. In *Land of sunshine: An environmental history of Greater Los Angeles*, ed. W. Deverell and G. Hise. Pittsburgh, PA: University of Pittsburgh Press, 2005, 52–66.

Collins, W. J. and Margo, R. A. (1999). *Race and home ownership, 1900 to 1990*. Washington, DC: National Bureau of Economic Research.

Cumming v. *Richmond County Board of Education* (1899). 175 U.S. 528.

Darity, W. A. and Myers, S. L. (1998). *Persistent disparity: Race and economic inequality in the United States since 1945*. Cheltenham: Edward Elgar.

Deverell, W. F. (1988). To loosen the safety valve: Eastern workers and western lands. *Western Historical Quarterly* 19 (3): 269–85.

Fairlie, R. W. and Robb, A. M. (2007). Why are Black-owned businesses less successful than White-owned businesses? The role of families, inheritances, and business human capital. *Journal of Labor Economics* 25 (2): 289–323.

Fetter, D. K. (2010). Housing finance and the mid-century transformation in US home ownership: The VA home loan program. Unpublished manuscript, Harvard University.

Finkelman, P. (2007). *Scott* v. *Sandford*: The Court's most dreadful case and how it changed history. *Chicago-Kent Law Review* 82 (3).

Finkelman, P. (2011). Coming to terms with Dred Scott: A response to Daniel A. Farber. *Pepperdine Law Review* 39: 49.

Gendzel, G. (2009). It didn't start with Proposition 187: One hundred and fifty years of Nativist legislation in California. *Journal of the West* 76.

Gordon, A. (2005). The creation of homeownership: How new deal changes in banking regulation simultaneously made homeownership accessible to Whites and out of reach for Blacks. *Yale Law Journal* 115 (1): 186–226.

Green, R. K. and Wachter, S. M. (2005). The American mortgage in historical and international context. *Journal of Economic Perspectives* 19 (4): 93–114.

Herbold, H. (1994). Never a level playing field: Blacks and the GI Bill. *Journal of Blacks in Higher Education* 6: 104–8.

Hillier, A. E. (2005). Residential security maps and neighborhood appraisals. *Social Science History* 29(2): 207–33.

Jackson, K. T. (1985). *Crabgrass frontier: The suburbanization of the United States*. Oxford: Oxford University Press.

Jelinek, L. J. (1998). "Property of every kind": Ranching and farming during the Gold-Rush era. *California History* 77 (4): 233–49.

Johnson v. *M'Intosh* (1823). 21 U.S. 543.

Kappler, C. J. (1904). *Indian affairs: Laws and treaties*, Volume 2. Washington, DC: Government Printing Office. Retrieved from http://digital.library.okstate.edu/kapler.

Katznelson, I. and Mettler, S. (2008). On race and policy history: A dialogue about the GI Bill. *Perspectives on Politics* 6 (3): 519–37.

Kim, C. and Kim, B. L. C. (1976). Asian immigrants in American law: A look at the past and the challenge which remains. *American University Law Review* 26: 373.

Krebs, A. V. (1995). Banishment from the "gold mountain." *Agriculture and Human Values* 12 (3): 45–54.

Lanza, M. L. (1999). *Agrarianism and reconstruction politics: The Southern Homestead Act.* Baton Rouge: Louisiana State University Press.

Lui, M., Robles, B., Leondar-Wright, B., Brewer, R., and Adamson, R. (2006). *The color of wealth.* New York: United for a Fair Economy.

Massey, D. S. (1993). *American apartheid: Segregation and the making of the underclass.* Cambridge, MA: Harvard University Press.

Morris, T. D. (1974). *Free men all: The personal liberty laws of the North, 1780–1861.* Clark, NJ: Lawbook Exchange.

Olson, K. W. (1973). The GI Bill and higher education: Success and surprise. *American Quarterly* 25 (5): 596–610.

Onkst, D. H. (1998). "First a negro … incidentally a veteran": Black World War Two veterans and the GI Bill of Rights in the Deep South, 1944–1948. *Journal of Social History* 31 (3): 517–43.

Painter, N. I. (1992). *Exodusters: Black migration to Kansas after reconstruction.* New York: W. W. Norton and Company.

Plessy v. *Ferguson* (1896). 163 U.S. 537.

Sawtelle, S. D., Kasdan, A. R., and Malcolm, J. (2004). Treaty of Guadalupe Hidalgo: Findings and possible options Regarding longstanding community land grant claims in New Mexico. *Rep* 59: GAO-04.

Shanks, T. R. W. (2005). The Homestead Act: A major asset-building policy in American history. In *Inclusion in the American Dream: Assets, poverty, and public policy,* ed. M. Sherraden. Oxford: Oxford University Press, 20–41.

Taylor, S. C. (1983). The Federal Reserve Bank and the relocation of the Japanese in 1942. *Public Historian* 5 (1): 9–30.

Turner, S. and Bound, J. (2003). Closing the gap or widening the divide: The effects of the GI Bill and World War II on the educational outcomes of Black Americans. *Journal of Economic History* 63 (1): 145–77.

U.S. Department of Veterans Affairs (n.d.). G.I. Bill: History and timeline. Retrieved from www.benefits.va.gov/gibill/history/.asp.

Wilson, C. (2015). *Freedom at risk: The kidnapping of free Blacks in America, 1780–1865.* Lexington: University Press of Kentucky.

Yinger, J. (1995). *Closed doors, opportunities lost.* New York: Russell Sage Foundation.

5

EVIDENCE OF WEALTH PRIVILEGE

Two contrasting narratives have long battled to offer the most convincing explanation of the American story. No doubt, both narratives capture some measure of reality, which explains their lasting appeal. On the one hand, we see our nation as a "land of opportunity" where one "by pluck and by luck" can rise from "rags to riches" and anyone can "be a millionaire." We aim to make a "level playing field" on which all may compete to fulfill their potential and gain the rewards due those who work hard and intelligently. On the other hand, we worry that we are actually a nation of "haves and have nots" in which "the rich get richer and the poor get poorer." In this narrative, opportunity is not universally shared, but rather selectively offered to the favored few. The debate between these two narratives persists largely because we have known little about the distribution of wealth across households and over time.[1] Social norms discouraged the disclosure of wealth in public while public authorities have declined to measure private wealth systematically. We now are able to discover which narrative is closer to the truth. Thanks to the Federal Reserve through its regular surveys of wealth over the past generation, we have a breadth and detail of evidence that permits unprecedented investigation of this issue.

Recall the Wealth Privilege model from Chapter 3. It considers the policies, practices, and behaviors that favor wealthier households in the wealth-accumulation process. The model predicts that as affluent households move along each pathway they will receive additional favors to ease their journey. Further, the Wealth Privilege model argues that these sources of privilege increase in an escalating manner, causing wealth disparities to expand over time. Less affluent households must contend with increased obstacles as well as reduced institutional help. The model predicts that below certain thresholds, the wealth pathways function as vicious, not virtuous, cycles. These very different circumstances and experiences suggest that absolute wealth mobility is much greater among the affluent than those without wealth.

In this chapter, I offer substantial evidence to discern whether and how the Wealth Privilege model operates, particularly along the three wealth pathways. To illustrate the escalating privileges, I consider how households, depending on their wealth status, experience key elements of each pathway. To do this, I examine these factors by household-wealth quintiles. Though this appraisal focuses on socioeconomic class, I do not neglect racialized status. I examine the evidence by racialized group to show how the forces of wealth privilege are deepening the racial wealth divide as well. One issue in Chapter 4 must await a later discussion: how current federal wealth policies influence the accumulation of wealth and its growing concentration. Given the complexity of these policies, it makes sense to devote a separate chapter to them.

In looking for evidence of wealth privilege, I could examine the most current snapshot, using the 2013 survey. Yet, I believe the 2007 survey serves this purpose better, for two reasons. First, the 2007 survey reflects an economy at the peak of a six-year expansion that raised both household income and wealth. In contrast, 2013 culminates a prolonged period of economic distress and financial turmoil. Though the Great Recession officially ended in June 2009, the economy was still languishing with high unemployment and mediocre economic growth several years after. Household wealth still remained 15 percent below its peak in 2007. Clearly, the earlier survey examines an economy in apparent good health. Second, both housing and stock prices were at near peak levels in 2007. By 2013, stock prices had fully recovered from their fall in 2008, while housing prices remained depressed. Since home values represent a far more egalitarian source of wealth, these disparate trends likely exaggerate the wealth disparities in 2013. On both counts, I believe the earlier survey better reflects a "normal" economy as well as a more representative snapshot of household wealth.

The evidence

As shown in Table 5.1, household net worth grew significantly from 1989 to 2007, even after making adjustments for inflation. Among all households, the median or "typical" household's real net worth grew from $85,000 to nearly $135,000,[2] a

TABLE 5.1 Household net worth

Households by net worth	Real median wealth ($ 2013)		Share of total wealth (%)	
	1989	2007	1989	2007
Bottom quintile	0	56	−0.1	−0.2
Lower quintile	18,863	29,668	1.3	1.1
Middle quintile	85,579	134,965	5.3	4.5
Upper quintile	210,793	335,734	13.2	11.3
Top quintile	658,682	1,018,955	80.4	83.2

Source: SCF 1989, 2007

striking 53 percent increase in a generation's time.[3] In addition, the typical household in each wealth quintile witnessed an increase in net worth, suggesting a widely shared prosperity. Yet, the trend in wealth shares offers a contrasting picture. The share of wealth held by the wealthiest households increased, while the shares of all the remaining groups fell.[4] The bottom households as a group fell further into debt as their household liabilities exceeded their assets. Despite the modest gains experienced by the middle three wealth quintiles, their relative shares of U.S. household wealth also declined. The absolute differences among each of the groups' median net worth increased significantly. During this period of substantial wealth accumulation, the evidence reveals rising disparities in wealth as predicted by the Wealth Privilege model.

Table 5.2 illustrates the impact of wealth accumulation on racialized groups. Over the period, each group experienced significant increases in real median household wealth. The catchall category, Asian or Others, witnessed the most dramatic gains, virtually wiping out the median wealth gap between themselves and White households. Similarly, Black and Latino households experienced a quadrupling of their median net worth, a rate that exceeded what White households experienced. Nonetheless, the absolute gaps between both Black and Latino households on the one hand and White households (as measured by the difference in median household wealth) rose substantially over the period, from about $120,000 to almost $160,000. Despite their substantial gains, Black and Latino households found themselves further behind in 2007 than in 1989. As for Asian or Other households, we shall see in Chapter 9 that their apparent parity with White households was somewhat transitory. However, the evidence suggests that Asian or Other households experienced the wealth pathways differently than the typical Black and Latino household. To help untangle these complications, we must examine the dynamics of wealth accumulation in more detail.

Household saving

As discussed in Chapter 3, the Household Saving pathway offers the most inclusive means to wealth accumulation; each household has the opportunity to save, in theory. Cultural allegories such as the "self-made" millionaire who raised himself

TABLE 5.2 Household net worth by racialized group

Households by racialized group	Real median wealth ($ 2013)		Percent of White wealth (%)	
	1989	2007	1989	2007
Asian or Other	65,976	170,441	51	93
Black	7,748	19,136	6	10
Latino	9,008	23,513	7	13
White	130,043	182,863	——	——

Source: SCF 1989, 2007

up by the bootstraps and attained his lofty position through acumen and thriftiness raises the profile of this pathway. Yet, a declining national savings rate over this period suggests its role may actually be more modest (Federal Reserve Bank of St. Louis, 2016). In any case, household saving offers the most available means to accumulating household wealth.

Unfortunately, the SCF interviewers do not ask households how much they saved, but whether and how they saved over the prior year. Their answers only partially reveal the link between household wealth and saving. As Table 5.3 indicates, there exist strong ties between household wealth, income, and savings rates. It is no surprise that wealthier households earned higher incomes and experienced higher rates of actual saving.[5] While only 24 percent of the bottom households reported *actually saving* in the prior year, nearly two thirds of the wealthiest households stated doing so.[6] What is curious is the reported savings behavior of households: a majority of households, regardless of income and wealth, purportedly saved a portion of their income on a regular basis. As indicated in the last column, there is no link between family wealth and the *intention* to save regularly. No doubt, unforeseen circumstances either eliminated or enhanced household savings, thereby explaining the differences between households engaged in regularly saving and those actually able to save. Seemingly, household savings is less about motive than opportunity.

Similar patterns emerge when we compare households across racialized groups. White, and particularly Asian or Other households, experience high household incomes relative to their Black and Latino counterparts, advantages that reflect enhanced wealth status.[7] Similarly, the pattern of actual savings rates clearly conforms to each group's income status. Nonetheless, there is little difference among the racialized groups regarding their intention to save on a regular basis. This corroborates other studies that find racialized status by itself has little impact on savings

TABLE 5.3 Households who reported saving in the prior year

Households by net worth	Median household income ($)	Actually saved (%)	Regularly saved (%)
Bottom quintile	23,017	24	57
Lower quintile	40,280	37	53
Middle quintile	55,241	46	48
Upper quintile	71,354	51	49
Top quintile	124,293	65	53
Households by racialized group			
Asian or Other	74,921	53	56
Black	34,526	35	52
Latino	40,280	39	54
White	57,543	46	51

Source: SCF, 2007

behavior (Bradford, 2003; Conley, 1999; Galenson, 1972; Gittleman and Wolff, 2000). Indeed, this evidence suggests that households, regardless of position, recognize the importance of regular household saving; it appears that disparities in circumstances make actual saving accessible for some while out of reach for others.

Certainly, it makes sense that increased saving becomes easier as household income rises. As explained in Chapter 3, institutional practices favor the affluent over the wealth-poor. Access to banking services, direct deposit, and electronic bill paying reduce the temptations caused by carrying cash. Homeownership offers an often overlooked source of saving. As homeowners make their mortgage payments, a portion reduces their outstanding debt and builds equity. This amount represents non-discretionary saving that is unavailable to renters paying comparable amounts. In addition, wealth gives households a reserve that permits wise purchases. The affluent can buy items in bulk without fear that they will run out of cash before payday. Prosperous households can afford to purchase fuel-efficient cars and energy-efficient appliances, rather than being forced to buy the cheapest, but not necessarily the most economical, choice. Even when they have insufficient wealth to make the investment themselves, their resources help increase their access to credit.

Moreover, all households are subject to fluctuating incomes and expenses, leading to periods of negative cash flow. Wealthier households can weather these periods by simply drawing upon their assets. Households without such resources must seek available credit to survive. Even then, their access to credit is limited as suggested by Table 5.4. Although most households, regardless of their net worth, requested credit sometime over the previous five years, there exists a clear pattern among which households had their requests for credit restricted (either denied or reduced). Households with lower net worth, along with Black and Latino households, experienced far higher rates of credit restriction than did others, despite their lower rates of credit requests.[8] Equally striking is the evidence regarding households who

TABLE 5.4 Access to credit

Households by net worth	Requested credit (%)	Restricted requests (%)	Feared rejection (%)
Bottom quintile	54	32	37
Lower quintile	66	32	24
Middle quintile	72	20	9
Upper quintile	70	10	5
Top quintile	69	4	1
Households by racialized group			
Asian or Other	73	19	11
Black	59	27	32
Latino	59	25	24
White	68	18	12

Source: SCF, 2007

chose not to apply for credit out of fear of being rejected. The less affluent, along with Black and Latino households, reported much higher rates of not applying for credit for this reason. To be sure, uneven access to credit likely results from differences in household resources and perceptions of credit worthiness. However, these figures illustrate that while all households share a common desire for credit, they do not have similar access.

Without personal wealth to draw upon or similar access to credit, poorer households have fewer means to buffer financial turmoil. They are more likely to miss payment due dates and even experience bankruptcy. As Table 5.5 depicts, less affluent households reported significantly higher rates of missed payments (two months or more), as well as higher rates of personal bankruptcy. (In either case, their credit rating will suffer, making credit ever more difficult to obtain.) Black and Latino households experienced late payments more frequently than White households, though the differences were surprisingly modest. Similarly, the incidence of bankruptcy among Black and particularly Latino households was much lower than one might expect, given their significant financial disadvantages.

Not only do wealthier households have greater access to credit, they also can obtain lower-cost loans. Most households purchase cars and trucks on credit. As Table 5.6 depicts, wealthier households typically paid lower interest rates on car loans than did less affluent borrowers. Perhaps they received cheaper interest rates because they took shorter loans that generate less risk for lenders; however, the evidence below suggests otherwise. This pattern is replicated when we consider racialized status. Black and Latino households paid higher interest rates on their car loans despite their shorter terms. Both factors raised their monthly payments. These differences do matter. Assuming a new car loan of $20,000, these interest-rate differences can yield an added annual expense of $240 for less affluent households.[9]

Disparities in borrowing costs do not end here. Wealthier households can obtain lower mortgage rates as well. Though Table 5.6 indicates smaller differences in

TABLE 5.5 Credit history

Households by net worth	Late (60-day) payments (%)	Personal bankruptcy (%)
Bottom quintile	13	17
Lower quintile	6	19
Middle quintile	5	14
Upper quintile	2	8
Top quintile	1	3
Households by racialized group		
Asian or Other	2	7
Black	8	15
Latino	7	9
White	5	12

Source: SCF, 2007

TABLE 5.6 Vehicle and mortgage loan terms

Household by net worth	Vehicle loans		30-year fixed mortgage loans	
	Median rate (%)	*Average loan term (months)★*	*Median rate (%)*	*Median loan balance ($)*
Bottom quintile	8.00	55	6.50	133,175
Lower quintile	7.00	56	6.50	89,530
Middle quintile	6.50	60	6.25	113,031
Upper quintile	6.00	57	6.00	130,937
Top quintile	5.90	53	5.90	177,939
Household by racialized group				
Asian or Other	6.00	59	6.00	167,867
Black	7.00	54	6.25	123,102
Latino	7.00	54	6.50	126,460
White	6.50	57	6.00	121,983

Source: SCF, 2007

Note: ★ In this instance I use the mean rather than the median value. The median value is similar across all wealth and racialized groups, 60 months. Using the average term shows that there is some variation among the groups. Moreover, the average is not skewed by the size of the loan, so it is not vulnerable to the problems that measures of average wealth might have.

typical mortgage rates, the consequences are actually more significant. Typically, wealthier households paid interest rates that were 0.5 percent below those of less affluent homeowners. Assuming a 30-year mortgage on a $120,000 loan, this difference translated into an annual saving of nearly $600. Similarly, White, as well as Asian or Other, households carried mortgage loans with lower interest rates, saving them several hundred dollars annually. In addition, households with the financial means to pay 20 percent down on their home purchase will avoid the cost of private mortgage insurance, saving them another $600 a year.[10]

The same patterns occur when one examines revolving debt like installment loans and credit cards. Wealthier households typically paid lower interest rates, usually 1 percent or more. Similarly, Black and Latino households reported paying higher interest rates despite having less access to these forms of credit. Even these nominal differences in interest rates underestimate the actual advantage. Since wealthier households have greater access to cheaper forms of credit, they rely less on these forms of unsecured debt and instead have greater latitude to borrow against their home. Not only is mortgage debt less costly, it is also tax deductible, making it cheaper still. Moreover, the interest rate on revolving accounts is irrelevant for some households. Unlike vehicle and mortgage debt, wealthy households frequently have the means to pay off their monthly balances, making the interest-rate issue moot. Indeed, some households might choose credit cards with higher interest rates due to other benefits they offer.

To be sure, little about this evidence is surprising or new. Most presume that wealthy borrowers get better terms as they likely offer a better credit risk.

Regarding race, the Boston Federal Reserve released a landmark study in the early 1990s on mortgage-lending practices in the local metropolitan area. After taking creditworthiness factors into consideration, it concluded that Black mortgage applicants were rejected at twice the rate of White applicants (Munnell et al., 1996). A more recent study titled "Risk or Race? Racial Disparities in the Sub-prime Refinance Market" found that in 2000, both Black and Hispanic mortgage applicants were much more likely to get a sub-prime mortgage—one that carried a higher interest rate—than White applicants with similar incomes (Bradford, 2002). According to Jacob Faber (2013), this trend continued through the height of the housing boom in 2006. Further, Melvin Oliver and Thomas Shapiro (2006) demonstrated how Black homeowners were charged higher mortgage rates than White homeowners. Their findings "confirm that even when one controls for other variables, race proves to be a powerful determinant of interest rates" (Oliver and Shapiro, 2006, p. 145). Whatever their cause, these disparities do demonstrate that both wealth and racialized status play significant roles in our contemporary credit markets.

Beyond greater access to cheaper credit, wealthy households suffer less exposure to health-related expenses. Though the SCF does not query households on their actual expenses, it does elicit information on health status and insurance coverage. Table 5.7 shows the results. Despite being older, wealthier households reported lower rates of health concerns for both themselves and their spouses.[11] On both counts, wealth-poor households disclosed health concerns at three times the rate of affluent households. Despite their elevated health problems, these households held private health insurance at one third the rate of wealthy households. The availability of government health insurance like Medicare and Medicaid does mitigate, though not eliminate, this disparity. Clearly, wealthy families receive greater protection, both medical and financial, against poor health.

TABLE 5.7 Health status and health insurance coverage

Household by net worth	Head health concern (%)	Spouse health concern (%)	Private health insurance (%)	Any health insurance (%)
Bottom quintile	35	30	32	60
Lower quintile	27	24	53	69
Middle quintile	26	23	68	80
Upper quintile	24	16	79	88
Top quintile	13	11	87	92
Household by racialized group				
Asian or Other	22	17	71	83
Black	29	26	50	72
Latino	30	26	41	53
White	24	18	68	82

Source: SCF, 2007

A familiar pattern emerges when we examine these measures from the vantage of racialized groups. White as well as Asian or Other households reported lower rates of health concerns that likely reflected their wealth advantages. They also benefited from greater access to private health insurance. Again, the availability of public forms of health insurance reduced this advantage, though not completely. As before, the very households that experienced better health outcomes also benefited from increased coverage, thereby insulating them from the financial challenges imposed by illness and injury.

Perhaps wealth-poor families report lower savings rates not because of challenging circumstances but rather from reckless attitudes toward credit. Poor financial decision making could explain why wealth-poor households experience higher rates of late payments and personal bankruptcies. Fortunately, the SCF does query households regarding their attitudes toward credit. Table 5.8 shows these results. When asking whether households believe it is okay to borrow to buy jewelry or furs, take a vacation, or purchase a car, wealth status or one's racialized group have little impact on household attitudes. There is a remarkable unanimity among the responses. In contrast, wealth status does seem to influence whether households believe it is okay to borrow as a response to an income loss. Given the other answers, these differences likely relate to household circumstances rather than to varied attitudes toward credit and its use. One would expect households possessing a wealth cushion to hold more circumspect attitudes toward borrowing than those with no cushion. The pattern of answers given by the racialized groups corroborates this explanation.

Family support

Given the broad definition of wealth offered in Chapter 2, the Family Support pathway is not simply about who receives family gifts and inheritances. Likely, all

TABLE 5.8 Attitudes toward the use of credit

Household by net worth	Believes it is okay to borrow money to			
	buy jewelry and furs (%)	take a vacation (%)	offset a loss in income (%)	purchase a car (%)
Bottom quintile	5	17	64	72
Lower quintile	7	11	58	80
Middle quintile	5	14	49	83
Upper quintile	4	14	46	82
Top quintile	4	12	41	82
Household by racialized group				
Asian or Other	7	12	47	78
Black	7	19	60	75
Latino	4	14	60	66
White	5	13	49	82

Source: SCF, 2007

parents offer their children life lessons and social contacts, though the extent and quality of these gifts vary immensely. As Lisa Keister (2005) notes in her book *Getting Rich*, "studies show that children learn about finances from their parents, and it follows that parents who are wealthy have lessons to teach that are more likely to help their children become wealthy as well" (p. 76). Yet, measuring the value of these informational transmissions is quite difficult. In one creative study, Ngina Chiteji and Frank Stafford (2000) demonstrate the power of transmitting financial literacy as they show that young parents are more likely to hold bank accounts and own stock if their parents did so. Parents can share not only their wealth, but also their learned experiences.

Even measuring the actual transmission of financial wealth across generations is problematic. To ascertain the significance and distribution of these gifts, the SCF asks respondents a variety of questions. Not only are they asked whether they have received an inheritance, but in what form it came, whether monetary, real estate, or business interests. The survey inquires whether they expect a future gift, as well as what amount they anticipate. Further, the SCF asks respondents whether they have given gifts to others in the past year, in what amounts, and to whom. While these questions offer an unprecedented look into intergenerational giving, this peek is not without limits. Relying on recall and memory means that any reported estimates are likely low. More importantly, some forms of family support are not viewed as "inheritances." In interviewing families, Thomas Shapiro (2004) found that "not one white or black family even mentioned parental payment of college expenses as inheritance. Almost all acknowledged the helpfulness of parental support; they just did not consider it part of an inheritance" (p. 65). He concludes that most respondents define inheritances as only those gifts received from deceased parents, even as he notes that one study estimates that 43 percent of such gifts are from living relatives (Gale and Scholz, 1994). This means that our estimates of gifts and inheritances may ignore crucial transfers during college or when buying a home. These problems aside, the 2007 survey indicated that only 21 percent of households reported receiving an inheritance while an additional 9 percent expected one in the future.[12] Another 10 percent of households reported giving financial help to other family members in the past year. Consequently, just under 40 percent of households have either given, received, or expect a family gift. Given this narrow view of family support, this pathway provides the least inclusive means to increased wealth.

Table 5.9 presents the key results. The wealthiest households were five times more likely to have inherited a family gift than those in the bottom wealth group. Further, the typical gift amount rose dramatically with each ascending wealth quintile. These two factors explain why over 90 percent of the inherited wealth has gone to the top two wealth quintiles. It appears that family background plays a substantial role in the current distribution of wealth.[13] Obviously, any examination of anticipated inheritances requires substantial caution. Still, the trends were similar, though less dramatic. Wealthier households have brighter prospects for future inheritances, both in their likelihood and in their expected median value.[14] Neither

TABLE 5.9 Past inheritances and expected future gifts

Household by net worth	Past inheritances			Expected inheritances		
	Received gift (%)	Median value ($)	Share of total (%)	Expect gift (%)	Median value ($)	Share of total (%)
Bottom quintile	7	12,624	1	8	80,114	4
Lower quintile	14	37,871	3	13	84,386	7
Middle quintile	21	49,736	5	13	129,250	22
Upper quintile	25	101,361	12	15	199,750	18
Top quintile	39	207,300	80	17	320,455	48
Household by racialized group						
Asian or Other	15	101,361	2	10	290,546	3
Black	9	84,468	3	6	106,818	3
Latino	4	113,036	2	9	106,818	3
White	26	84,468	94	15	160,227	91

Source: SCF, 2007

of these disparities reaches the levels just witnessed with past transfers. One explanation is the advanced age of many wealthy households; they likely have fewer ancestors still alive to offer future bequests. Nonetheless, the wealthiest three quintiles anticipate receiving nearly 90 percent of all future gifts. Interestingly, the evidence offers hope of upward mobility for some households in the bottom two groups. For the fortunate few whose expectations are realized, receiving one of these median gifts can elevate them immediately into a higher wealth quintile.

There are striking patterns when we consider family inheritance by racialized group. White households benefited from family help at nearly twice the rate of Asian or Other households, nearly three times the rate of Black households, and six times the rate of Latino households. This pattern makes sense given our country's racial history. Curiously, the value of the typical inheritance was remarkably similar across the racialized groups. Nonetheless, White households still captured 94 percent of the inherited wealth, a figure that results from both demographics and history.[15] Similarly, White households reported greater optimism regarding the likelihood and size of future gifts, particularly when compared to Black and Latino households. Despite their considerable wealth, White households expected to inherit more than 91 percent of all future inheritances, suggesting a continuing dominance over inherited wealth.

SCF interviewers also inquire whether households have *given* financial support to family or friends in the past year. They ask not only for the amounts of these gifts, but the recipient as well. This level of detail offers additional insight into the flow of funds within families, as it reminds us that transfers can run both ways across the generations. Gifts of money to one's parents, grandparents, or siblings likely reflect different motivations than gifts made to one's children and grandchildren. Thus, I label the former gifts as *distress gifts* and the latter as *bequest gifts*. By making this distinction, I can examine not only the impact of wealth and racialized status on family giving, but also which type of giving.

At first glance, the evidence in Table 5.10 linking household giving and net worth appears unsurprising. Across the board on all five measures, wealthier households engaged in more family giving than did less affluent households. The very wealthy were more than twice as likely to offer financial support to other family members as the bottom group, and their average giving was substantially higher. Yet, interesting patterns emerge as we consider the recipients of these gifts. Considering *distress gifts* only, these disparities largely disappear. Less affluent households gave nearly as frequently and as much as their wealthier neighbors, particularly when one accounts for differences in wealth. *Bequest giving* explains the large disparities in family giving. The wealthiest households were more than four times as likely to make these gifts and their average gift was 20 times what the bottom households could offer. The age of households can explain some of this disparity. Less affluent households are generally younger and more likely to have children too young to require such gifts. Nonetheless, one cannot ignore the role that wealth status plays in permitting this form of giving. As the burden of *distress giving* falls disproportionately on wealth-poor households, it drains their meager resources and reduces what aid they might offer their own children.

The pattern of giving among the racialized groups is even more startling. Curiously, White households were less likely to offer financial help of any kind to other family members, despite having deeper pockets. Distinguishing between the two types of giving offers further insight. Although fewer White households engaged in *distress giving*, they led in *bequest giving*. This dichotomy is starkly evident when we compare the average giving levels. Despite their greater wealth, White

TABLE 5.10 Types and amounts of family assistance

	Household donors			Among donors	
Household by net worth	Providing support (%)	Distress help (%)	Bequest help (%)	Average distress help ($)	Average bequest help ($)
Bottom quintile	11	8	4	1,256	786
Lower quintile	12	8	5	2,074	1,395
Middle quintile	15	8	8	1,883	3,591
Upper quintile	17	9	9	1,765	4,737
Top quintile	25	11	16	5,893	21,599
Household by racialized group					
Asian or Other	25	21	6	4,263	1,835
Black	19	13	9	5,922	3,001
Latino	17	12	7	2,773	1,604
White	15	7	9	2,346	11,644

Source: SCF, 2007

households gave the least amount of distress help, nearly one third of what the average Black donor gave. Conversely, they led all groups in their giving of bequest aid, by a large margin. Largely free of the burden of supporting parents and siblings, White households funneled nearly all of their largesse to their kids. Among households of color, the bulk of their giving went overwhelmingly to helping siblings, parents, and grandparents.

Past research has documented the potential drag on wealth accumulation from needy family members. In comparing Black and White middle-class families, Ngina Chiteji and Darrick Hamilton (2002) showed that Black families suffered a wealth gap that could not be explained by differences in household income, educational attainment, or occupational status. Instead, they concluded that differences in family background, including the presence of needy parents and siblings, could account for over one quarter of the racial wealth gap. In this way, the past is continuing to assert its influence on the present. Past policies cause households of color to experience very different giving patterns than White households. Families of color are much more likely to offer support to their elders than to their children. This need to help their parents diverts precious resources required to support their own kids, causing the pattern to repeat itself.

One might wonder if these patterns of interfamily giving are the result of different attitudes toward leaving a legacy. Perhaps individuals raised in a wealthy family recognize more clearly the importance of leaving an inheritance, causing them to do so at higher rates. Fortunately, the SCF asks households about their attitudes and expectations toward leaving a sizeable legacy. Table 5.11 provides these results. Interestingly, wealth appears to have little impact on the importance attached to leaving a legacy. Households reported rather uniform attitudes, regardless of their wealth. In contrast, wealth status did raise the expectation of leaving an actual legacy. The wealthiest households were twice as confident about

TABLE 5.11 Attitudes toward leaving a legacy

Household by net worth	Believe legacy is important (%)	Likelihood of leaving a legacy (%)
Bottom quintile	56	32
Lower quintile	55	39
Middle quintile	51	38
Upper quintile	50	45
Top quintile	58	68
Household by racialized group		
Asian or Other	58	51
Black	66	46
Latino	66	49
White	50	43

Source: SCF, 2007

doing so compared to the bottom households. Taken together, these figures suggest that varied capacity, not dissimilar interest, explain differences in legacy giving.

Table 5.11 illustrates a curious link between attitudes toward leaving a legacy and racialized group. Black and Latino households attach greater importance to leaving a legacy than do Asian or Other and, especially, White households. One must wonder if those who benefited most from such gifts are more inclined to underestimate their importance. Indeed, as he interviews various households, Thomas Shapiro in *The Hidden Cost of Being African American* found that families who had inherited wealth "rationalized handed-down advantages as deserved by attributing success to their own endeavors and hard work" (2004, p. 76). Due to their discomfort with this undeserved advantage, recipients have possibly downplayed the importance of these gifts.

Equally surprising are the expectations about leaving a sizeable legacy. Despite their substantial advantage in wealth, White households held lower expectations about leaving a legacy than did the other groups of color. Taken collectively, the evidence suggests that households of color, despite their diminished means, attach a greater value and report an increased motivation in leaving a legacy to their children.

Asset appreciation

As households acquire assets, they access a third pathway to increased wealth through asset appreciation. Financial assets like savings accounts, CDs, bonds, and stocks generate either interest or dividends that will supplement the balance, if left untouched. Real assets like homes, other real estate, and business assets can appreciate, sometimes requiring patience alone. These increases, called *passive saving*, enable households to experience substantial increases in their net worth. Table 5.12 depicts the typical amount of household assets held by each group, as

TABLE 5.12 Asset ownership

Household by net worth	Median household assets ($)	Share of total assets (%)
Bottom quintile	5,394	1
Lower quintile	58,753	3
Middle quintile	218,843	7
Upper quintile	439,700	13
Top quintile	1,185,143	77
Household by racialized group		
Asian or Other	327,677	4
Black	55,061	4
Latino	60,096	4
White	287,613	88

Source: SCF, 2007

well as their share of the total. The evidence offers no surprises as it shows a wide gulf in median household assets across the wealth quintiles. Whereas the typical household from the top wealth group had over $1 million in assets, those at the bottom held almost none. Similarly, White and Asian or Other households typically own about five to six times the assets held by Black and Latino households. Assuming for the moment that all assets appreciate uniformly, we would expect these disparities to expand in the future. For example, using a standard 5 percent rate of return on all assets, the wealthiest households would gain $50,000 annual increases in their holdings while the least wealthy would gain increases of $250. This trend is mitigated somewhat as households approach their end of life. Yet, in the absence of huge dissaving by the wealthy, it is hard to imagine the wealth gap doing anything but grow.

Of course, different assets appreciate at dissimilar rates. To understand fully the Asset Appreciation pathway, we must investigate the pattern of asset ownership. Table 5.13 examines asset ownership by wealth and racialized group. According to the table, 64 percent of the bottom quintile owned vehicles while only 16 and 2 percent owned stocks and business assets, respectively. In comparison, 87 and 34 percent of the wealthiest households owned stocks and business assets. Roughly speaking, these selected asset categories range from low risk return to higher risk return, moving left to right.[16] Not only did wealthier households own each asset with greater frequency, but also their leads in ownership rates increased as we consider the higher risk-return assets. Similarly, a much higher proportion of White and Asian or Other households owned homes, stocks, and business assets than did Black and Latino households. These disparities in ownership rates suggest that Black and Latino households typically will find it difficult to keep up with their White and Asian or Other neighbors during periods of rising asset values.[17]

TABLE 5.13 Asset ownership rates

Household by net worth	Vehicles (%)	Liquid account (%)	Real estate (%)	Stocks (%)	Business assets (%)
Bottom quintile	64	72	12	16	2
Lower quintile	90	92	58	38	5
Middle quintile	93	98	91	54	11
Upper quintile	93	99	95	70	15
Top quintile	94	100	98	88	34
Household by racialized group					
Asian or Other	91	97	65	65	14
Black	73	81	52	33	6
Latino	84	79	52	28	8
White	89	95	77	59	16

Source: SCF, 2007

Several obstacles make it difficult for some households to gain ownership over certain assets. Both real-estate and business ownership generally require significant down payments or initial investments that are beyond the means of most households. Ownership of these assets remains fairly concentrated in relatively few hands. At the same time, past policies have limited opportunities for households of color to buy homes and start businesses. Even today, Black entrepreneurship remains at one third of the rate among Whites, a figure that has held steady for over a century (Fairlie and Meyer, 2000).

Table 5.14 demonstrates the significance of asset ownership even more clearly. It lists the share of each group's wealth invested in the various asset categories. For example, the least affluent held 28 percent of their wealth in vehicles while the wealthiest households parked only 1 percent. This allows the rich to invest almost exclusively in assets that appreciate while wealth-poor households suffer declining values in one quarter of their portfolio. This represents a major impediment facing the less affluent as they attempt to "keep up with the Joneses." Wealthier households devote more of their portfolio into higher-return assets such as real estate, stocks, and businesses. At the same time, they can diversify their portfolios more fully. As Table 5.14 shows, the wealthiest households experienced the greatest balance in their asset selections. Similarly, White, as well as Asian or Other households, had greater balance in their portfolios than did Black and Latino households, whose wealth was largely concentrated in real estate. Given what occurred after 2007, this distinction will carry substantial consequences.

In his clearly titled article "Why Is Wealth Inequality Rising?" James Smith (2001) concludes that different asset portfolios among the affluent versus the wealth-poor offer the most convincing explanation. Over the ten-year period he studied, 1984–94, stock prices rose two and half times. Given their concentrated ownership among the rich, he argued that differences in asset ownership best

TABLE 5.14 Asset portfolio choice

Household by net worth	Vehicle value (%)	Liquid accounts (%)	Real estate (%)	Stocks (%)	Business assets (%)
Bottom quintile	28	5	53	4	0
Lower quintile	15	5	61	5	1
Middle quintile	8	5	66	6	2
Upper quintile	5	6	60	11	3
Top quintile	1	7	34	21	25
Household by racialized group					
Asian or Other	3	5	48	10	24
Black	5	4	60	8	8
Latino	5	3	65	6	13
White	3	5	38	20	20

Source: SCF, 2007

explain the rising wealth gap. Consequently, the differences in asset portfolios as shown in Table 5.14 signal a warning. We should expect wealth disparities to increase during periods of rising asset values. Less affluent households have a greater share of their wealth tied up in depreciating assets, and a much smaller portion in high-reward assets like stocks and business assets. As some assets are subject to cyclical fluctuations, we will witness some exceptions to this rule. During periods of rising real estate values, we might see some reductions in the wealth gaps, as less affluent, along with Black and Latino households, benefit disproportionately from these increases. This point also reveals their vulnerability to declines in real estate values.

The Wealth Privilege model argues wealthier households will invest a greater share of their wealth in high risk-return assets because they can tolerate more risk. Their increased wealth offers more opportunities for asset diversification, as well as a financial cushion that can protect them from unexpected reversals of fortune. Further, they have connections to a better-endowed social network that they may call upon in dire emergency. Each of these links presumably functions in a self-reinforcing manner. Table 5.15 corroborates this point. Wealthier households reported a higher likelihood of getting emergency funds or a "safety net" of $3,000 from family or friends. Equally consistent is the relationship between increasing wealth and a willingness to accept higher risk for greater rewards. The richest households were twice as risk tolerant as the bottom group; their accumulated wealth offers opportunities that their less fortunate neighbors cannot prudently take. Likewise, White, as well as Asian or Other households, tolerated more risk than did Latino or Black households. However, these differences disappear if one controls for household wealth.

The benefits of wealth extend beyond increasing risk tolerance. One must consider whether different households have access to higher-yielding assets within a given asset class. Presumably, all households can obtain information on which car

TABLE 5.15 Attitudes toward risk

Household by net worth	Safety net (%)	Risk tolerant (%)
Bottom quintile	42	38
Lower quintile	59	51
Middle quintile	70	54
Upper quintile	76	68
Top quintile	86	80
Household by racialized group		
Asian or Other	71	67
Black	49	47
Latino	47	41
White	72	62

Source: SCF, 2007

models depreciate the least. Similarly, all households can purchase the stocks of their choice and select the next rising star. Yet, wealth conveys some privileges. Affluent households can attract higher savings rates given their capacity to offer larger deposits. Real estate deals require minimum investments that most households cannot meet. Wealthy households rub elbows with other investors who share expertise and tips. While all of these examples suggest added advantages of holding wealth, they are difficult to document.

One exception emerges from this obscurity. Unlike most other investments, homeownership retains a rigid pattern of segregation when considering both wealth and racialized group. Discerning whether any pattern of privilege exists is significant given the importance homeownership plays for most households. Fortunately, the SCF queries homeowners on the purchase price, length of tenure, and current value of their home. Table 5.16 summarizes these results. Looking first at the role of wealth status, the results are unsurprising. As wealthier households are older on average, it makes sense that they have lived longer in their current home. There exists an equally strong link between wealth status and typical rates of home appreciation. Indeed, the richest households experienced annual appreciation rates that were triple what the least affluent homeowners earned. With their deeper pockets, wealthy homebuyers can purchase homes in select neighborhoods that likely will experience greater appreciation.[18] Often, they must pay more to gain access into these desired neighborhoods. All of these factors—longer tenure, higher purchase price, and faster appreciation—explain why the wealthy have so much more unrealized capital gains in their homes, giving them one more advantage in the race for greater wealth.

The evidence related to racialized groups is somewhat more complicated. The longer tenure for White homeowners is unsurprising given their past wealth advantages and higher homeownership rates. However, Latino as well as Asian or

TABLE 5.16 Tenure and price appreciation of principal residence

Household by net worth	Median tenure (years)	Median annual increase (%)	Median total appreciation ($)
Bottom quintile	4	1.8	8,545
Lower quintile	6	3.7	21,364
Middle quintile	9	4.9	59,818
Upper quintile	11	5.2	114,296
Top quintile	13	6.2	238,205
Household by racialized group			
Asian or Other	7	6.6	82,250
Black	9	4.5	48,068
Latino	7	6.4	64,091
White	11	5.1	88,659

Source: SCF, 2007

Other homeowners experienced home-appreciation rates above what one might expect given their wealth status. In both cases, they realized home-appreciation rates above those earned by the typical White homeowner. One plausible explanation for this curious result is geography.[19] According to the Case-Shiller Home Price Indices, home prices rose much faster in Florida, the Far West, and New York than in the Midwest and South (Standard and Poor Dow Jones Indices, 2016). Latino, as well as Asian or Other households, live disproportionately in these boom markets, thereby skewing their numbers. Despite their stellar appreciation rates, neither Latino nor Asian or Other homeowners kept abreast of typical White homeowners in terms of total appreciation. At the same time, Black homeowners experienced the lowest appreciation rates and the smallest gains, despite their rather long tenure in their homes. These rates likely reflect the extent of residential segregation and racial prejudice that still exists (Holloway et al., 2012; Iceland and Weinberg, 2002). As few White homebuyers look to purchase houses in predominantly Black neighborhoods, this reduced demand reduces the appreciation of home values in these neighborhoods.

Conclusion

Through its detailed and comprehensive set of questions, the SCF reveals new insights in the acquisition of wealth in America. Though the survey cannot examine directly how a given household accumulates wealth over time, it does illuminate the opportunities and challenges confronting different households as they strive for financial security. Most importantly, the survey enables us to investigate the circumstances different households face on the three pathways. The overwhelming evidence gives proof to the old adage that "it takes money to make money." The survey results illustrate a collection of systemic advantages and institutional practices that favor the wealthy, giving proof to the concept of wealth privilege. To be sure, few of these advantages are particularly surprising, while many result from understandable business practices. What is startling is the breadth and extent of advantages available to wealthy households. Moreover, given the self-reinforcing nature of these systemic advantages, we can only expect they will deepen over time.

According to the evidence, affluent households are far more likely to benefit from an inheritance than less wealthy households are; the size of their gift is much larger as well. Their family background not only offers them a source of direct support, but also protects them from the burden of supporting aging family members. Freed of this burden, they can support their own children more generously to secure their future prospects. Although the opportunity to save is open to all households, there are systemic advantages that make this easier for the wealthy. Many forms of wealth generate their own income streams, thereby easing the sacrifices of saving. With their superior financial resources, wealthy households have greater access to credit and pay lower borrowing costs, allowing them to finance purchases that can limit future expenses. Sitting on a sizeable nest egg, wealthier households can take greater risks as they manage their diversified invest-ment portfolio. They can devote a larger share of their assets to higher-return investments. All of these advantages and more demonstrate how wealth confers its privileges. The weight of this evidence offers a compelling explanation for why wealth inequality has grown during times of prosperity.

Not only does wealth offer special benefits, but the lack of wealth also generates obstacles. Households with few assets have more trouble getting credit that could allow economical purchases with high upfront costs. Even when they gain approval for credit, they endure higher interest rates and shorter terms. Rather than antici-pate a future inheritance, they often witness parents and other family members in financial need. Their primary asset, a car or truck, will depreciate over time and eventually require replacement. Limited financial security means they must keep their meager resources as liquid as possible, though the returns may be low. With negligible resources, households must overcome all of these challenges and more before they experience the forward momentum of wealth accumulation.

Largely due to historical circumstances and policies discussed in the previous chapter, households of color, particularly Black and Latino households, find themselves with much less wealth than the typical White household.[20] Even in the absence of any contemporary racial discrimination, these historical circumstances influence their experiences today. Fewer Black and Latino households have accu-mulated sufficient wealth to benefit fully from its privileges. They are far more likely to have minimal assets, causing them to face the financial obstacles just described. Given these conditions, it is unsurprising that the racial wealth gap is expanding.

People often argue our wealth disparities result from different attitudes and behaviors that distinguish wealthier households from those less fortunate. They claim that the wealthy exert better financial discipline and view credit more prudently. Others contend the affluent have greater interest in leaving a legacy to their kids. Lastly, some maintain the rich are simply less risk averse, enabling them to grasp opportunities many of us would duck. Yet, the evidence suggests a somewhat dif-ferent picture. There is little support for the belief that the wealthy have different attitudes toward the use of credit or leaving a legacy. The unanimity of attitudes on these two issues is clear. There is substantial evidence that the wealthy are less risk averse, though it is unclear whether this results from personality or from circum-stances. Wealth disparities result less from differences in household attitudes than in circumstances and opportunities.

Though this chapter has documented numerous benefits of wealth, the list is still incomplete. All of the benefits discussed focus on how wealth produces more wealth in a prosperous economy. Yet, all economies suffer reversals and one important benefit of acquiring wealth is the financial security it provides during times of distress. Its capacity to insulate households from the worst consequences that accompany financial turmoil gives further cause for the widening wealth gaps. The years after 2007 offer such a period of economic distress, though my analysis of this period must wait until Chapter 7. In addition, current federal wealth policies also operate to promote increased wealth. Understanding how these policies widen the wealth gap must await its own investigation in Chapter 8.

Before moving to these issues, we must investigate further an issue that remains unresolved. The Wealth Privilege model argues that each wealth pathway offers households very different circumstances depending on their wealth status. The evidence reviewed in this chapter certainly confirms this view. For households with few assets, the Asset Appreciation pathway offers little reward while for others it is extremely fruitful. Some households find themselves assisting other family members in need while others receive generous gifts. While households report similar intent to save, actual savings rates reflect the very different circumstances that households face. In most cases, the sources of wealth privilege apparently swell with increased household wealth. Both the model and the evidence suggest that households may find themselves in very different conditions as they strive to improve their financial well-being. Examining this possibility more closely is the focus of the next chapter. Discerning whether different circumstances do exist can illuminate the extent to which the American Dream is truly under assault.

Notes

1 Shammas (1993) provides an excellent analysis of what we do know about wealth inequality throughout U.S. history.
2 In this case, I'm using the median household of the middle wealth quintile as my measure of "typical" wealth.
3 Even more stunning, average real household wealth increased over 75 percent over this same period.
4 This apparent puzzle can be explained as follows. While less affluent households experienced some gains over the period, their gains were disproportionately modest, causing their share of total wealth to fall.
5 Given the question, the SCF is asking about *active saving* as opposed to *passive saving*.
6 The reader may wonder why the saving figure is so low for the wealthiest households. Not all wealthy households have high incomes and some are in retirement. The link between actually saved and household income is even stronger.
7 In the other seven SCF surveys starting in 1989, median household income for Asian or Others households ranged between 80 percent and 110 percent of White median household income. In the 2007 survey, the ratio stands at 130 percent. Given that this racialized group is the smallest demographically, as well as the broadest in diversity, it likely suffers from sampling problems.
8 One would expect higher credit-restriction rates among groups that tend to request credit in greater numbers, other things being equal. Higher credit-request rates mean that less qualified borrowers are asking for credit and are therefore more likely to receive a negative response.
9 Author's calculation based on a 60-month term and a 2 percent difference in interest rates.
10 Though the cost of private mortgage insurance varies according to the loan balance and length, an annual payment of 0.5 percent of the outstanding balance is a realistic figure. The above figure is based on a $120,000 loan.
11 This is based on the percentage who respond that their health is either "fair" or "poor" as opposed to "excellent" or "good."
12 The actual results are 21.0 percent of households report receiving an inheritance and 13.0 percent expect to receive one in the future. Since some households are benefactors

in both cases, the percentage of households receiving either past or future inheritance is 29.9 percent.

13 Using different data sources and methodologies, past researchers have concluded that anywhere from 20 percent to 80 percent of household wealth is due to family gifts and bequests. Wolff and Gittleman (2011) offer a recent review of this literature.

14 While households may be able to predict accurately whether they will receive a gift or not, I do question how well these recipients can guess its size.

15 If inherited wealth were equally spread across the racialized groups, White households would receive only 74 percent.

16 Strictly speaking, the asset category, cars and vehicles, actually depreciates over time.

17 One wonders if echoes of the Japanese internment experience can still be evidenced in this table. While Asian or Other households hold similar assets to White households, their ownership rates lag behind White households in real asset categories while they lead in financial assets. Perhaps this pattern reflects the losses of two generations back, as well as an aversion to returning to these forms of assets.

18 Wealthier homeowners have more funds to make improvements and additions to their home, thereby providing another reason for why they may witness greater appreciation.

19 One casualty of the SCF's desire to protect the anonymity of respondents is their unwillingness to share geographical information.

20 Much of the evidence in this chapter suggests that Asian or Other households have largely erased the wealth gap relative to White households. This conclusion is less certain than might otherwise appear. What is clear is that the wealth status for the typical Asian or Other household is different than the status for either Black or Latino households. As this explanation requires more than a paragraph or two and it relies on evidence that goes beyond what is provided in this chapter, I direct the interested reader to Appendix B for this discussion.

Bibliography

Bertrand, M. and Mullainathan, S. (2003). *Are Emily and Greg more employable than Lakisha and Jamal? A field experiment on labor market discrimination.* Washington, DC: National Bureau of Economic Research.

Bradford, C. (2002). *Risk or race? Racial disparities and the subprime refinance market.* Washington, DC: Center for Community Change.

Bradford, W. D. (2003). The wealth dynamics of entrepreneurship for Black and White families in the US. *Review of Income and Wealth* 49 (1): 89–116.

Brimmer, A. F. (1988). Income, wealth, and investment behavior in the Black community. *American Economic Review* 78 (2): 151–5.

Charles, K. K. and Hurst, E. (2002). The transition to home ownership and the Black–White wealth gap. *Review of Economics and Statistics* 84 (2): 281–97.

Chiteji, N. S. and Hamilton, D. (2002). Family connections and the Black–White wealth gap among middle-class families. *Review of Black Political Economy* 30 (1): 9–28.

Chiteji, N. S. and Stafford, F. P. (2000). *Asset ownership across generations.* Ann Arbor: Population Studies Center.

Coate, D. and Schwester, R. W. (2011). Black–White appreciation of owner-occupied homes in upper income suburban integrated communities: The cases of Maplewood and Montclair, New Jersey. *Journal of Housing Research* 20 (2): 127–39.

Conley, D. (1999). *Being Black, living in the red: Race, wealth, and social policy in America.* Berkeley: University of California Press.

Faber, J. W. (2013). Racial dynamics of subprime mortgage lending at the peak. *Housing Policy Debate* 23 (2): 328–49.

Fairlie, R. W. and Meyer, B. D. (2000). Trends in self-employment among White and Black men during the twentieth century. *Journal of Human Resources* 35 (4): 643–69.

Federal Reserve Bank of St. Louis (2016). Personal Savings Rate, April 29. Retrieved from https://research.stlouisfed.org/fred2/series/PSAVERT.

Gale, W. G. and Scholz, J. K. (1994). Intergenerational transfers and the accumulation of wealth. *Journal of Economic Perspectives* 8 (4): 145–60.

Galenson, M. (1972). Do Blacks save more? *American Economic Review* 62 (1/2): 211–16.

Gittleman, M. B. and Wolff, E. N. (2000). *Racial wealth disparities: Is the gap closing?* Annandale-on-Hudson, NY: Bard College, Jerome Levy Economics Institute.

Holloway, S. R., Wright, R., and Ellis, M. (2012). The racially fragmented city? Neighborhood racial segregation and diversity jointly considered. *Professional Geographer* 64 (1): 63–82.

Iceland, J. and Weinberg, D. H. (2002). *Racial and ethnic residential segregation in the United States 1980–2000.* Washington, DC: Bureau of Census.

Keister, L. A. (2005). *Getting rich: America's new rich and how they got that way.* Cambridge: Cambridge University Press.

Logan, J. R. (2003). Ethnic diversity grows, neighborhood integration lags. In *Redefining urban and suburban America,* ed. B. Katz and R. E. Lang. Washington, DC: Brookings Institution, 235–56.

Munnell, A. H., Tootell, G. M., Browne, L. E., and McEneaney, J. (1996). Mortgage lending in Boston: Interpreting HMDA data. *American Economic Review* 86 (1): 25–53.

Oliver, M. L. and Shapiro, T. M. (2006). *Black wealth, White wealth: A new perspective on racial inequality.* New York: Taylor and Francis.

Ross, S. L. and Yinger, J. (2002). *The color of credit: Mortgage discrimination, research methodology, and fair-lending enforcement.* Cambridge, MA: MIT Press.

Shammas, C. (1993). A new look at long-term trends in wealth inequality in the United States. *American Historical Review* 98 (2): 412–31.

Shapiro, T. M. (2004). *The hidden cost of being African American: How wealth perpetuates inequality.* Oxford: Oxford University Press.

Smith, J. P. (2001). Why is wealth inequality rising? *Causes and consequences of increasing inequality* 2: 83–116.

Standard and Poor Dow Jones Indices (2016). S&P/Case-Shiller 20-City Composite Home Price Index. Retrieved from www.standardandpoors.com/indices/sp-case-shiller-home-price-indices/en/us/?indexId=spusa-cashpidff-p-us——.

Turner, M. A. (2002). *Discrimination in metropolitan housing markets: National results from phase I of HDS2000.* Washington, DC: Urban Institute.

Wolff, E. N. and Gittleman, M. (2011). Inheritances and the distribution of wealth or whatever happened to the great inheritance boom? *Journal of Economic Inequality* 12 (4): 1–30.

6

THREE VIEWS OF THE
AMERICAN DREAM

In the abstract, each of us has the opportunity to become a millionaire. Every household may regularly save some portion of its current income. Each can purchase assets and experience rising values. All households can receive as well as share financial help with family members. The wealth pathways are open to all comers—but circumstances matter. All three pathways feature a threshold that households must cross. Beyond this threshold, each pathway functions as a virtuous cycle offering households the prospect of ever expanding wealth. Short of the threshold, however, households experience a vicious cycle that works to undermine their financial position. For those with meager incomes, continual dissaving can lead to mounting debts, not rising wealth. Until households collect adequate savings to purchase a home, other real estate, or stocks, their primary investment—their cars—will depreciate, not appreciate. Households of limited means are restricted in what help they can provide their children and may require aid from them instead. Until households can cross these thresholds, they will face resistance rather than assistance in their efforts to accumulate wealth.

Circumstances vary even among those households that have crossed these thresholds. According to the evidence reviewed in Chapter 5, the very wealthy earn substantially higher incomes and report significantly higher savings rates. They also report greater access to credit and pay lower interest rates on their debt. Over one third of the wealthiest households have received an inheritance and many expect to collect even bigger gifts in the future. The wealthy have the means and opportunity to offer larger gifts to their children. They enjoy far greater diversification in their financial portfolios and thus greater financial security. Willing to absorb more risk, they invest in higher-yielding assets. Their wealth allows them to cherry pick the most lucrative investments, including homes in the most desirable neighborhoods. Not unlike those households that occupy the basement floors of our wealth skyscraper, those households residing in the building's upper floors occupy a world with vastly different opportunities than those residing in the middle floors.

Others have argued that wealth status influences household attitudes, behaviors, and decisions. From his interviews of various families, Thomas Shapiro concludes that families view and use wealth differently depending on their circumstances. He argues that "(w)orking-class and poor families use wealth for life support, to cushion bad times, and to meet emergencies. Middle-class families, in contrast, use their assets to provide better opportunities that advantage them" (2004, p. 35). Similarly, John Karl Scholz and Ananth Seshadri (2009) contend that middle-class and low-income families hold different motivations for saving. While middle-class families emphasize savings for college and retirement, low-income families view Pell grants and Social Security better able to meet these longer-term needs. Instead, these families target saving that can buffer the anticipated instabilities caused by job loss, illness, and other emergencies. Others have accepted Oscar Lewis's "culture of poverty" argument to contend that the poor suffer from impulsive, hedonistic, and fatalistic values that trap them in poverty (Jordan, 2004). According to this view, it is not so much their external circumstances, but rather their shared attitudes that differentiate the poor from other families.

All of this suggests that households of varied wealth status, whether from different opportunities or motivations and values, likely pursue dissimilar strategies in augmenting their wealth. In this chapter, I examine households at three different places along the wealth spectrum and compare how certain attitudes, behaviors, and opportunities affect wealth accumulation at each point. To what extent do the wealth-building strategies reflect the disparate circumstances faced by households along the wealth continuum? Do the same strategies work for households regardless of their wealth status? Alternatively, do the specific circumstances radically alter the options and opportunities faced by households at different locations along the wealth spectrum?

Understanding the wealth continuum

To discern whether and how wealth status affects wealth-building strategies, I take the following steps. First, I continue to focus on households during 2007. As the peak in household wealth over the past generation, it offers the best choice in discerning which circumstances best explain wealth accumulation. Second, I exclude households headed by seniors. Before age 66, most households are building their net worth in anticipation of retirement while after this age they are working to mitigate its decline. They may employ the same wealth-building strategies as before, but will likely witness a decline in their net worth now that they are retired. To limit this shift, I omit those households headed by seniors.

Third, I return to the Wealth Privilege model to investigate whether differences in wealth status affect wealth accumulation. That model describes three distinct groups operating under substantially different circumstances. Wealth-poor households will likely experience difficulty in traversing the thresholds that separate the vicious from the virtuous cycles along each wealth pathway. Affluent households can avoid these difficulties and benefit from many of the privileges of wealth. However, the full benefits of wealth privilege are reserved for the rich. Thus, the Wealth Privilege model suggests a three-tiered approach: bottom, middle, and top; coincidentally, this resembles our usual convention of socioeconomic class, in which we speak of working, middle, or upper class.[1]

To illustrate these differences, I divide the households into one of three terciles, based on their net worth. Table 6.1 depicts the different circumstances that each group faces. With a median household net worth of $6,290, the bottom tercile represents households whose assets barely exceed their accumulated debt. Indeed, a significant number of households in this group have zero or negative net worth. Further, their relatively low rates of household saving (30 percent) and home-ownership (28 percent) suggest that most households in this group have yet to cross any thresholds. In contrast, the middle tercile has a median household wealth of over $240,000 and includes households that have achieved some measure of financial security and wealth. The vast majority of households in this group have crossed some, if not all, of the thresholds. Lastly, households in the top tercile have a median net worth of over $4.6 million, thereby representing households that have attained substantial endowments.[2] Virtually all are homeowners and the vast majority earn an income that permits household saving. Their circumstances indicate these households have long since crossed over the thresholds and experience the full benefits of wealth privilege. By investigating these different conditions, we can discover how the circumstances, decisions, and behaviors vary across the wealth spectrum.

It is worthwhile examining Table 6.1 in some detail. The first group of variables is simply demographic information. Persons of color head over 40 percent of the households in the bottom tercile while the percentages for the middle and top terciles drop to 20 and 8 percent, respectively. Curiously, Asian or Other households are spread evenly across the three groups, while Black and Latino households are concentrated in the bottom group. Just as the higher terciles have more White households, they also include dramatically higher numbers of college graduates. Further, households in the top tercile are older and much more likely to be married. Taken collectively, the evidence shows that wealthier households are older, better educated, more likely to be married, and White.

The next nine variables offer insight into the specific circumstances each group faces along the Household Saving pathway. As expected, both median employment income and reported saving rates increase across the wealth terciles.[3] Consistent with common sense, economists have demonstrated a strong link between household income and actual saving behavior (Browning and Lusardi, 1996, p. 1811). Yet, other factors matter here as well. Although the LCH model argues that households base their savings behavior on normal income, periods of prolonged unemployment may disrupt this link. The evidence suggests less affluent households experienced higher rates of unemployment in the prior year than did wealthier households, by a wide margin.[4] Among these affected households, their *actual* incomes over the prior

TABLE 6.1 Describing the wealth terciles

	Bottom tercile	Middle tercile	Top tercile
Net worth ($)	$6,290	$241,228	$4,644,415
Demographic			
Asian or Other (%)	4	5	4
Black or Latino (%)★	37	15	4
White (%)★	59	80	92
Age★	38	47	53
Married (%)★	47	72	88
Children (no.)	1.04	1.02	1.07
College educated (%)★	22	46	80
Household saving			
Normal salary income	$27,766	$62,174	$118,262
Did save (%)★	30	51	77
Has health insurance (%)★	60	83	96
Late pay (%)★	11	03	01
Unemployment (%)★	28	12	04
Bankruptcy (%)★	19	13	02
Credit for vacation Ok (%)	16	15	12
Long-run horizon (%)★	27	50	73
Legacy important (%)	57	52	61
Life remain (years)★	42	35	32
Asset appreciation			
Owns vehicle (%)	80	95	93
Homeowner (%)★	28	90	97
Holds home mortgage (%)★	23	76	66
Owns other real estate (%)★	04	25	68
Owns stock (%)★	06	21	60
Business owner (%)★	04	20	72
Risk taker (%)★	16	27	44
Family support			
Has education debt (%)★	23	16	05
Amount inherited ($)★	$5,880	$27,318	$990,885
Value of expected inheritance★	$18,520	$82,606	$963,057

Note: ★ Differences among terciles are statistically significant at 0.05 level. These are simply the result of a difference-between-means test.

year would have challenged their capacity to save. Further, households in the bottom tercile experienced higher rates of making late payments and suffering bankruptcy at some point in their past. Both events would lower their credit rating and raise their interest costs. Low earnings combined with higher interest costs would limit their actual saving, regardless of any desire to save. Given these factors, it is unsurprising that the reported savings rates rise with household wealth.[5] Perhaps the only surprise is that the differences are so narrow.

Lastly, four attitudinal variables may affect household saving. The "Credit for vacation Ok" measures household attitudes toward the use of installment credit to finance vacations. Households that rely more on installment credit will likely report less saving and experience lower wealth since their "saving" will come after the purchase as they pay down their credit line. Though attitudes toward credit appear rather uniform across the wealth terciles, differences within each group may still emerge as significant. Wealthier households reported having a longer-term planning horizon than did less wealthy households. No doubt, such a perspective would encourage patience and an increased willingness to save for one's future.[6] Notably, there existed little difference among the three wealth groups regarding the importance of leaving a financial legacy. These uniformly high percentages suggest that this portion of the American Dream still has broad support. Lastly, households with a longer life expectancy will desire a larger nest egg that they may rely upon. Largely due to the age differences already noted, those in the bottom tercile reported a longer life expectancy that should increase the urgency for saving today.[7] Given the likely impact of each of these attitudinal variables on household saving, it is worth investigating whether they influence the wealth-building efforts of different households.

The next seven variables compare circumstances along the Asset Appreciation pathway. For most households, vehicle ownership represents the first substantial step. The evidence in Table 6.1 demonstrates that it is the most widespread form of asset ownership. But, recall that vehicles depreciate over time, making them less effective investments. More important is the role played by homeownership. Owning one's home, other rental property, stocks, or a business are the four primary ways that households can benefit from asset appreciation. As the evidence shows, ownership of these assets varies widely with one's wealth status. While not quite one third of households in the bottom tercile own their own homes, over 90 percent of the other two groups do. Though not as disparate, ownership rates among the other selected assets indicate a similar pattern. Just as asset ownership should increase wealth, so will holding a home mortgage tend to diminish net worth. Certainly, owning a home free and clear of any mortgage debt offers the greatest benefits. As expected, the share of homeowners free of mortgage debt rises in each wealth tercile, offering these households the full benefits of homeownership. The remaining variable, Risk taking, indicates that wealthier households tolerate greater risk than do less affluent households.

The last group of variables characterizes the Family Support pathway for the wealth terciles. The first variable offers indirect evidence regarding family support.

Since many parents who are capable of offering financial assistance to their children's education will do so, the existence of such debt is a measure of available family support. Despite the much higher college attainment rates among the wealthier terciles, the incidence of education debt declined with wealth.[8] Similarly, the remaining two inheritance variables offer little surprise. Both variables measure how much inheritance households in each group, on average, either received or expect to receive in the future. Both corroborate the significant role that family inheritances may play in the wealth–accumulation process.

Taken collectively, these statistics generate little surprise. Wealthier households are older, better educated, and more likely to be White. They earn higher incomes, experience fewer misfortunes, and report greater capacity to save. Wealthier households own the listed assets in much greater numbers and report substantially less aversion to risk. Lastly, households in the middle and top terciles benefit much more extensively from financial help from their families. Given what we have seen in prior chapters, none of this is remarkable. With few exceptions, these differences are statistically significant as indicated in Table 6.1 by the asterisks.[9] Consequently, these results demonstrate how different the circumstances are that confront households in each of these wealth terciles. While it may be true that the wealth-building pathways are open to all households, these figures corroborate how disparate their experiences are depending on their position along each pathway. Sharpening the focus on this issue is the aim of the remainder of this chapter.

Quantile regression results

To deepen this investigation, I employ quantile regression analysis. Though similar to OLS (ordinary least squares) regression, quantile regression offers two distinct advantages. First, it focuses on *median* as opposed to *mean* net worth. In doing so, it reduces the impact that extreme outlying variables might have on the analysis. Given the high concentration of household wealth, this offers a substantial advantage. Second, quantile regression allows one to investigate the circumstances anywhere along the wealth spectrum. In this way, I can target the analysis and assess which variables impact wealth accumulation across the wealth spectrum. To compare households at the bottom, middle, and top of the wealth continuum, I return to the full sample of non-senior households and apply the analysis at the 16th, 50th, and 84th percentiles of household net worth. I choose each of these because they represent the center of the three wealth terciles just discussed.

This analysis offers us two critical insights. It measures the singular impact of each predictor variable on household wealth even as it considers the effects of the other included variables.[10] For example, quantile regression analysis can estimate the importance of homeownership to household net worth at each level of wealth. We can learn whether homeownership generates comparable or widely disparate rewards for households, depending on their wealth status. I can extend this comparison across all of the behaviors or circumstances that might encourage or inhibit wealth accumulation. In addition, the analysis estimates to what extent we can trust these results. In any statistical analysis, random chance always influences the outcomes. Fortunately, I can measure its likely role and generate some level of certainty (called statistical significance) that the calculated results truly reflect reality.[11] I have shared both sets of information in Table 6.2, the regression coefficients as well as which ones are statistically significant.

To understand which factors influence wealth accumulation at the selected quantiles, we must interpret the various coefficients. Interpreting most of these coefficients is straightforward, since nearly all of the variables are dichotomous (e.g. either/or conditions). Their coefficients simply measure how much the specific circumstance raises or lowers (positive or negative number) household wealth at the selected location. For example, simply having the head of household as Asian or Other instead of White decreases household wealth by $17,029 among households at the 16th percentile of wealth, holding all other variables fixed. Being Asian or Other will reduce household net worth by $70,098 among the affluent (at the 50th percentile) and only $19,462 among the wealthy (at the 84th percentile). When considering the impact of being Black or Latino, we see that it raises household wealth across all three quantiles, though of modest amounts. Before we conclude that this proves we have finally achieved a post-racial society, we must assess how certain these results are, an issue I address shortly.

Seven variables, Age, Age squared, Children, Normal salary income, Life remain, Amount inherited, and Expected inheritance, require a slightly different interpretation of their coefficients. In their cases, the coefficient measures the impact of a one-unit increase in any of these variables on net worth at the particular quantile. For example, for every $1 increase in the amount inherited, household net worth at the 16th percentile rises by $0.47, while the same $1 increase will boost net worth at the 50th and 84th percentiles by $1.09 and $2.02, respectively. The Age and Age squared variables are simply a methodological device to capture the non-linear way that household wealth is expected to rise over time as households age and approach retirement.

As mentioned earlier, not all of these results are trustworthy.[12] Statistical tests can calculate *p-values*, which estimate how likely a particular result is attributable to random sampling error. The lower the *p-value* the more we can trust the estimated result. *P-values* below 0.05, 0.01, and 0.001 represent the bronze, silver, and gold standards of statistical significance. I have identified the standard for each coefficient as indicated by one, two, or three asterisks, respectively.

Demographic variables

Now we are ready to examine fully the quantile regression results. Starting with the initial demographic variables, the age variables (Age and Age squared) are reliably credible across all three quantiles. Taken together, these two coefficients suggest older households have more wealth, holding other factors constant, and that the disparity does grow with increasing age. The specific values of these coefficients suggest this effect is greatest as households near retirement age, results that

TABLE 6.2 Quantile regression results

Variables	16th percentile Coefficient	50th percentile Coefficient	84th percentile Coefficient
Household net worth			
Demographic			
Asian or Other	−17,029	−70,098	−19,462
Black or Latino	4,667	17,592	12,997
Age (years)	−17,381★	−43,984★★★	−76,476★★★
Age squared	247★★	614★★★	1,054★★★
Married	−24,511	−130,031★★★	−179,731
Children (no.)	23,852★★★	46,682★★★	48,046★★
College graduate	9,877	−9,000	−111,922
Household saving			
Normal salary income ($)	2.55★	7.97★★★	12.36★
Did save	46,576★★	16,472	19,341
Health insurance	21,789	9,700	−11,919
Late pay	−5,176	26,568	61,179
Unemployment	−38,647★	5,537	45,746
Bankruptcy	−70,014★★	−62,388★	−19,217
Credit for vacation Ok	−16,318	−96,732★★	−53,577
Long-run horizon	32,683★	16,262	4,611
Legacy important	5,797	45,869	52,461
Life remain (years)	149	341	138
Asset appreciation			
Owns vehicle	−45,865★★	−127,347★★★	−100,714★
Homeowner	134,235★★★	339,451★★★	20,251,198★★★
Holds home mortgage	−142,726★★★	−531,882★★★	−20,476,080★★★
Owns other real estate	124,720★★★	307,909★★★	2,140,518
Owns stock	100,901★★★	215,867★★★	8,334,597
Business owner	258,112★★★	1,552,802★★★	12,913,720★★★
Risk taker	−9,686	22,004	124,777
Family support			
Has education debt	−122,930★★★	−188,069★★★	−170,823★★★
Amount inherited ($)	.47★★★	1.09★★★	2.02
Expected inheritance ($)	.30	.67	2.11
Constant	103,378	546,962★★★	1,223,088★★

Note: ★ = p <0.05; ★★ = p < 0.01; ★★★ = p < 0.001

corroborate the LCH. While these results do not predict that households will necessarily experience absolute mobility over their lifetimes, they certainly suggest that it is possible.[13]

Family structure plays a role in wealth accumulation. Curiously, married households have less net worth than do unmarried ones while households with more children have higher net worth. Both results appear somewhat surprising, though in the case of marriage, they are only partially significant. Regarding the marriage coefficient, the key issue is whether both spouses are earning incomes or not. Married families with two adult earners will witness higher household income that will undoubtedly boost their net worth. However, the marriage coefficient compares households having the same income based simply on whether there are married partners or not. In this case, having a spouse who is not earning an income appears to lower family net worth, at least among affluent households. At the same time, households that have more kids do experience increased net worth. Apparently, the parental motivation to provide for their children exceeds the financial drain imposed by their presence.

Lastly, neither of the race variables appears to have any direct impact on wealth accumulation. It's unclear whether this result is meaningful, since racialized status can function through other variables, most notably household income and inheritance. The remaining variable, attaining a college education, has a mixed, though ultimately insignificant, effect on household net worth. While this may be surprising, the explanation here is similar to the marriage argument. Gaining a college education usually leads to higher household income, thereby boosting household wealth over time. Simply having a college diploma without any increase in income clearly will likely reduce wealth given its substantial cost.

Household saving variables

Among this group, only one variable, Normal salary income, is consistently significant across all three quantiles. Clearly, increases in wage and salary income will raise net worth and substantially so.[14] As we saw with the age variables, the coefficients suggest that increases in household income generate substantially larger payoffs for the affluent and rich households. This result suggests that periods of economic growth that generate rising household income will simply continue to exacerbate the expanding wealth gaps. While households who reported saving last year did experience increased net worth, the results are significant only at the 16th percentile. Apparently, wealth accumulation among the rich is more the product of rising asset values and inherited gifts than from unspent current income.[15]

While this evidence suggests that many wealth-poor households experience the benefits of the virtuous savings cycle, two other variables remind us of their stark reality. For wealth-poor households, avoiding the dire consequences of either bouts of unemployment or personal bankruptcy are real concerns. Households that suffered unemployment during the past year or experienced bankruptcy sometime in their past could expect reductions in net worth of \$38,647 or \$70,014, respectively.

Even households from this group, when forced to make late payments, could face further declines in net worth, though this result is not statistically significant. Notably, each of these threats diminishes dramatically for affluent households.

We should not ignore the four remaining attitudinal variables in this group. According to the results, attitudes toward the use of installment credit, the importance attached to leaving a legacy, the length of one's planning horizon, or one's remaining life expectancy have no discernible impact on wealth accumulation, with two exceptions. Among wealth-poor households, those families able to plan more long term saw a sizeable increase in their net worth. While such patience and discipline caused household net worth to increase across the board, the impact is not statistically significant among affluent households. Similarly, a liberal attitude toward the use of credit depresses net worth across the wealth spectrum, but only at the median is this link significant. While the remaining two variables largely influence household wealth in ways that make sense, none does so at levels that generate any confidence. It is certainly striking that these attitudinal variables, along with the savings behavior already discussed, play such an insignificant role in determining household wealth.

Asset appreciation variables

In contrast, the asset appreciation variables broadly influence household-wealth building. Across the first two quantiles, six out of the seven variables attain statistical significance; among the very wealthy, the figure falls to four. The Risk taker variable aside, all six remaining variables offer a consistent pattern across the three quantiles. Among these six, four provide opportunities for substantial advancement. Owning a home as well as other real estate, running a business or investing directly in stocks each produces significant increases in household wealth, even to wealth-poor households. Though these households face major obstacles in making these investments, the results demonstrate their value, nonetheless. Of course, the rewards of asset ownership rise significantly, as we move up the wealth spectrum.

These results offer a cautionary tale as well. Owning a vehicle, often the first investment for any household, actually reduces net worth, across the board. Although this setback is not onerous for the affluent, it represents a major challenge to those households unable to secure other assets. Since so many wealth-poor families can only afford a car or truck, their experience on the Asset Appreciation pathway appears limited to holding depreciating assets only. Even those able to purchase a home may find it a mixed experience, since households normally take out a mortgage to purchase the home. As the evidence indicates, holding a mortgage uniformly reduces net worth, regardless of wealth status. The assumption of mortgage debt reflects the inherent risk of homeownership and reminds us that prudence and patience are often needed before it reaps much reward.

The remaining variable from this group, Risk taker, plays little role in wealth accumulation. At no point does it attain statistical significance nor does it produce a consistent result across the groups. Curiously, only among wealthier households does risk taking seem to lead to increased wealth. Given the perception of its importance to wealth accumulation, it is remarkable that it has no apparent influence.

Family support variables

All three family support variables attempt to measure family background and support through different means. Of the three variables, only past inheritances provide direct evidence of family support.[16] The expectation of a future inheritance suggests the family has some resources to give; it is likely that these families have provided past help to their children in ways not measured by the survey. The existence of education debt also offers indirect evidence of family resources. Normally, we would expect parents to assist their college-educated children to graduate with little or no debt, if they can. Interestingly, all of the variables show consistency across the three groups. The existence of education debt consistently and significantly reduces net worth across the board. At the same time, both past and the expectation of future gifts increase net worth, although the link is not always statistically significant. With both inheritance variables, their impact appears greater as we move along the wealth continuum. Regarding family inheritances, it certainly makes sense that a "bird in the hand is worth two in the bush," which is supported by the larger coefficients and the presence of statistically significant results in two of three quantiles.

It is worthwhile to investigate one issue more closely. The coefficients for both inheritance variables, both gifts past and expected, suggest the rich are better able to leverage these gifts for their gain. In both cases, a comparable family gift generates twice the gain as we move from the 16th to the 50th and again to the 84th percentile. Two explanations for this come to mind. Given the very wealthy are older, they received many of these gifts more distantly in the past, giving them an opportunity to invest and grow these gifts over a longer period. Even more importantly, the very wealthy recipient likely used these gifts to invest in ventures that are more fruitful. Whereas gifts to the wealth-poor may have financed the purchase of a car or truck or even repayment of existing debt, the affluent could use their gifts to invest in real estate or a new business venture. Although these coefficients are not wholly significant, they do suggest another venue in which wealth privilege may operate.

Analytical insights

Before discussing the broader implications of these results, it makes sense to identify the limitations of this analysis. Due to the underlying survey methodology, these results offer only a limited and indirect understanding of how much wealth mobility households experience. To grasp this fully, we need data on how specific households accumulate wealth over time. Unfortunately, the SCF does not follow the same households over time; instead, it surveys different households every three years.[17] The evidence underlying this analysis is simply a one-time snapshot of household wealth. Nonetheless, the evidence is sufficient to produce results that can help us understand the circumstances that either encourage or discourage wealth mobility at various points along the wealth spectrum. Returning to the metaphor introduced in Chapter 1, this analysis does not explain how households arrived at different parts of the American Wealth building, whether penthouse, basement, or somewhere in between. Instead, it provides insight into the factors that permit households at different heights of the building to rise or fall a few floors. Rather than illuminate how much wealth mobility is actually experienced, these results clarify which opportunities allow incremental mobility. This analysis elucidates which behaviors, attitudes, and opportunities either encourage or discourage wealth accumulation at different floors and by how much.

As this analysis uses the unweighted sample of households queried by the SCF, the results are not representative of the 16th, 50th, and 84th percentiles of American households at large. Nonetheless, the results do suggest what circumstances American households face if they are wealth-poor, comfortably affluent, or quite wealthy.

Perhaps the most visible insight of Table 6.2 is the crucial role of asset owner-ship, as demonstrated by the preeminent part played by the Asset Appreciation pathway. The six asset variables are largely significant across all three quantiles. The lone variable from this group that does not attain this standard is an attitudinal variable (Risk taker), not an asset ownership variable. Somewhat startling is the importance that asset ownership plays for even wealth-poor households. The results in Table 6.2 suggest an important public policy issue—the importance of identifying ways to expand asset ownership among this group. Yet, these oppor-tunities are not without risk. As the single most important wealth-building asset for most households, homeownership also entails significant mortgage debt that can sink households when circumstances go awry. Nonetheless, the results clearly demonstrate the importance of asset ownership and suggest substantial potential for programs that effectively diffuse asset building across the wealth spectrum.

In contrast, Table 6.2 offers revealing evidence regarding the role played by the Household Saving pathway in building wealth. Of the ten, only one variable, Normal salary income, attains statistical significance across all three quantiles. Among the remaining variables, only five achieve any level of credibility. Of course, increases in expected income will augment household wealth. What is surprising is that households who actually saved part of their current income over the past year did not witness statistically significant increases in their net worth, except among wealth-poor. This curious result corroborates our previous realization that wealth accumulation among the wealthy is less about *active saving* and more about *passive saving* that results from asset appreciation. Among the wealthy, wealth accumulation is not so much about discipline and frugality, but rather about asset ownership and their resultant capital gains.

This insight is corroborated by the relative unimportance of the four attitudinal variables: Credit for vacation Ok, Long-run horizon, Legacy important, and Life remain. We would expect that households who are careful about their use of credit, consider future consequences, want to leave a legacy, and expect to live for many more years would each lead to rising net worth. As such, the coefficients in Table 6.2 make sense.[18] However, with two exceptions, these four attitudinals do not credibly influence wealth accumulation. Household attitudes toward saving appear to have a modest impact on wealth accumulation at best.

At the same time, three variables among the ten represent obstacles to household well-being. Falling behind on bill paying, suffering unemployment, or experiencing a bankruptcy can challenge households trying to augment their wealth. Among the wealth-poor households, two of these obstacles, unemployment and bankruptcy, pose real and significant obstacles. Working in tandem, they can drain over $100,000 in household wealth from these households. Even for households adjacent to the 50th percentile, the experience of bankruptcy substantially lowers net worth. Among the very wealthy, none of these three obstacles poses a significant threat.

The empirical findings of Table 6.2 suggest the Family Support pathway plays a moderate and somewhat nuanced role in household wealth. Of the three variables, only the presence of education debt affects household wealth across the board. As this variable serves as an indirect measure of parental wealth, it suggests that family financial support for college represents a principal way that families transfer wealth across generations. This is particularly notable since few respondents will likely report this help as an inherited "gift." Even among the wealthiest households, the presence of this debt reduces household wealth by a substantial amount. The wealth of one's parents does matter. Indeed, past gifts have a clearly identifiable impact on household net worth at the 16th and 50th percentiles. Across the wealth spectrum, the anticipation of future gifts does lift household wealth, but not to a level that attains statistical significance.

Not only do these results offer evidence on the relative importance of each wealth pathway, they also corroborate elements of the Wealth Privilege model. Each wealth pathway contains an obstacle that deters household efforts, particularly among the wealth-poor. For this group, avoiding the hardships caused by unemployment or bankruptcy remain substantial challenges. These threats decline as households gain affluence. Similarly, the initial step in asset ownership, purchasing a car or truck, produces a substantial penalty to households. For those who might experience only this form of asset ownership, the Asset Appreciation pathway will appear quite unwelcoming. Lastly, the impact of holding education debt shows clearly the value of having parents whose resources can pay for college. This drag on wealth accumulation will hamper wealth-poor households far more than their affluent neighbors. This hindrance not only disproportionately reduces their net worth, but recalling Table 6.1, it also affects far more of these households.

Following the lead of Oliver and Shapiro's (2006) emphasis on the sociology of wealth, the Wealth Privilege model argues that the primary reason for the widening wealth gaps are the different opportunities and privileges accorded to wealth. In contrast, some argue that what differentiates the poor from the affluent is a different set of attitudes and behaviors. Many argue that poor households are saddled with imprudent attitudes toward credit, poor saving habits, short planning horizons, little stomach for taking risks, and little hope for leaving a legacy, thereby explaining their current position. With two exceptions, none of these attitudinal or behavioral variables played a statistically significant role in building household wealth. The results in Table 6.2 demonstrate that opportunities, much more than attitudes, influence household net worth.

The findings reported in this chapter offer insight regarding the dimming of the American Dream. Overcoming the obstacles and challenges facing our young and wealth-poor households is less about character and more about capacity building. The evidence offered here suggests that teaching different attitudes toward credit or longer planning horizons will likely bear modest fruit. Instead, these results offer a different source of hope. Programs that assist households in acquiring assets like a home or even starting a business could help them gain better access to the Asset Appreciation pathway. As the results show, this pathway offers these households the greatest promise of a financial nest egg. At the same time, these programs must be designed to mitigate the risks that asset ownership necessarily entails. In the next chapter, I examine some of these risks as they increased the vulnerabilities of households to the financial turbulence of the Great Recession.

Notes

1　As discussed in Chapter 3, Wolff (1981) also suggests that the very wealthy and wealth-poor households build wealth in ways very different from the "middle" that conforms to the LCH model.
2　Consistent with the later analysis in this chapter, I use an unweighted version of the sample. As such, these net worth figures reflect terciles of the sample, but are not representative of comparable wealth terciles in the U.S. population at large. Using these three values of net worth, they reflect household wealth found at the 22nd, 67th, and 98th percentiles of households at large.
3　I use wage and salary income as my measure of household income since it is less likely to suffer reverse causality between net worth and income. As the SCF queries households not only about their actual, but also normal income, I use the ratio of these two answers to normalize their wage and salary income. Though the differences are modest, the LCH argues that household saving reflects expected income rather than actual.
4　These rather high unemployment rates reflect two issues. Typically, an unemployment rate measures a particular point in time while this figure measures the experience of unemployment at any time during the past 12 months. Also, the measure here reflects "household" unemployment, not simply "individual" unemployment.
5　These rates refer to the percentage of households who reported active saving in the prior year, not the percentage of income saved.
6　In more technical terms, households that report a longer planning horizon likely have a lower time discount, making them less focused on the present.
7　This masks an important difference. If one adds the median age along with the life-remaining variable, it is clear that households in the bottom tercile have a significantly lower life expectancy than their wealthier peers.
8　Certainly, the relative youth of the bottom and middle terciles plays some role here.
9　Statistical significance means these differences are sufficiently large that we can plausibly exclude sampling error as a possible cause. In this case, we can view the differences as meaningful.
10　The dependent variable is measured by household net worth. This measure includes the full range of assets and debts discussed in Chapter 2.

11 I use bootstrapping to estimate the standard errors of the coefficients, which makes the use of sample weights problematic. Consequently, I am using an unweighted sample in this analysis. This means that the results are reflective of the SCF sample, but not representative of the broader U.S. society at the measured quantiles. This analysis is based on 200 bootstrap replications.

12 Recall that most survey respondents are randomly selected. The positive coefficients for the Black or Latino variable could be the result of the SCF inadvertently selecting wealthier Black or Latino households than their general population warrants. The positive coefficient could result from this possibility thereby influencing the results. Thus, we calculate standard errors, t statistics, and p-values to estimate this possibility.

13 This reflects a very complicated and technical point. Since this analysis does not examine specific households over time, these results do not demonstrate that households do experience absolute wealth mobility. Since age alone does appear linked to increased net worth, this could easily explain that absolute mobility is occurring.

14 These coefficients are consistent with what others have found including Blau and Graham (1990), Menchik and Jianakopolos (1997), and Oliver and Shapiro (2006).

15 Presumably, some if not most of those in the upper two terciles who reported "not saving" in the prior year experienced increases in net worth nonetheless, due to rising asset values or family gifts. Most economists would disagree with these householders and argue that saving did occur.

16 As the SCF generally asks not only for the size of any gifts and inheritances as well as the date received, I calculated the present value of these gifts using a 6 percent nominal discount rate. In those cases where the date of the gift was not provided, I took an average of the other dated gifts. As the wealthy might employ these gifts in investments that yield higher rates of return, it is possible that this uniform discounting will underestimate the role of these gifts in raising the net worth of the very wealthy.

17 The SCF made an important exception to this practice, which will be the focus of the next chapter.

18 The Credit for vacation Ok actually measures credit indulgence, the negative signs of the coefficients make sense.

Bibliography

Altonji, J. G. and Doraszelski, U. (2005). The role of permanent income and demographics in Black/White differences in wealth. *Journal of Human Resources* 40 (1): 1–30.

Altonji, J. G., Doraszelski, U., and Segal, L. (2000). Black/White differences in wealth. *Economic Perspectives: Federal Reserve Bank of Chicago* 24 (1): 38–49.

Angrist, J. D. and Pischke, J. S. (2008). *Mostly harmless econometrics: An empiricist's companion.* Princeton, NJ: Princeton University Press.

Barsky, R., Bound, J., Charles, K. K., and Lupton, J. P. (2002). Accounting for the Black–White wealth gap: A nonparametric approach. *Journal of the American Statistical Association* 97 (459): 663–73.

Blau, F. D. and Graham, J. W. (1990). Black-White differences in wealth and asset composition. *Quarterly Journal of Economics* 105 (2): 321–39.

Browning, M. and Lusardi, A. (1996). Household saving: Micro theories and micro facts. *Journal of Economic Literature* 34 (4): 1797–855.

Deaton, A. (1997). *The analysis of household surveys: A microeconometric approach to development policy.* Washington, DC: World Bank.

Hao, L. and Naiman, D. Q. (2007). *Quantile regression.* New York: Sage.

Hurst, E., Luoh, M. C., Stafford, F. P., and Gale, W. G. (1998). The wealth dynamics of American families, 1984–94. *Brookings Papers on Economic Activity*: 267–337.

Jordan, G. (2004). The causes of poverty cultural vs. structural: Can there be a synthesis? *Perspectives in Public Affairs* 1: 18–34.

Kennickell, A. B. (1998). Multiple imputation in the Survey of Consumer Finances. In *Proceedings of the section on business and economic statistics*. Dallas, TX: Citeseer, 63–74.

Lindamood, S., Hanna, S. D., and Bi, L. (2007). Using the Survey of Consumer Finances: Some methodological considerations and issues. *Journal of Consumer Affairs* 41 (2): 195–222.

Menchik, P. L. and Jianakoplos, N. A. (1997). Black-White wealth inequality: Is inheritance the reason? *Economic Inquiry* 35 (2): 428–42.

Oliver, M. L. and Shapiro, T. M. (2006). *Black wealth, White wealth: A new perspective on racial inequality*. New York: Taylor and Francis.

Scholz, J. K. and Levine, K. (2004). US Black-White wealth inequality. In *Social inequality*, ed. K. Neckerman. New York: Russell Sage Foundation, 895–929.

Scholz, J. K. and Seshadri, A. (2009). The assets and liabilities held by low-income families. In *Insufficient funds: Savings, assets, credit, and banking among low-income households*, ed. R. M. Blank and M.S. Barr. New York: Russell Sage Foundation, 25–65.

Shapiro, T. M. (2004). *The hidden cost of being African American: How wealth perpetuates inequality*. Oxford: Oxford University Press.

Smith, J. P. (2001). Why is wealth inequality rising? *Causes and Consequences of Increasing Inequality* 2: 83–116.

Wolff, E. N. (1981). The accumulation of household wealth over the life-cycle: A microdata analysis. *Review of Income and Wealth* 27 (1): 75–96.

7

RESILIENCE AND WEALTH PRIVILEGE

Given the privileges that accompany wealth, it is clear how a growing, prosperous economy can lead to widening wealth disparities. Economic growth generates higher incomes that foster increased household saving, particularly among the affluent. More importantly, economic prosperity produces rising asset values that benefit the wealthy disproportionately. Affluent parents can offer greater educational and financial support to their children as they mature and start their own lives with a comfortable head start. In this way, economic prosperity expands the opportunities and eases the choices faced by affluent households. Expanding wealth disparities is a predictable outcome of a prosperous U.S. economy. Our nation's success is undermining the remaining semblance of shared, economic opportunity.

As we know, bad stuff happens. Violent tornadoes and hurricanes destroy property and devastate communities. Powerful earthquakes level cities without notice. Less violent but more widespread, economic calamities shutter businesses, eliminate incomes, and shrink asset values. These threats arguably encourage the most basic reason for accumulating wealth: to overcome such disasters with minimal deprivation. Curiously, wealth functions as a double-edged sword in times of disaster. The possession of wealth generates greater exposure to financial harm during these periods. Simply stated, the wealthy have more to lose. At the same time, wealth provides increased resilience. It serves as a safety net that can limit the damage and suffering during periods of crisis. Further, wealth offers individuals and even communities the means to rebuild damaged properties and recover from whatever mayhem occurs.

Financial resilience, or the capacity to endure and even overcome adverse conditions, depends on several factors. These include the ability to mitigate harm as well as the means to recover quickly and fully while avoiding unwanted structural changes (Holling and Meffe, 1996). Wealth offers households the power to endure and recover from much greater levels of external disturbance. Not all assets suffer uniformly in periods of calamity. As the wealthy tend to have more diversified asset portfolios, they benefit from increased protection (Keister, 2005, p. 72). Wealthy households suffer fewer bouts of unemployment; even those that do suffer job losses have other sources of income to draw upon. Better covered by health and property insurance, affluent households can recover their health and rebuild damaged assets more quickly. Under dire circumstances, the wealthy have two other avenues for help. According to Mullainathan and Shafir (2009), the wealthy experience greater financial slack. Given their pattern of consumption, reducing their spending to weather an emergency is easier since these goods are more discretionary than necessary. In addition, the wealthy have greater access to external resources. The affluent can obtain credit more easily and pay lower interest rates. In most cases, their friends and families have greater means to offer financial support as needed. Lastly, deeper pockets limit the need to sell assets under duress, thereby giving the wealthy the opportunity to recover as assets recoup lost values. In contrast, less affluent households often must sell homes, other real assets, and stocks to weather the storm. In doing so, they desperately meet immediate needs at the expense of longer-term recovery. Wealth offers protection and revitalization during bad times that complement the privileges enjoyed during good times.

These advantages of wealth clearly have racial consequences as well. Showing real foresight, Melvin Oliver and Thomas Shapiro (2006) highlight the precarious position of the Black middle class. While greater numbers of aspiring Black households have achieved many of the benefits of middle-class status, these accomplishments mask an important vulnerability, their relatively low wealth. Taking up this point, Dalton Conley (1999) offers a vivid image when he argues that the evidence "shows that the white middle stands for the most part on the two good legs of good earnings and substantial assets while the black middle class stands for the most part on the earnings leg alone" (p. 92). In both cases, they warn that the low levels of wealth in the Black community make recent economic gains vulnerable to loss.

We can now investigate financial resilience as an additional and important source of wealth privilege. Remember that the SCF normally queries different households in each survey, which precludes any examination of how specific households experience calamities. Recognizing the extraordinary times, the Federal Reserve decided to alter this tradition.[1] Aware that the 2007 survey captured household wealth just as the Great Recession was unfolding, the Federal Reserve returned to these households two years later during the depths of the turmoil. Nearly 90 percent of the original households responded again, offering broad and detailed data about how individual families fared during this period. By comparing household outcomes, we can examine the intersection of financial resilience and wealth privilege. In particular, we can assess how the Great Recession harmed households across the wealth spectrum. While this two-year period is too short to investigate the full recovery of households, it does enable us to ascertain the harm and initial recuperation experienced by them. Further, it allows us to examine whether households merely suffered financial losses due to declining asset values or experienced structural declines that result from the sale of these assets. In other words, are the losses temporary and recoverable or longer lived and enduring?

The timing of these surveys aptly captures the shock waves triggered by the financial collapse. The 2007 SCF interviewed households mostly from June to December 2007 while the follow-up interviews occurred during the same months two years later. Over the last half of 2007, the bulk of economic news was still positive. The stock market continued its climb, peaking in October, and declined only modestly through the end of the year. The economy as measured by GDP grew throughout the year. According to the National Bureau of Economic Research (NBER), the U.S. economy peaked in December 2007 while the unemployment rate stayed below 5 percent throughout the year. Only housing prices foreshadowed the impending crisis. After years of strong growth, housing prices peaked in 2006 and declined 10 percent during 2007 (Standard and Poor Dow Jones Indices, 2016). Two years later, the stock market had fallen by one third and housing prices had declined an additional 20 percent. According to the NBER, the economy ended its recession during the summer of 2009, though unemployment peaked at 10 percent in October. As much as one could hope, the 2007 survey queried households just as the Great Recession was unfolding and the 2009 survey questioned them just as the economy was reaching its nadir.

What happened?

Unsurprisingly, most households suffered a decline in wealth over those two years. According to the Federal Reserve's own estimates (Bricker et al., 2012), nearly two thirds of American families endured some decline in net worth, with the typical loss being 18 percent. Even among non-senior households, the results were equally calamitous as indicated in Table 7.1.[2] Interestingly, only a bare majority among the bottom wealth tercile experienced a decline while almost three quarters of the

TABLE 7.1 Lost wealth, 2007–2009

Group	Lost wealth	Median 2007	Abs. change	Percentage change
All < 66	*62%*	*$101,281*	*−$10,088*	*−19%*
Wealth tercile				
Bottom	52	7,974	−647	−9
Middle	68	247,611	−45,912	−21
Top	75	1,432,542	−316,397	−21
Racial group				
Asian or Other	62	163,624	−10,207	−19
Black	61	17,502	−5,060	−31
Latino	65	23,612	6,060	−31
White	61	141,774	−12,103	−17

Source: SCF, 2007–9

wealthiest households did so. Perhaps this simply indicates it is hard to lose what you do not have. As Table 7.1 shows, wealthier households suffered larger absolute and relative declines in their net worth.[3] While households in the bottom wealth tercile typically lost 8 percent of their fortunes, affluent households typically saw their net worth decline by one fifth.

Across the racialized groups, the percentages of decline are remarkably similar. At first glance, this might suggest the Great Recession was colorblind. However, there is more to the story. Given their lower wealth status, it is surprising that Black and Latino households experienced losses in their net worth at rates slightly higher than the wealthier White and Asian or Other households. Even more telling is the typical losses suffered among each group. In absolute terms, White and Asian or Other households lost more than their Black or Latino peers did. However, on a percentage basis, the comparisons are reversed. Black and Latino households typically lost much greater portions of their net worth, almost double the rate borne by White households. These disparities become even more striking as we consider the reduced wealth held by Black and Latino households. Understanding how they suffered disproportionately despite their limited wealth is a major focus of this chapter.

Understanding why the Great Recession fell disproportionately on the wealthy is straightforward. It is simply an example of the taller one is, the farther one falls. The very assets that lost substantial value during this period—homes, real estate, business assets, and stocks—are the ones largely owned by the wealthy. Their heavy investment in these areas made them particularly vulnerable to economic loss. Less affluent households, either unable or unwilling to invest in these riskier assets, endured the decline in asset values largely unscathed. The penalty of unemployment, though less frequent among the wealthy, could inflict greater harm given their high salaries. Faced with the loss of employment income, affluent households likely consumed their accumulated savings at a rapid clip. Of course, their wealth offered a substantial cushion to mitigate this fall. Having more to lose, the wealthy did lose more during this period.

Understanding the disproportionate impacts of the Great Recession on Black and Latino households requires a more nuanced examination. We already know that Black and Latino households hold far less wealth than their White and Asian or Other peers. This disparity explains why they suffered smaller absolute losses, but not why they experienced larger relative declines. To understand this puzzle, we must examine how Black and Latino households entered the period more vulnerable financially, why the adverse conditions disproportionately harmed them, and how their circumstances forced them to make structural accommodations that damaged their prospects for recovery. Only then can we comprehend the consequences of the Great Recession and its impact on future wealth disparities. Further, we must untangle the threads of wealth status and racialized group to discern fully these disparate impacts. While affluent Black and Latino households certainly gain access to the privileges of wealth, one might wonder whether they gain the full measure of these privileges. In separating these two issues, we can answer this question.

TABLE 7.2 Lost wealth in detail, 2007–9

Tercile	Percentage lost	Median 2007 ($)	Abs. change ($)	Percentage change
Bottom				
Asian or Other	53	12,116	−304	−15
Black	51	4,142	−159	−6
Latino	58	7,591	−1,528	−23
White	51	10,149	−525	−3
Middle				
Asian or Other	62	272,466	−27,171	−12
Black	82	235,184	100,616	−51
Latino	79	205,670	−69,706	−38
White	66	252,893	−39,704	−18
Top				
Asian or Other	87	1,381,847	−436,740	−36
Black	90	939,805	−399,028	−46
Latino	78	1,062,523	−350,572	−27
White	73	1,578,251	−287,400	−19

Source: SCF, 2007–9

To untangle the entwined threads of wealth status and racialized group, I use similar wealth terciles to those presented in Chapter 6.[4] In this way, I can compare the circumstances of Black and Latino households with others of similar wealth, thereby distinguishing the impact of racialized background from wealth status. Table 7.2 reprises the same variables as Table 7.1, though in a detail that offers interesting insights. For each wealth tercile, households of color generally fared worse than White households. This is particularly true for affluent Black and Latino households while the results are more ambiguous for Asian or Other households. Almost without exception, greater numbers of Black and Latino households suffered declines in net worth, and they typically lost more wealth, both in absolute and relative terms. Black and Latino losses were particularly high in the middle and top wealth terciles. For reasons to be determined, their wealth status gave them less protection than their White peers. Despite starting with less wealth, affluent Black and Latino households experienced substantially larger reductions in their net worth. In fact, they suffered devastating losses during this period. Further investigation of the evidence reveals even worse harm.

Financial vulnerability

A household's financial resilience begins with the extent of its financial vulnerability. Households with greater financial security can suffer increased injury before they must make desperate decisions. The depth and breadth of household assets, the capacity to save out of current income, and the ability to get help from family and friends all reduce financial vulnerability. Each of these three avenues offers households the means to mitigate the harm done by damaging circumstances. Unfortunately, households of color, especially Black and Latino households, experienced systemic disadvantages in utilizing these privileges.

That Black and Latino households experience greater financial vulnerability is not simply the result of their lower levels of household wealth. As Table 7.3 suggests, their vulnerability manifests itself in several ways. Even within each wealth tercile, Black and Latino households hold less wealth and fewer liquid assets to draw upon in times of trouble. Further, they experience lower rates of health insurance coverage and are less likely to have a retirement account. In the case of cash life-insurance policies, Black and Latino households differ. Among the racialized groups, Black households are the most likely to have this form of life insurance while Latinos lag far behind. Nonetheless, Black and Latino households entered the Great Recession with fewer resources to draw upon. Of course, Table 7.3 illustrates some of the protective roles that household wealth plays. Wealthier households hold greater amounts of liquid assets, have higher rates of health coverage, are more likely to have a retirement account as well as life insurance, and with a cash balance to draw upon as needed.

Increased wealth offers households the opportunity to diversify their portfolio and limit their financial vulnerability. Table 7.4 illustrates the degree of diversification as it depicts the proportion of assets typically invested in a given asset *among*

TABLE 7.3 Levels of financial protection in 2007

Tercile	Net worth ($)	Liquid assets ($)	Health insurance (%)	Retirement account (%)	Cash life (%)
Bottom					
Asian or Other	12,116	2,693	76	41	11
Black	4,142	409	65	29	16
Latino	7,591	414	49	18	2
White	10,149	932	69	41	11
Middle					
Asian or Other	272,466	9,424	93	80	13
Black	235,184	5,178	86	74	49
Latino	205,670	3,625	69	61	16
White	252,893	6,939	87	77	27
Top					
Asian or Other	1,381,847	48,673	92	90	33
Black	939,805	14,498	83	64	48
Latino	1,062,523	16,570	80	72	19
White	1,578,251	38,628	95	91	43

Source: SCF, 2007–9

TABLE 7.4 Median share of total assets among different asset holders

Tercile	Vehicle owners (%)	Homeowners (%)	Landlords (%)	Shareholders (%)	Business owners (%)
Bottom					
Asian or Other	46	77	4	5	21
Black	52	82	29	9	2
Latino	63	86	64	7	2
White	33	81	33	8	3
Middle					
Asian or Other	5	72	28	7	10
Black	4	71	23	7	9
Latino	5	79	35	3	22
White	6	61	16	11	9
Top					
Asian or Other	2	33	25	16	17
Black	2	25	44	6	57
Latino	3	42	51	13	53
White	2	27	17	19	19

Source: SCF, 2007–9

owners of that asset. For example, among households in the bottom group, the typical (or median) White household that owns a vehicle holds 33 percent of their total assets in this way.[5] For cars and homes, the share of total assets declines as we move from poorer to wealthier families, thereby giving affluent households further protection against declining asset values. Though this trend is less apparent with the remaining assets, each offers added safety since wealthier households likely own multiple properties, stocks, and business interests. In most cases, Black and Latino owners experience increased dependence on certain assets, especially their homes, rental properties, and businesses. Declining asset values in these areas can translate into greater harm to net worth. The exception to this pattern is stock ownership. In this case, White households that own stock typically have a higher share of their net worth tied up in equities. Given the ease of diversifying stock portfolios, this distinction likely exaggerates their exposure to risk. Nonetheless, this disparity is significant since stock values rebounded more quickly than did real estate prices.

Wealth offers an additional advantage in limiting financial vulnerability. To investigate this, we must examine the principal asset for most households, their home. Table 7.5 provides this opportunity. With mounting affluence, households attain homeownership at increasing rates, purchase pricier homes, live in them for longer periods, and accumulate more equity. This latter point is significant since any fall in home value causes a disproportionate decline in net equity and therefore net worth.[6] As wealthier households usually have more equity in their homes, they

TABLE 7.5 Home values and home equity

Tercile	Homeowner rates (%)	Median home ($)	Median equity ($)	Median equity (%)	Median tenure (years)
Bottom					
Asian or Other	28	103,560	27,961	39	3
Black	25	95,275	17,605	19	7
Latino	24	82,848	20,711	29	4
White	39	103,560	20,712	21	5
Middle					
Asian or Other	83	269,255	134,628	52	6
Black	90	217,476	93,204	51	6
Latino	93	295,145	114,951	53	8
White	92	227,831	111,845	53	9
Top					
Asian or Other	93	724,918	466,019	64	7
Black	100	403,883	265,113	69	16
Latino	89	621,359	453,952	71	12
White	97	517,799	363,495	78	12

Source: SCF, 2007–9

will suffer a smaller relative decline in their household wealth, even if they experience an equivalent price reduction.

When we examine these issues in terms of racialized groups, we find both expected and surprising patterns. On the one hand, homeownership rates among households of color in the bottom wealth group clearly lag behind those of White households. One could easily argue this reflects the historical disparities discussed in Chapter 4. Moving to the two higher wealth groups, these gaps largely disappear given the universal appeal of homeownership. Somewhat unexpectedly, Latino as well as Asian and Other households generally owned higher-priced homes and held comparable levels of equity in 2007 as compared to their White peers. Black homeowners tended to lag behind all others in both categories, despite longer tenure in their current homes. Two factors explain these puzzles. As discussed previously, Latino as well as Asian and Other households largely reside in regions that experienced substantial increases in home prices (Taylor et al., 2011). In 2007, they stood on the peak of a housing bubble just beginning to burst. Their financial vulnerability was much greater than their balance sheet would suggest. In contrast, Black homeowners were largely unaffected by the housing bubble as their longer tenures and lower home-equity margins would suggest. Embedded patterns of residential segregation across the country can account for their lower appreciation rates. With lower home-equity margins, Black homeowners entered the Great Recession with greater vulnerability to sliding home prices.

During times of trouble, households also can tap any surplus income. They might divert current saving or prune discretionary expenses to offset declines in income or respond to pressing needs. Of course, not all households have the same capacity to address financial reversals. As Table 7.6 corroborates, wealthier households earn higher (normal) incomes giving them greater means to respond to adverse circumstances. Among homeowners, median mortgage payments do rise with wealth status, but not as fast as income. As a result, wealthier households expend a lower share of their income on mortgage payments, as measured by the mortgage-burden variable. Moreover, they experience lower debt burdens, suggesting less income is claimed by pre-existing commitments. Fewer affluent households have monthly debt payments that exceed 40 percent of their income, as measured by the high risk category. With lower debt burdens on higher incomes, affluent households have much greater flexibility in using their current income to offset financial setbacks, giving them another source of financial resilience.

We find the usual racialized patterns in Table 7.6. Black and Latino households earn significantly lower incomes than their White and Asian or Other peers for each wealth class. Yet, Black and Latino homeowners generally pay the same or more each month in mortgage payments as compared to White mortgage holders.[7] Therefore, both groups experience increased debt and mortgage burdens. Unsurprisingly, many more Black and Latino households entered the Great Recession

TABLE 7.6 Median household income, mortgage, and debt burden in 2007

Tercile	All	Among homeowners only			
	Normal income ($)	Mortgage payment ($)	Mortgage burden (%)	Debt burden (%)	High risk (%)
Bottom					
Asian or Other	38,339	932	41	49	85
Black	28,754	880	25	36	44
Latino	33,014	808	21	35	39
White	37,274	839	20	31	27
Middle					
Asian or Other	85,198	1,346	19	22	9
Black	70,288	1,243	20	30	20
Latino	63,899	1,553	25	33	38
White	77,743	1,139	17	23	14
Top					
Asian or Other	160,811	2,796	13	17	19
Black	123,537	1,657	17	23	11
Latino	149,097	2,278	21	27	16
White	169,331	1,905	12	15	12

Source: SCF, 2007–9

already financially vulnerable as their current debt payments exceeded 40 percent of their current income. With a greater share of their income already claimed by fixed commitments, these households had much less flexibility in using their current income to respond to any financial reversals. Lastly, Table 7.6 suggests that many non-affluent Asian or Other homeowners entered this period in a very vulnerable position as well.

While the above discussion and evidence focuses on homeowners alone, the situation for renters is remarkably similar. Despite their reduced incomes, Black and Latino tenants made monthly payments similar to those paid by White tenants; consequently, their rent and debt burdens are substantially heavier. Similarly, a greater proportion of Black and Latino (as well as Asian or Other) tenants started the Great Recession with debt burdens above the 40 percent mark.

Households experience decreased financial vulnerability if they have access to help from family and friends. Table 7.7 examines this issue and corroborates previous patterns. Wealthier households affirmed higher rates of receiving past inheritances as well as greater optimism regarding future gifts. Each gives evidence of a wealthier family network to draw upon. More directly, affluent households reported an easier time getting $3,000 from family or friends if circumstances warrant. Conversely, affluent households offered distress gifts to siblings and parents in greater numbers, suggesting contrary evidence. Yet, it is important to note the racialized pattern in this last column. Among White households, giving rates rose only modestly with increased wealth while those among households of color jumped substantially.

TABLE 7.7 Typical family and network resources

Tercile	Past family gifts (%)	Expect gift (%)	Has safety net (%)	Distressed giver (%)
Bottom				
Asian or Other	16	16	62	22
Black	6	4	42	7
Latino	1	8	40	11
White	15	14	60	6
Middle				
Asian or Other	14	3	75	22
Black	21	9	64	26
Latino	3	14	64	16
White	24	21	80	7
Top				
Asian or Other	14	12	73	33
Black	15	16	83	33
Latino	44	11	65	22
White	43	26	89	12

Source: SCF, 2007–9

Likely, this pattern results from the recent improvements in wealth experienced by many affluent households of color. Raised in families with limited means, their own prosperity enables them to be generous givers to less fortunate family members. This pattern largely repeats itself among the other variables of Table 7.7 as well. For each wealth class, Black and Latino households reported much lower inheritance rates and access to an external safety net. Once again, households of color experienced another source of vulnerability at the outset of the Great Recession.

The extent of harm

Just as households entered the Great Recession with very different financial resources, so did the financial maelstrom affect households in disparate ways. The assault on American household wealth was savage, yet surprisingly narrow in focus. Over a mere two years, household wealth fell by an average of $100,000 per household. Yet, over 95 percent of the lost wealth was caused by declining values in three areas: real property, business assets, and stock ownership. Lost income due to rising unemployment completes the damage generated by the Great Recession. Households without real estate, business interests, or stock ownership and fortunate enough to stay employed were unscathed and even prospered during these two years. This explains how so many households in the bottom wealth triad witnessed an increase, however modest, in their household net worth during this period. Even the majority of households that suffered during this period did not do so uniformly.

To survey the damage, let us focus first on the American home. During the Great Recession, housing prices tumbled in virtually all markets across the country. Table 7.8 measures the impact of this decline on those homeowners that maintained ownership of the same property.[8] Among this group, the typical homeowner experienced a 13 percent decline in their home value and a 20 percent reduction

TABLE 7.8 Impact of falling home values

Group	Lost value ($)	Lost value (%)	Net equity (%)	Tenure (years)
All under 66	−25,136	−13	−21	8
Wealth tercile				
Bottom	−7,492	−10	−14	5
Middle	−27,120	−13	−23	9
Top	−75,178	−16	−21	12
Racial group				
Asian or Other	−48,543	−16	−25	6
Black	−25,136	−16	−40	7
Latino	−42,799	−20	−34	7
White	−23,138	−12	−18	9

Source: SCF, 2007–9

in net equity. For many households, the decline in home equity represented their most important loss suffered during the period.

However, the injury caused by falling home prices was not shared equally. As Table 7.8 illustrates, wealthier households lost more, whether one considers the absolute decline in value, its percentage decline, or the relative loss in net equity. In this particular instance, wealth did not offer its claimants a special advantage. The market simply took away what it had given earlier during the housing bubble. More interesting are the results along racialized lines. All homeowners of color suffered disproportionately, no matter which measure one chooses. Two likely explanations come to mind. As mentioned previously, the concentration of Latino and Asian or Other households in regions that experienced the most volatile shifts in home prices explains some of the disparity. In addition, the persistence of residential segregation by race across the country could explain the remaining differences in declining home values. Property values in neighborhoods of color fell more precipitously likely due to higher foreclosure rates experienced by neighbors as well as reduced buyer demand due to rising unemployment and tightening credit. As a result, Black and Latino homeowners suffered greater losses in their home values and therefore experienced a disproportionate fall in net equity and net worth.

Black and Latino homeowners suffered more than simply watching their home values plummet. The financial turmoil forced many of them to lose their homes, causing the homeownership gap to widen further. Table 7.9 records their difficulties. Over the two-year period, Black and Latino homeowners were less likely to remain in their current home. While Americans are constantly on the move, Black and Latino homeowners suffered higher rates of selling their home due to distress or bankruptcy.[9] These figures suggest they experienced higher rates of financial and emotional stress during this period. Lastly, Black and Latino homeowners were less

TABLE 7.9 Impact on 2007 homeowners

Group	Homeownership rate 2007 (%)	Unchanged residence (%)	Distress sale (%)	Experienced bankruptcy (%)	Homeowner in 2009 (%)
All under 66	66	93	2.7	2.5	96
Wealth tercile					
Bottom	34	89	6.6	6.0	91
Middle	91	94	1.6	1.7	97
Top	96	94	1.5	0.8	99
Racial group					
Asian or Other	66	95	2.8	1.2	97
Black	46	88	4.4	3.1	90
Latino	49	92	5.0	2.6	94
White	72	93	2.3	2.5	97

Source: SCF, 2007–9

likely to remain in their homes two years later, placing them at a disadvantage whenever housing prices began to rebound.

Although relevant to a smaller number of households, investment properties affected their owners in much the same way. Most properties suffered price declines over the two-year period, with the typical property owner losing 8 percent of net value, an amount smaller than the volatile residential market. Table 7.10 offers a broader picture of those investors who maintained their investment properties. Generally, less affluent property owners lost more than their wealthier peers. Once again, owners of color experienced heavier losses than White property owners. To the extent that investors invest within their own communities, the same forces described above can explain these disparities as well. No doubt some of the volatility of these numbers also reflects the relatively small numbers who own investment properties.

Yet, Table 7.10 captures just some of the damage suffered by investment property owners. As Table 7.11 depicts, almost half of all investment property owners in 2007 had divested their holding by 2009. Of those still holding property, over 4 percent recently had experienced bankruptcy while another 4 percent owned properties whose debt exceeded their market value, known as being *under water*. Although still property owners, they are highly vulnerable to further financial distress and future divestment. Clearly, the Great Recession took its toll. Among the bottom wealth group, most property holders had divested their holdings or experienced bankruptcy. Similarly, the period savaged most property owners of color. A majority liquidated their holdings while many of the remainder experienced bankruptcy or suffered properties under water.

The Great Recession ravaged businesses as well. Collapsing financial institutions created a contagion of fear causing banks to restrict their lending in order to preserve cash. Money-starved businesses faced difficulties in paying suppliers and lenders on time. Simultaneously, business sales plummeted due to declining consumer

TABLE 7.10 Investment property losses among those who maintained their portfolio

Group	Net value ($)	Loss in value ($)	Relative decline
All under 66	85,000	−4,000	−8
Wealth tercile			
Bottom	15,000	−5,000	−20
Middle	54,000	−2,000	−3
Top	200,000	−10,000	−10
Racial group			
Asian or Other	45,000	−6,400	−60
Black	150,000	−40,000	−27
Latino	130,000	−7,000	−8
White	82,000	−1,000	−2

Source: SCF, 2007–9

TABLE 7.11 Status of investment property owners

Group	Property ownership		Among remaining owners	
	Property ownership rate (%)	Percent divested (%)	Experienced bankruptcy (%)	Under water in 2009 (%)
All under 66	8	48	4	4
Wealth tercile				
Bottom	1	61	44	0
Middle	10	55	5	3
Top	27	37	0	5
Racial group				
Asian or Other	10	68	0	0
Black	6	47	21	11
Latino	5	69	23	1
White	9	45	2	4

Source: SCF, 2007–9

spending, creating additional challenges. Many businesses responded by dismissing workers and even closing their doors. Some owners sold some of their business interests to generate cash to supply the others. Taken together, business owners suffered greatly as the value of their assets fell.

Table 7.12 documents the damage. Among those households that managed a business, the median value of their holdings declined by half. Nearly 3 percent of these households experienced bankruptcy during this period while another 25 percent simply liquidated all of their holdings. Of those still in business, nearly 15 percent owned businesses with no measurable value while nearly one third

TABLE 7.12 Impact on owners of actively managed businesses

Group	Among all business owners in 2007					Still owners	
	Owns business (%)	Median value 2007 ($)	Median decline in value (%)	Recent bankruptcy (%)	Divested business (%)	No business value (%)	Credit restrict (%)
All under 66	14	78,000	−50	3	25	15	31
Wealth tercile							
Bottom	4	5,000	−100	8	36	36	77
Middle	16	50,000	−42	2	23	14	30
Top	47	500,000	−46	2	24	11	25
Racial group							
Asian or Other	13	56,000	−73	0	34	13	88
Black	7	25,000	−100	13	30	30	100
Latino	9	107,000	−45	5	11	14	10
White	16	90,000	−43	2	25	14	28

Source: SCF, 2007–9

experienced credit restrictions. As Table 7.12 depicts, business owners endured financial harm regardless of their wealth or racialized status. Yet, certain business owners suffered egregious damage. Among those in the bottom wealth tercile, half had no business interests of value two years later. Black-owned businesses experienced similar devastation. Already underrepresented, nearly one third of Black business owners divested their holdings while another third held valueless enterprises. For their efforts, Black business owners endured double-digit bankruptcy rates as well. All of the remaining Black-owned businesses operated under credit restrictions imposed by lenders. While their losses were not as devastating, Asian or Other business owners suffered disproportionately as well.

Some of the losses depicted in Table 7.12 result from business owners selling their interests, in some cases even for a profit. To exclude this possibility, Table 7.13 examines only those owners that neither added nor reduced their business ventures.[10] Doing so reduces the losses suffered. Among this group, the typical business owner lost 14 percent of their business value. Yet, as we consider both wealth and racialized status, we find the same pattern. Less affluent owners generally witnessed a larger relative decline in their business value, with one notable exception. In addition, Black as well as Asian or Other business owners experienced devastating declines in the value of their business holdings. This evidence suggests that while some members of these groups might have sold their business interests before the floor collapsed, most did not. For whatever reasons, Black as well as Asian or Other businesses suffered dramatic reversals during this period.

The last major source of declining wealth stemmed from falling stock values. Table 7.14 summarizes the results. A bare majority of households, just over 55 percent, reported owning stock, either directly or through mutual funds and retirement plans. Over the two years, the typical household lost almost $3,000 or about 26 percent. About one in eight of stock-holding households divested their

TABLE 7.13 Median losses without divestiture

Group	Median business value ($)	Median loss experienced ($)	Median percentage loss (%)
All under 66	80,000	−3,999	−14
Wealth tercile			
Bottom	7,100	−999	−47
Middle	56,000	0	0
Top	500,000	−31,200	−26
Racial group			
Asian or Other	56,000	−39,100	−71
Black	25,000	−17,999	−91
Latino	120,000	−1,799	−25
White	91,000	−1,999	−9

Source: SCF, 2007–9

TABLE 7.14 Impact of declining stock values

| Group | Owns stock 2007 (%) | Among those households holding stock in 2007 | | | |
		Median value of holdings 2007 ($)	Median change in stock ($)	Median change (%)	Percentage divested
All under 66	55	32,621	−2,900	−26	12
Wealth tercile					
Bottom	30	4,142	−264	−24	24
Middle	72	39,197	−4,453	−23	10
Top	91	298,252	−68,260	−35	5
Racial group					
Asian or Other	70	32,621	57	3	13
Black	35	14,498	−1,367	−49	23
Latino	27	12,945	−932	−12	16
White	62	38,317	−4,009	−26	11

Source: SCF, 2007–9

funds by 2009. When examining the experiences of households based on their wealth status, no startling patterns appear. Wealthier households held larger stock portfolios and suffered greater losses, perhaps reflecting their inclination to hold riskier stock portfolios. When we consider households by racialized status, their experiences exhibit curious patterns. Black and Latino households lag behind others in stock ownership, largely reflecting their reduced wealth status. Yet, the similarities end there. Black households typically lost almost half of their stock holdings while Latino investors lost only a tenth. Over the two years, nearly one fourth of Black households liquidated their stock holdings while 16 percent of Latino households did so. Lastly, Asian and Other households saw little change in their holdings; undoubtedly, some liquidated their portfolios while others must have bought stock during the period.

To some extent, the figures cited in Table 7.14 might overstate the losses experienced by households. In some cases, the declining stock portfolios are not simply reductions in stock values, but also decisions to sell shares. Some households fearful of future declines sold their stock shares and invested the proceeds elsewhere in their portfolio. Thus, these percentage losses likely overstate the impact of these changes on household net worth. In addition, stock divestiture does not have the same implications of possible distress as the sale of one's home, other real property, or businesses. While reversing these latter decisions can be costly in time and money, reinvesting in the stock market is relatively easy. Thus, the rather high divesture rate among Black stockholders may not preclude future opportunities. Nonetheless, it corroborates a broader pattern in which Black households, in particular, find themselves less able to profit from the ensuing expansion since their asset ownership has declined.

TABLE 7.15 Unemployment and its impact on household net worth

Group	Experienced unemployment in 2007 (%)	Experienced unemployment in 2009 (%)	Experienced net worth loss (%)	
			No unemployment in 2009	Yes unemployment in 2009
All under 66	18	25	60	66
Wealth tercile				
Bottom	26	33	49	59
Middle	12	20	66	78
Top	8	14	75	74
Racial group				
Asian or Other	15	26	59	70
Black	23	33	60	64
Latino	28	35	62	72
White	16	22	60	65

Source: SCF, 2007–9

Lastly, the Great Recession imposed the burden of rising unemployment on many households, causing them to liquidate their net worth. As Table 7.15 illustrates, the incidence of mounting unemployment affected all household groups, though not uniformly.[11] Over one quarter of all households reported experiencing some spell of unemployment over the previous year. The burden fell heaviest upon the least affluent as well as Black and Latino households. Obviously, households experiencing a bout of unemployment saw their household income decline. This loss caused many households to use savings or increase debt to finance household expenses. In this way, unemployment increased the likelihood that a household would experience declining net worth. Further, unemployment increased financial vulnerability in ways not documented in Table 7.15. During bouts of unemployment, households saw their monthly rent, mortgage, or total debt payments exceed 40 percent of current income. Households experiencing unemployment doubled their rates of late payments and bankruptcy. That Black and Latino households as well as wealth-poor households experienced higher unemployment rates only added to their other challenges.

Structural harm

So far, I have discussed which attributes caused households to suffer disproportionately during this period. Households without property or stock ownership largely survived the period unharmed, especially if they kept their jobs. In contrast, wealthier households with substantial holdings in property, businesses, and stocks were particularly vulnerable, as declining asset values ravaged their net worth. Though the wealthy frequently suffered substantial absolute losses, their diversified portfolios often limited these losses to smaller relative declines than those experienced by less affluent households. One notable exception is the primary residence in which the most affluent households experienced absolute and relative losses greater than others did; by definition, one cannot diversify one's primary residence.

Though wealthy households certainly lost more wealth, they suffered less long-term harm. Greater financial reserves gave them increased protection against the financial mayhem. Affluent households with lower debt burdens had increased flexibility in responding to sudden financial reversals. Homeowners with greater home equity could withstand steeper declines in home values before facing the dilemma of a home under water. Similarly, well-diversified households could better withstand drastic declines in portions of their financial portfolio. Their deeper reserves offered added protection against the likelihood of making late payments, selling one's assets, experiencing foreclosure, or declaring bankruptcy. Despite their substantial losses, affluent owners of real property and businesses experienced lower divestment rates. Retaining ownership allowed them to benefit readily once these assets began to appreciate again.

Despite their modest wealth, households of color experienced surprising vulnerability to asset declines. Black and Latino homeowners witnessed the steepest declines in their home values and home equity. Turning to investment property, Black as well as Asian or Other property owners endured the largest losses. Similarly, business owners from these two groups suffered catastrophic losses. Lastly, Black shareholders experienced the deepest decline in their holdings, though Latino as well as Asian or Other households fared better than Whites did overall. Nonetheless, this pattern of racialized disparities suggests that these privileges of wealth do not extend fully to affluent households of color.

Sharply declining asset values posed acute challenges to Black and Latino households in particular. Their limited wealth and shallower pockets offered less protection, causing them to make tougher choices. Further, their lower incomes and higher debt burdens gave them less financial flexibility in their responses. Lastly, the pattern of racialized disparities extended to the incidence of unemployment. While the Great Recession raised the specter of unemployment for all, it did so disproportionately on households of color. For all of these reasons, Latino and especially Black households suffered severe structural harm. Black households experienced higher bankruptcy and property divestment rates than Whites, making them less capable of benefiting once the economy began to recover.

A quick scan of three assets important to most households can demonstrate the pattern of structural harm. Table 7.16 depicts key circumstances surrounding homeownership and suggests that the decline in homeownership will continue. Among all homeowners in 2007, fully one out of six households experienced housing and debt payments that exceeded 40 percent of household income. As indicated, the rates were higher for low-wealth families as well as households of color. The same groups experienced lower persistence rates in retaining homeownership just two years later. In addition, almost one tenth of those still owning their home found their mortgage debt exceeding their current home value. It is notable that the rate of homes under water was higher for less affluent homeowners and

TABLE 7.16 Structural conditions in homeownership

Group	Among homeowners in 2007		Still homeowners in 2009	
	Homeownership rate 2007 (%)	High debt burden (%)	Persistence rate 2009 (%)	Under water in 2009 (%)
All under 66	66	17	96	10
Wealth tercile				
Bottom	34	27	91	17
Middle	91	15	97	9
Top	96	10	99	3
Racial group				
Asian or Other	66	18	97	17
Black	46	24	90	17
Latino	49	30	94	15
White	72	15	97	8

Source: SCF, 2007–9

doubled among homeowners of color. These figures suggest that the home divestment rate will continue along the familiar patterns even after 2009.

Although not as important as one's home, retirement accounts and vehicles represent two other key assets in most households. In 2007, 59 percent of U.S. households held some type of retirement account. Two years later, over 10 percent of those households (all under age 66) had emptied their accounts. As Table 7.17 illustrates, affluent households were less disposed to take this action. More pointedly, financial demands compelled many more Black and Latino households to take this step than Whites. Likely, pressing needs required them to sacrifice their retirement

TABLE 7.17 Divestment of retirement and vehicular assets

Group	Has retirement account 2007 (%)	Still has one in 2009 (%)	Owns vehicle in 2007 (%)	Still owns vehicle in 2009 (%)
All under 66	59	89	89	95
Wealth tercile				
Bottom	35	80	81	92
Middle	76	92	96	97
Top	89	97	95	97
Racial group				
Asian or Other	68	96	95	96
Black	43	79	78	89
Latino	35	82	87	91
White	65	91	92	97

Source: SCF, 2007–9

nest eggs. Table 7.17 depicts a similar pattern regarding vehicle ownership. For low-wealth households, losing their car limits their employment opportunities, as they must depend on the reliability and coverage of public transportation. Once again, it is the least affluent as well as households of color that suffered the greatest declines in vehicle ownership. As in the case of homeownership, these patterns demonstrate that low wealth as well as households of color largely suffered substantial reductions in their ability to benefit from the wealth pathways.

Sorting through the issues

Although the previous discussion identifies those factors that permit households to experience greater financial resilience, two questions remain unanswered. Which of these factors offered households the most protection from financial harm? Is it possible to distinguish which attributes played the leading roles? In addition, can we differentiate between wealth and racialized status to discern whether wealth privilege did not fully apply to affluent households of color? To answer these questions, I turn now to the following logit regression model whose results are presented in Table 7.18.

These results indicate which factors offered households the greatest protection against financial harm during the Great Recession. To do this, the analysis examines whether or not a household increased its net worth during the period and which household attributes as measured in 2007 best correspond to this outcome. Each coefficient estimates the specific impact of a given variable on whether or not households increased their net worth over the two-year period. For example, households that entered the Great Recession in the middle wealth tercile had a 70 percent less chance of experiencing wealth gains than did a comparable household in the bottom tercile. In contrast, households that reported regular saving in 2007 were 26 percent more likely to gain wealth over the period. As before, the asterisks reflect how confident we can be regarding the findings and reflect the same standards of statistical significance. I report the both the logit regression coefficients and the p-values for the weighted sample results in Table 7.18.[12]

As the results demonstrate, household circumstances certainly mattered. These findings corroborate earlier evidence that suggested wealthy families were more likely to experience financial reversals during the Great Recession. Having wealth alone, particularly a moderate amount, increased the likelihood that households would suffer financial losses by a wide margin. Similarly, homeowners were far more likely to suffer losses than renters were. Interestingly, homeowners with a longer tenure in their home gained some protection as indicated by the positive coefficient; however, this defense did not attain the standard of statistical significance. Unlike owning a home, simple ownership of rental property, business, or equity shares did not lead unequivocally to financial decline. Though somewhat surprising, these ambiguous results can be explained by how exclusive owning these assets is. Plenty of non-owners lost wealth during the period making ownership of these assets less important.

TABLE 7.18 Logit regression that examines which households increased net worth between 2007 and 2009

Variable	Coefficient	P-value
Increased net worth		
Wealth and ownership		
Middle wealth tercile	−.70★★★	.000
Top wealth tercile	−.44★	.031
Homeowner	−.30★	.039
Years owned home	.01	.129
Landlord	−.12	.370
Business owner	.07	.603
Shareholder	.03	.835
Financial vulnerability		
Has health coverage	.15	.224
Saved regularly	.26★	.011
High payments	−.28	.096
Unemployed	−.37★★	.001
Family background		
Gave distressed help	−.32	.075
Expect inheritance	.13	.366
Attitudes		
Long-run horizon	.05	.667
Risk taker	−.05	.676
Credit vacation is Ok	.04	.778
Other		
White	.26 ★	.033
Constant	−.28	.040
F-statistic	5.51	.000

The next four variables examine the impact of financial vulnerability on wealth outcomes. Health-insurance coverage offered families some protection against financial losses, though the evidence is fully conclusive in just the unweighted sample results reported in Appendix C. Families who entered the period with sufficient means to save regularly were more than 26 percent more likely to prosper over the two years. Perhaps, their capacity to save enabled them to overcome any asset declines. In contrast, those households already financially strapped by housing and debt payments that exceeded 40 percent of their income experienced greater difficulties, although not conclusively so. Without a doubt, bouts of unemployment wreaked havoc on family finances. Among those households experiencing unemployment, they saw their prospects of getting ahead fall by over one third. As these results suggest, financial vulnerability did make a discernible difference in how households fared during the period.

Certainly, family background could affect one's fortunes. As discussed, both the need to offer a distress gift as well as the expectation of getting some future inheritance offers us indirect measures of potential family support. However, the evidence is modest. While the coefficients suggest that households who engaged in distress giving suffered losses while those who expect future gifts did not, neither of these results is conclusive.

Throughout this book, I have examined the role of key attitudes to discern their impact on household wealth. The next three variables offer an insight into how such attitudes might affect household fortunes. One would expect that households adopting the longer view in their financial planning, taking fewer risks, and avoiding installment credit would fare better over the period. While the coefficients for these variables generally take the expected sign, the evidence suggests that none of these were linked conclusively to family fortunes.[13]

Lastly, we turn to racialized status. In this case, being White as opposed to Black, Latino, or Asian or Other, offered families a 26 percent boost to whether they prospered or not during the period. Likely, this result captures the systemic advantages conferred on Whites given their access to greater wealth. At the same time, it undoubtedly includes the benefits that accrued to Whites as homeowners, rental property, and business owners as they experienced lower asset-value declines than did their Black, Latino, and Asian or Other peers. The interpretation of the constant term simply corroborates the role of racialized status as it suggests that households of color with none of the other attributes included in the model would likely suffer a wealth loss over the period.

Concluding remarks

In prior chapters, I investigated how wealth begets further wealth during times of prosperity. In this chapter, we examined the protections offered by wealth during times of calamity and crisis. Clearly, the possession of wealth does not insulate households from all harm caused by a financial collapse and severe recession. During the two-year period under investigation, wealthy households lost much of their net worth. Yet, their deeper pockets did protect them from the worst consequences the period delivered. They largely avoided a foreclosure or distressed sale of their home. They suffered lower rates of divestment of other real property, business assets, and stock holdings. They avoided the calamity of bankruptcy and they continued to experience lower debt burdens. Despite losing more, the wealthy were arguably harmed less by the Great Recession. As prosperity returned and asset prices reverted upward, they were ready to take advantage. In contrast, less affluent households experienced higher rates of property divestment, creating greater disparities in asset-ownership rates. Although the Great Recession may have caused wealth disparities to decline initially, these growing disparities in asset ownership will simply expand future wealth gaps once real property and business assets resume their normal ascent.

As we consider the sources of wealth privilege raised in this chapter, some give us little reason to be outraged. Wealth protects families from the trap of high debt burdens and enables them to engage in regular saving; we should cultivate this opportunity across all households. Having deeper pockets and an increased safety net protects affluent households against difficult dilemmas; rather than discouraging this, we should offer this security to all households. That the rich can diversify their wealth is not an attribute we want to eliminate, but emulate. These sources of wealth privilege are opportunities we might wish all households had the means to adopt.

More alarming are the disparate impacts and uneven protection that families have against the scourges of unemployment and poor health. Both job loss and illness afflict the wealthy at lower rates than they do wealth-poor households. Yet, the affluent have much better access to both health and unemployment insurance. While the Affordable Care Act has expanded health coverage to more households, the gaps remain substantial. Only by offering universal health insurance along with a more comprehensive and generous unemployment insurance system can we redress these disparities.

Most disturbing is the evidence that wealth does not inoculate households of color from contemporary racism. Despite having much less to lose, Black and Latino households suffered disproportionately large losses during the Great Recession. Among the moderate and highly affluent, Black and Latino households generally lost at twice the rate of their White counterparts. Worse, these losses are not simply paper losses that are easily recoverable. Their depth caused far greater numbers of Black and Latino households to experience significant structural harm. In disproportionate numbers, Black and Latino families lost their homes, retirement savings, vehicles, stock portfolios, and businesses. In particular, Black homeowners, property owners, and business owners were forced to declare bankruptcy at highly elevated rates. Both the asset divestiture and the experience of bankruptcy will leave these households poorly positioned once prosperity does return. No doubt, these disparities result from persistent race prejudice as manifested in our high levels of residential segregation as well as more subtle forms of institutionalized racism. Whatever the source, the privileges of wealth don't appear to offer equal protection to all households.

As the American Dream presupposes a period of expansive prosperity, one might wonder at the relevance of this short but destructive period. The economic decline experienced during the Great Recession produced circumstances not seen in over a generation. Yet, this period holds a foreboding shadow over our future. The consequences of this period, particularly the widening gap in asset ownership across American households, suggest that future economic expansion will benefit even more narrowly the fortunate few. Households that gained some measure of middle-class status through homeownership as well as professional jobs only to lose these during the Great Recession may find their retrieval elusive. One lasting consequence of this period may be even greater tendencies toward the concentration of wealth among the rich.

Notes

1 There actually is a precedent for this. Many years prior, the Federal Reserve used the 1986 survey to question the 1983 households a second time. Starting with the 1989 survey, the Federal Reserve implemented its standard practice of creating a new panel of households with each survey.

2 Like the last chapter, I am interested in examining the capacity of households to accumulate wealth, or resist wealth declines. As such, I include only households headed by those 65 years of age or younger. Households older than this traditional retirement age operate under different circumstances.

3 Kennickell (2011) argues that the largest relative decline was among households below the 30th percentile, somewhat the reverse of what these results show. One difference is the sample population. I have excluded households headed by seniors. On the other hand, the results in Table 7.1 are similar to those found by Wolff et al. (2011).

4 In this case, I include only those households surveyed in 2007 that responded again in 2009.

5 The careful reader of Table 7.4 might wonder why the percentages along each might add up to more than 100 percent. Since not every household is both a homeowner and a landlord, each column is examining a slightly different sub-group. Typically, White homeowners among the bottom wealth tercile have 81 percent of their net worth tied up in their home equity. Among those Whites from this group that own rental property, they typically have a third of their wealth tied up in their rental property. Likely, most of these landlords rent their own principal residence.

6 A simple example makes the point. Assume a homeowner who owns a house valued at $100,000 and has 20 percent or $20,000 of net equity. A decline of $10,000 in the value of the home translates into a 10 percent decline in value, but a 50 percent decline in one's net equity. The latter figure is more important to the household's net worth than is the former. The same price decline will harm a homeowner with 50 percent equity in their home to a much smaller extent.

7 There are a number of likely reasons for this. For reasons already discussed, Black and Latino mortgage holders pay higher interest rates. To the extent that many of these buyers have purchased homes recently in a rising market, their monthly payments will reflect the increased cost of a home. Lastly, residential segregation has remained remarkably impervious to any shift in attitudes or behaviors. As such, Black and Latino buyers will likely find themselves steered toward specific neighborhoods, thereby limiting their home-buying choices.

8 Table 7.8 and those that follow offer a more truncated view than the tables shown previously in the chapter. Showing household experience by both wealth and racialized group offers too many cells with thin, if any, results.

9 Although the bankruptcy rates appear similar, the rates before rounding are 3.1, 2.7, and 2.5 percent for Black, Latino, and White households, respectively.

10 Of course, by simply comparing those business owners that had the same number of business interests does not preclude owners who exchanged more or less valuable businesses for businesses already in their possession.

11 These figures appear higher than the usually reported rates. They represent household rates (either respondent or spouse), they reflect any point in prior year, and they include some "discouraged" workers.

12 According to Lindamood et al. (2007), the best practice is to provide the results for both the weighted and unweighted sample along with the p-values. In this case, the results for both are quite similar. For the interested reader, I have supplied the p-values for both logit runs as suggested in Appendix C.

13 One would expect that households who take a liberal attitude toward the use of credit would have witnessed a decline in their net worth.

Bibliography

Bricker, J., Bucks, B., Kennickell, A., Mach, T., and Moore, K. (2011). *Surveying the aftermath of the storm: Changes in family finances from 2007 to 2009*. Washington, DC. Division of Research and Statistics and Monetary Affairs, Federal Reserve Board.

Bricker, J., Bucks, B., Kennickell, A., Mach, T., and Moore, K. (2012). The financial crisis from the family's perspective: Evidence from the 2007–2009 SCF Panel. *Journal of Consumer Affairs* 46 (3): 537–55.

Conley, D. (1999). *Being Black, living in the red: Race, wealth, and social policy in America*. Berkeley: University of California Press.

Deaton, A. (1997). *The analysis of household surveys: A microeconometric approach to development policy*. Washington, DC: World Bank Publications.

Holling, C. S. and Meffe, G. K. (1996). Command and control and the pathology of natural resource management. *Conservation Biology* 10 (2): 328–37.

Keister, L. A. (2005). *Getting rich: America's new rich and how they got that way*. Cambridge: Cambridge University Press.

Kennickell, A. B. (2011). *Tossed and turned: Wealth dynamics of US households 2007–2009*. Washington, DC: Federal Reserve Board.

Lindamood, S., Hanna, S. D., and Bi, L. (2007). Using the Survey of Consumer Finances: Some methodological considerations and issues. *Journal of Consumer Affairs* 41 (2): 195–222.

McKernan, S. M., Ratcliffe, C., Steuerle, E., and Zhang, S. (2013). *Less than equal: Racial disparities in wealth accumulation*. Washington, DC: Urban Institute.

McKernan, S. M., Ratcliffe, C., Steuerle, E., and Zhang, S. (2014). *Impact of the Great Recession and beyond*. Washington, DC: Urban Institute.

Mullainathan, S. and Shafir, E. (2009). Savings policy and decision-making in low-income households. In *Insufficient funds: Savings, assets, credit, and banking among low-income households*, ed. R. M. Blank and M.S. Barr. New York: Russell Sage Foundation, 121–45.

Oliver, M. L. and Shapiro, T. M. (2006). *Black wealth, White wealth: A new perspective on racial inequality*. New York: Taylor and Francis.

Real Capital Analytics (2015). *Commercial property price indices*. Retrieved from www.rcana lytics.com/Public/rca_cppi.aspx.

Standard and Poor Dow Jones Indices (2016) *S&P/Case-Shiller 20-City Composite Home Price Index*, April 26. Retrieved from www.standardandpoors.com/indices/sp-case-shiller-home-price-indices/en/us/?indexId=spusa-cashpidff-p-us——.

Taylor, P., Kochhar, R., Fry, R., Velasco, G. and Motel, S. (2011). *Wealth gaps rise to record highs between Whites, Blacks, and Hispanics*. Washington, DC: Pew Research Center.

Wolff, E. N., Owens, L. A., and Burak, E. (2011). How much wealth was destroyed in the Great Recession? In *The Great Recession*, ed. D. B. Grusky, B. Western, and C. Wilmer. New York: Russell Sage Foundation, 127–58.

8

THE SPIRAL OF PRIVILEGE AND POLICY

Given how household wealth anchors economic security and well-being for American households, it is unsurprising that our government takes great interest in sponsoring its expansion. Consistent with its constitutional mandate to "promote the general welfare," the federal government offers a variety of policies and tax deductions to assist households in their pursuit of wealth. What is surprising is the tilt to these policies. In earlier chapters, I examined assorted advantages and systemic privileges that aid affluent households in their quest for additional wealth. Given their range and extent, we might expect our wealth-building policies would target those households struggling to supplement meager bank accounts, buy a home, or set up a retirement plan. Rather than buttress the efforts of households with the greatest need, much of our public largesse benefits our wealthiest citizens. Further, the design of these programs emulates the self-reinforcing pathways already identified. Ostensibly open to all households, these programs funnel the greatest help to wealthier families. Since these policies generally offer open-ended assistance, their generosity rises with household wealth without limit. In this way, they reinforce the growing disparities in wealth that are undermining the reality of the American Dream.

Our federal wealth policies include a mixture of income tax deductions and tax credits along with our system of estate and gift taxes. American households gain hundreds of billions of dollars annually through various tax exemptions that help them as they journey along the wealth pathways. Conversely, our estate and gift taxes function to limit the transfer of wealth from one generation to the next. To describe how this system works, I must explain certain features of our tax policy, including the differences between tax deductions and credits. We must understand these tax policies in order to appreciate how their design reveals the intent of our policymakers as well as their long-term consequences. Understanding these details enables us to consider other policy designs that might redirect the assistance toward those households struggling to build their financial nest egg.

Previous research has documented these wealth-building policies. Starting in 2003, Lillian Woo and her colleagues at the Corporation for Enterprise Development examined 13 tax exemptions that targeted household wealth accumulation. According to their estimates, these 13 tax breaks offered households $334 billion of aid, with 84 percent of this going to the top 20 percent of taxpayers (Woo et al., 2004).[1] Five years later, Woo and colleagues found little change as the vast bulk of this assistance still targeted the most affluent households (Woo et al., 2011). More recently, the Tax Policy Center examined nearly three dozen tax expenditures that subsidized asset building among families. The researchers estimated that these tax policies offered U.S. households $384 billion in help to own homes, afford a college education, save for retirement, as well as other needs. Like the earlier studies, they found "that the design of current tax subsidies channels the majority of savings incentives, especially those for homeownership and retirement saving, to upper income households who likely require less incentive to save" (Tax Policy Center, 2014, p. 31). In 2013, the Congressional Budget Office (CBO) analyzed ten of the largest tax expenditures, whether explicitly asset building or not. Using a less conservative measure of the help offered by these tax exemptions,[2] they estimated these policies assisted households to the tune of $900 billion, with over half being funneled to the top quintile of before-tax income earners (CBO, 2013).

Although these different studies vary in time, estimation methodologies, and the specific tax expenditures they examine, they all reach a similar conclusion: the vast bulk of our wealth-building subsidies assist our most affluent households. Even Gervais and Pandey (2008), who criticize the underlying methodology used in several of these studies, conclude that the mortgage deduction given to homeowners largely assists the affluent. To understand this consensus, we must examine how the specific designs of these tax expenditures accommodate the preferences of the wealthy. Yet, the above studies neglect two issues. First, what is happening to these tax expenditures over time? Are recent policy changes making them more or less egalitarian in their generosity? For example, Looney and Moore (2015) examine the changes to the capital gains exclusion and conclude these changes have contributed to increased wealth inequality. One wonders what effect other changes might have had. Second, these cited studies all examine their distributional benefits based on household income. It makes sense to reconsider their impact on the distribution of wealth, especially given the differences in income and wealth disparities. Looking solely at those provisions that give preferential treatment to homeownership, Cho and Francis (2011) conclude they contribute to wealth inequality as well. Again, one wonders about the effects of the other tax expenditures that promote wealth accumulation. Answering these questions is the focus of this chapter.

Key facets of our tax policy

I suspect many of us suffer from an involuntary response whenever the discussion turns to the finer distinctions between a tax deduction and a tax credit; our eyes may glaze over and our brains may shut down. Yet, the differences are real and quite important, as I will show. Tax deductions lower taxable income, or the amount that is subject to taxation, while tax credits reduce one's tax liability, or payment, directly. As an example, a $1,000 tax deduction lowers one's *taxable income* by an equal amount while a $1,000 tax credit reduces your *tax bill* by that amount. Although tax deductions lower each taxpayer's taxable income equally, the value of the deduction depends on one's tax bracket. For a taxpayer in the 35 percent tax bracket, a $1,000 tax deduction decreases their taxes by $350.[3] To another taxpayer in the 10 percent bracket, the same deduction is worth only $100 in lower taxes. Consequently, tax deductions are worth far more to high-income than to lower-income households. The value of any tax deduction rises as households earn more income and land in higher tax brackets. Further, changes in the tax code unrelated to the deduction itself can alter its value substantially to affected taxpayers.

Generally, tax credits function impartially as they reduce the outstanding tax bill of all eligible taxpayers, regardless of their tax bracket. Yet, sometimes their specific design limits their evenhandedness. Some households earn so little income that their federal tax liability is smaller than the tax credit. Other households earn even less and pay no federal income taxes. Various tax credits treat these circumstances in different ways. Some tax credits are designed as *non-refundable*. Eligible households who pay no income taxes will receive no tax credit. For those who pay taxes, they will receive a credit equal to the credit limit or their tax liability, whichever figure is smaller. Alternatively, tax credits can be designed as *fully refundable*. In this case, every taxpayer eligible for the credit will receive its full value, either as a reduction to their tax bill or as a tax refund. Lastly, some tax credits are designed as *partially refundable*. Taxpayers who pay little or no federal income taxes may recover a portion of their eligible credit, based on some formulae. The refund policy determines how equitably a tax credit treats households across the income spectrum.

The issue of indexing complicates the picture. Frequently, tax policy designers use specific income limits to regulate which households can utilize a tax deduction or credit. For example, the Omnibus Budget Reconciliation Act of 1990 restricted households earning above $100,000 from taking certain tax deductions. Similarly, the Economic Growth and Tax Relief Reconciliation Act of 2001 created a tax credit to households whose income is below $55,000. In both cases, Congress designed these tax policies to limit participation by higher-income households. It is important to not only recognize these limits, but also understand how they function over time. As Congress refrains from revisiting taxes each year, specific limits and thresholds languish over time. In the case of the 1990 law, the income thresholds were subject to inflation indexing while the comparable thresholds in the 2001 law were not. Thus, as inflation boosts most incomes, these income limits function differently. In the case of the 1990 law, indexing these limits for inflation means they will largely keep pace with rising incomes over time, thereby limiting the number of households that might lose the deduction. In the case of the 2001 law, rising incomes means fewer and fewer households will be eligible for this tax credit, even though inflation is taking most of their income gains. Not only do these differences have budgetary implications, they also affect who benefits from these provisions over time.

In contrast, estate and gift taxes function to limit wealth accumulation, particularly as households transfer wealth from one generation to the next. Enacted 100 years ago, the estate tax was created to limit the corrosive power of concentrated wealth. In particular, supporters feared that unequal wealth in one generation would undermine the role of merit and opportunity in subsequent generations. As a society, we expect and encourage parents to give their children every advantage in preparation for their careers and adult lives. Yet, parents who accumulate vast sums can offer their kids huge amounts of unearned wealth, thereby relieving them of their obligation or need to earn their own way. To limit these wealth transfers to the next generation, the estate tax reduces only the largest estates of the deceased. Later, Congress created the gift tax to discourage those trying to avoid the estate tax by transferring their wealth prior to death. This tax limits the amount of gifts that can be transferred across generations untaxed. More recently, Congress enacted a Generation Skipping Trusts (GST) tax to assess those using trust accounts to exploit tax loopholes and avoid taxation. These three taxes represent the only wealth taxes in the federal tax arsenal to limit the passage of wealth across generations. Along with various tax deductions and credits that support household efforts to preserve and increase their wealth, these taxes comprise our current federal wealth policy.

Federal wealth policy in 1989

Virtually all components of our current federal wealth policy existed a generation ago. Nearly all survived the groundswell for tax simplification that culminated in the Tax Reform Act of 1986 (TRA 1986), a law that eliminated numerous exemptions, deductions, and credits from the U.S. Tax Code.[4] Their survival testifies to their strong political support. In addition, virtually all of the tax deductions listed in Table 8.1 can trace their roots back to the early twentieth century to the creation of the federal income tax. As such, this list includes the most venerated and popular exemptions in our tax system.

The debate over the size and influence of government dominates our political discourse. How much government spends and how many employees it hires are the subjects of constant political quarrels. Less discussed is the size and influence exerted by the range of federal tax deductions and credits, which constitute a much

TABLE 8.1 List of key tax deductions and credits in 1989

Health insurance deduction	Pension exclusions	Local taxes exclusion
Charitable contributions	Home mortgage deduction	Home property tax deduction
Home sales exclusion	Capital gains exclusion	Tax exempt bonds
Estate step-up exclusion	Life insurance exclusion	Earned income tax credit

less visible, but potent, form of government intervention. Fortunately, federal law requires annual government estimates of the value of these exemptions, either as a benefit to the recipient taxpayers or as a loss to the federal treasury. From these estimates, we can observe the relative size of each exemption listed in Table 8.1 as well as their collective share of all such federal help. In 1989, about 100 tax exemptions, exclusions, or credits directly benefited individual taxpayers to the tune of over $213 billion. The 12 tax exemptions listed represent the "who's who" of federal tax deductions; collectively, they account for over 80 percent of the total deductions offered that year to individual taxpayers.[5] Further, we can estimate the distribution of these tax benefits as they accrue to different households by wealth status. As Figure 8.1 illustrates, the bulk of the benefits from these 12 programs go to the wealthiest households, even using extremely conservative assumptions.[6] Indeed, over half of the estimated benefits assisted the wealthiest households. Rather than tilt government assistance to those households with the greatest need, public policy in 1989 mostly helped those with the most wealth. Let me explain how this worked.[7]

Among the largest tax deductions in 1989 were those exemptions for health insurance and medical care premiums paid by employers and the self-employed. As important fringe benefits, these premiums represented a source of non-cash "income" that was not subject to federal income tax, unlike normal wage and salary income. Households covered by these plans paid no taxes on these benefits, thereby boosting their after-tax income and their capacity to engage in household saving.[8] As wealthier households have much higher rates of private health-insurance coverage, they benefit disproportionately from this tax deduction. Since not all health insurance plans are alike, wealthier households likely have better policies with broader coverage and lower co-payments, skewing the disparities further. Unfortunately, the SCF simply asks whether households have insurance coverage and ignores qualitative differences. For this reason, the estimate of benefits likely understates the actual value to wealthier households.

The next largest group of tax deductions supported household saving and asset appreciation through retirement savings accounts, to the tune of $56 billion.[9] Like

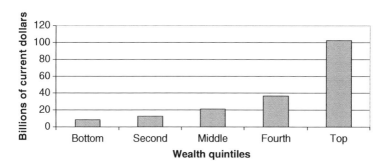

FIGURE 8.1 Distribution of tax expenditure benefits, 1989
Source: Joint Committee of Taxation, SCF 1989, and author's calculations

health insurance premiums, the IRS viewed employer contributions to qualified pensions as a non-income fringe benefit, exempting them from taxation. To encourage retirement saving further, contributions to qualified pension plans and IRAs (individual retirement accounts) were made tax deductible as well. Further, as funds in these accounts gained in value, all appreciation was exempt from taxation until withdrawn during retirement.[10] This tax deferral enabled households to save unimpeded by federal taxes. Even then, households could withdraw these funds as their other income sources declined, thereby reducing their tax liability further due to their lower tax bracket.

Though open to all taxpayers, these exemptions on retirement savings attracted wealthier households. The restrictions limiting the use of funds deterred many less affluent households; their more desperate circumstances caused "rainy-day saving" to supersede their need for retirement saving. Having met this latter need already, affluent households had both the interest and means to use these vehicles to fund their retirement plans. Further, their higher tax brackets made the tax exemptions even more generous. As a result, affluent households have taken much greater advantage of these tax exclusions.

Another tax deduction targeted a different retirement asset. The exclusion on investment income in life insurance and annuity contracts allows these assets to appreciate without generating a tax liability. Like the pension exemption, these earnings are taxed only as they are withdrawn. As before, wealthier households made much greater use of this exemption, providing them with another vehicle to build their financial nest egg.

Two more tax deductions permitted households to lower their federal taxes. The deduction for state and local taxes allowed households to reduce their taxable income in equal amounts to their non-federal income and personal property taxes. Similarly, the charitable contributions deduction permitted taxpayers to subtract these outlays from their taxable income. As exemptions for cash outlays, these provisions were less valuable to wealth building. Yet, both allowed taxpayers to support local efforts, public or private, to expand services in their community, effectively boosting their own "income" and, in some cases, wealth.[11] The reduction in federal taxes increased after-tax income, from which taxpayers may supplement their household saving. As affluent households are subject to higher state and local taxes and make greater charitable donations, they benefited more fully from these tax deductions. Further, since Glaeser and Shapiro (2002) find that many lower-income households do not itemize their deductions, they were even less likely to gain from these tax provisions than Figure 8.1 suggests.

Three additional tax deductions benefited homeowners at the expense of renters.[12] First, the mortgage interest deduction allowed homeowners to deduct up to $1 million of mortgage interest from their taxes each year. This provision did not simply provide homeowners with extra cash to save for the future: it encouraged homebuyers to leverage their purchases and earn higher rates of return on their reduced down payments.[13] With the advent of home equity lines, homeowners could borrow money more cheaply than those who rented.[14] They could use these funds to purchase other properties, buy stocks, or pay college tuition.[15] The second exemption, the homeowners' property tax exclusion, permitted homeowners to deduct property taxes paid on their homes, offering further tax savings that could supplant their household saving efforts. Higher property taxes could fund better schools and neighborhood parks that would then boost property values. The third provision sheltered any capital gains earned on one's home. The exclusion of home sales exempted from taxation any realized capital gains as long as households used the earnings to purchase a new home. After age 55, homeowners could keep tax-free gains from the sale of their home, up to $125,000. Together, these three deductions offered homeowners substantial assistance based on the size of their mortgage debt, the extent of their property taxes, and any appreciation earned on their homes. On all counts, these factors benefited wealthier households disproportionately.

In 1989, all other capital gains, other than those earned on one's home, were taxed as normal income, thereby offering no special exemption. However, households did have access to the exclusion of interest on tax-exempt bonds. Since these bonds offer lower interest than regular bonds, they appeal only to high-income households whose high tax rates make their tax-exempt status attractive.

The last tax deduction, the estate step-up exclusion, favored the heirs of those who left behind a substantial estate. This exclusion exempted any unrealized capital gains residing in the portfolio of a deceased person's estate from current or future capital gains taxation. It did so by treating the assets at their current market value (stepped-up basis) rather than their (usually) lower purchase price (cost basis). This treatment of the estate's assets had double-edged consequences for the heirs. On the upside, the heirs were liable only for any capital gains above the step-up basis. Thus, death eliminated any tax liability on the unrealized capital gains. On the downside, this treatment increased the value of the estate, potentially subjecting it to increased estate taxes. No doubt, this side effect intensified the desire among the wealthy to reduce the federal estate tax.

Among the tax exemptions in Table 8.1, only one tax credit made the list in 1989. The earned income tax credit (EITC) targeted the working poor as it offered a maximum benefit of $910 to households earning under $10,240 annually. As a fully refundable tax credit, even households whose earned income was insufficient to trigger federal taxes benefited from the credit.[16] The credit diminished as household incomes increased above the $10,240 threshold and reached zero for households earning more than $19,340. Unlike all of the tax exemptions discussed to this point, this tax credit neglected the wealthy. Its objective was to assist households of modest means and mitigate the possibility that such households would fall into the trap of rising debt. To ensure its effectiveness over time, the tax law required annual inflation adjustments to offset the effects of rising incomes and household expenses.

The third part of the federal wealth policy is composed of the estate and gift taxes levied directly on intergenerational transfers of wealth. In 1989, the laws treated intergenerational gifts, whether made before or after one's death, as the same. The estate tax only considered estates larger than $600,000. The law sub-jected larger fortunes to taxation rates that ran from 18 percent to a top rate of 55 percent, the latter on holdings that exceeded $3 million. Just a decade earlier, the top rate on the largest estates had been 77 percent. Similarly, one could provide gifts tax free as long as the annual gift did not exceed $10,000 (or $20,000 if each spouse offered a gift) nor the lifetime sum exceed $600,000. To avoid these taxes, the wealthy employed GSTs. In skipping a generation, one could transfer one's wealth untaxed. Skilled attorneys designed these trusts so that one's children could benefit from the income generated but would not have access to the principal. At the death of the children, control of the trust would pass to one's grandchildren. Only at this point would the trust be subject to any estate taxes, after it had supported tax free the deceased's children throughout their lives. To limit this possibility, the GST tax assessed the value of these trusts at the maximum estate tax rate, with an exemption of $1 million (or $2 million if both spouses worked in concert). In 1989, this patchwork of taxes provided a modest bulwark against the transfer of wealth from one generation to the next.

Perhaps it is helpful to visualize these different pieces of our federal wealth policy, taxes, tax credits, and deductions, as the three legs of a stool. In 1989, the 11 tax deductions totaled more than $175 billion in federal assistance to households. During that same year, the estate and gift taxes raised under $9 billion while the sole tax credit aimed at helping struggling households cost just $6 billion. Given this disparate treatment, one might observe that the legs of our stool are uneven and wobbly. Further, nine of the 11 tax deductions placed no ceiling on how large a deduction one could take. The exceptions were the mortgage-interest deduction that restricted its largesse to $1 million and the home sales exclusion capped at $125,000. The other nine deductions offered unlimited generosity as household wealth (or income) rose. By design, the bulk of our federal wealth policy provided the same self-reinforcing qualities already witnessed in the wealth pathways. To be sure, the second largest leg of our stool, the estate and gift taxes, operated in a similar manner. Rising wealth would generate larger estates and gifts that in turn would exceed the thresholds and trigger higher rates of taxation. Yet, the disparities between these two legs in 1989—$175 billion versus $9 billion—indicate they would function at very different levels of scale and effectiveness. Nonetheless, the estate and gift taxes offered modest protection in 1989 against the wholesale transfer of wealth from the generation that earned it to subsequent generations.

Policy changes since 1989

Our federal wealth policy reflected several, sometimes conflicting, impulses. Most importantly, the policy signaled an overwhelming desire to help households build wealth and gain financial security. Three deductions rewarded those able to gain homeownership. Two others deferred taxes paid on retirement and life insurance accounts as they appreciated. Collectively, these five exemptions directly assisted households build value in their homes and pensions, for most the primary sources of financial well-being. Yet, another impulse powers this public generosity as well. The different tax deductions were designed to funnel their assistance to those households who had already achieved some level of affluence. The 11 tax deductions only helped households that paid federal income taxes. Three deductions directly assisted homeowners, but none targeted those unable to afford a home. Nine of the 11 deductions placed no caps on how much a household might benefit. In 1989, our federal wealth policy reflected a desire to reward the affluent and to maintain their privileged position within society. Although the policy encouraged wealth building in the generation in which it is "earned," it reflected a concern regarding its wholesale transfer to heirs where it would be clearly "unearned." The web of estate and gift taxes illustrates this impulse. Lastly, the policy revealed a limited desire to help the "working poor" as evidenced by the EITC. This tax credit helped struggling households make ends meet and reduced pressures to liquidate scarce household assets.

Beyond simply recognizing each of these impulses, we can discern their importance by considering the relative size and specific design of these policies. The evidence from 1989 demonstrated a clear set of priorities among them. Yet, policies change over time, usually in reaction to shifting political and social values. Perhaps, the recognition of rising wealth disparities has spread alarm and generated perceptible shifts in our wealth policy. Possibly, the concern over rising wealth disparities has redirected more assistance to wealth-poor households and less to the wealthy. To investigate these issues, I examine the changes in federal wealth policy over the past generation to discern how the underlying impulses have evolved.

Changes in tax deductions

Since 1989, six of the initial 11 tax deductions have remained largely unchanged.[17] That is not to say that they have remained static in terms of relative importance. Tax policy changes that altered the marginal tax rates (or tax brackets) affected the benefits of each deduction, including the "static six." In 1990 and again in 1993, Congress raised the top marginal tax rate on individual incomes; these actions increased the value of these six deductions to the wealthiest households. The reverse occurred for many households with the lowering of marginal tax rates in 2001. Further, escalating health-care costs and proliferating home equity loans have raised the relative value of both the health-coverage deduction as well as the home-mortgage deduction. Though these shifts are significant, they reveal little about the underlying values in our wealth policy.

Interestingly, the 1990 law that initially raised the top tax bracket also resurrected a long-standing tax deduction. This law raised the top tax rate to 31 percent on most forms of income while maintaining the cap on long-term capital gains at 28 percent. Later laws retained this cap even as the top tax rate climbed to 36 and even 39.6 percent. Since the wealthiest households realize a lopsided share of any capital gains, this exemption shielded the rich from much larger tax increases. Further relief to the rich came just four years later. The Taxpayer Relief Act of

1997 cut tax rates on capital gains from 15 and 28 percent to 10 and 20 percent; it reduced rates even lower for assets held over five years.[18] In 2003, rates fell even further, to 0 and 15 percent. Given that the wealthiest quintile of households earned over 80 percent and the top two quintiles accounted for over 95 percent of all unrealized capital gains in 1989, these changes clearly favored those already wealthy. Though non-existent in 1989, the exclusion on capital gains earnings became the largest tax deduction in 2013.[19]

Tax reform in 1997 also expanded the home-sales exclusion. Historically, homeowners could exclude $125,000 of any home appreciation from taxation. Due in part to rising home values, Congress raised this limit to $500,000 for an individual and $1 million for a couple. Among all homeowners at that time, the typical or median amount of unrealized gain in one's house was about $30,000. Pressure to raise this cap could only have come from those already well off, living in high-priced homes. According to the 1995 SCF, only 7 percent of households had met or exceeded this cap.

Tax reform also brought expanded opportunities for retirement saving. Initially, Congress created traditional IRAs only for those who could not benefit from an employer-based pension plan; lawmakers later ended this restriction though with limits. Households with access to an employer-based plan could contribute up to $2,000 annually only if their income was below $35,000 if single and $50,000 if joint return. The 1997 act raised these thresholds to $60,000 and $100,000. Equally important, the law created Roth IRAs. Unlike traditional IRAs, contributions to Roth IRAs are not tax deductible; however, these funds and any earnings are fully exempt from taxation, even at withdrawal. This tax-exempt feature is particularly attractive to very affluent households that will likely experience high tax rates, even in retirement. Both changes offered affluent households broader and more appealing rewards for their saving. Subsequent legislation raised the annual contribution limits from $2,000 to $3,000 and later to $6,000. All but the most affluent households could now stash $12,000 annually, if a married couple, into tax-sheltered funds.[20]

Not all of the changes made during this period expanded the tax-sheltered options for the wealthy. Two tax deductions, the exclusions on homeowners' property taxes as well as other state and local taxes, endured what the financial world calls a "haircut." Both deductions suffered income phase-outs as part of the 1990 tax increase to reduce growing budget deficits. In both cases, households earning above $100,000 annually would lose their tax deductions incrementally, up to 80 percent of the expected deduction. Recent legislation reversed these phase-outs and fully restored the deductions in 2010.

As this review suggests, not all of the policy changes to our federal tax exemptions have favored the wealthy; yet, the benefits accruing to the affluent have far exceeded the restrictions placed on their participation. Indeed, the restoration of the capital gains exclusion, by itself, easily offset any disadvantages borne by the wealthy.[21] Moreover, all of the changes unfavorable to wealthy households occurred in the early 1990s, mostly in response to the rising budget deficits. Since 1993, the policy changes have all favored the wealthy, as evidenced by the continual reductions in the capital gains tax and the restoration of the financial "haircut." Whatever political force existed early in the period to limit benefits to the wealthy appears to have evaporated over the past decade and a half. All but two of the cited tax deductions benefit wealthier Americans without limit while one of the remaining witnessed a rise in its cap. These policy shifts clearly demonstrate that wealthy households are the prime beneficiaries.

Changes in tax credits

Turning to the tax-credit leg of our three-legged stool, the EITC received regular attention from policymakers. Both in 1990 and 1993, Congress vastly expanded the program. In the first makeover, Congress boosted the tax credit and enacted an additional amount for families with two or more children. Three years later, it raised the credits again and added a modest credit for households without children. Both times, Congress enacted changes that enabled low-earning households to receive more assistance at lower income levels. These legislative changes transformed the EITC from a small and insignificant program to one that offered substantial help to a broad range of low-income, working households. More recently, the program received two additional increases in benefit levels. In 2001, Congress raised the credit to married households in order to offset the marriage penalty existing in the tax code. In 2009, households with three or more children saw their credit increase. Only one other change to the program is worthy of note. In 1997, new provisions mandated that fraudulent claims to the program would result in termination from future benefits. What is most striking about this provision is not simply its harshness, but also its exceptional nature. No doubt, most of the programs discussed earlier suffer some measure of fraudulent claims. Only this program merits such an explicit penalty.

In 1997, Congress created the Child Tax Credit to help households raising children. Initially set at $400 per qualifying child, Congress upped the ante to $1,000 per child in 2003, where it has remained. The original law made the credit partially refundable only to households with three or more children; in 2001, this provision was expanded to include all households with children. Under the law, households could receive no more than 10 percent of any earnings above $10,000. This provision effectively excluded all households earning less than $10,000 and limited its help to households earning below $20,000. Further, the 2001 law indexed this threshold to inflation, thereby ensuring the credit would not expand its reach over time to help those struggling financially. Households earning either $55,000 individually or $110,000 jointly received the full credit; above these income levels, their credit was moderately reduced. Clearly, this tax credit targeted its help toward middle-income and affluent households to assist them in raising their children. Two recent changes did direct more help to poorer households as Congress lowered the income threshold to $3,000 and raised the credit-refund rate from 10 to 15 percent. Both changes enabled many more low-income parents to get assistance.

The second tax credit created during this period is the Saver's Tax Credit. This provision offers qualified households a 50 percent tax credit up to $2,000 annually for every dollar deposited into a qualifying savings account. This generous benefit falls to 20 percent for households jointly earning above $30,000 (but below $33,000) and then falls to 10 percent to households jointly earning under $50,000. Thus, the tax credit targets low- and moderate-income households exclusively. Yet, it does so quite ineffectively. Since it is a non-refundable tax credit, only households paying substantial income taxes can make use of the credit. While lower-income households expend a sizeable share of their limited income on pay-roll, excise, and sales taxes, they frequently pay little or no federal income tax. As the law indexes the income thresholds for inflation, the credit could become useful to low-income households, but only if it ever becomes refundable.

Tax credits offer the most effective means to target wealth-building help to where it is needed most: disadvantaged households. At best, the changes just discussed deserve a mixed review. Expanded benefits and broader guidelines enable the EITC to offer greater help to more households in need. With this aid, households can avoid the cycle of increasing debt when they fall behind mounting bills. Similar to the pattern witnessed earlier, significant improvements to the EITC largely ended in 1993. More recently, the introduction of the Child Tax Credit and the Saver's Tax Credit have brought new opportunities for struggling households. However, their restrictions on credit refunds cause both to neglect those house-holds with the greatest needs. These limits reflect a prevailing reluctance to assist the most vulnerable in their efforts to stabilize their financial circumstances and engage in wealth-building efforts. Only in 2009 with the lowered income thresh-old for the Child Tax Credit has there been a targeted effort to help these households.

Changes in wealth taxes

We now turn to the last leg of our stool and examine how our system of estate and gift taxes has changed over the past generation. For nearly a decade, all was quiet with inheritance laws until the Tax Reform Act of 1997 shattered this calm. This law raised from $600,000 to $1 million the threshold under which estates could pass untaxed, phased in over a ten-year period. Similarly, the legislation boosted the exemption of cumulative gifts from parent to child by the same amount to keep the two consistent and unified. Already set at the $1 million mark, the threshold on gifts made to GSTs would now be indexed to inflation. In addition, the law adjusted the annual gift limit of $10,000 to reflect future inflation. Lastly, the special exemption given to farms and businesses would also receive annual inflation adjustments. Each of these changes permitted more wealth to transfer untaxed from one generation to the next.

The changes wrought in 1997 pale in comparison to those made in 2001. Congress raised the exemptions on the estate tax and the GST tax to $3.5 million over the course of the decade and then eliminated each in 2010 in hope of ending the "death tax." Curiously, the law left the exemption on cumulative gifts given *in vivo* unchanged. Showing concern for the plight of the very rich, Congress lowered the top rates on all three taxes; the top rate fell from 55 to 45 percent for the estate tax and GST tax while the gift tax fell to 35 percent. For one year, these changes effectively eliminated our system of estate and gift taxation, as simple patience could elude the gift tax.

In 2012, Congress acted again with the American Taxpayer Relief Act. Rather than allow the estate exemptions return to their 2001 level of $1 million, Congress created a unified threshold of $5 million that would allow virtually all estates and gifts to pass through untaxed. Starting in 2012, this limit would receive an annual inflation adjustment. Congress also selected 40 percent as a compromise top tax rate for all three taxes.

The changes made to our federal wealth policy over the past generation reveal stark shifts in the underlying values that formed this policy. Most clearly, the weakening of the estate and gift tax system demonstrates a disregard for the consequences of concentrating wealth. This represents a startling shift in values for a society that historically has placed such importance on the difference between "earned" and "unearned" wealth. The changes made to our tax deductions show an equivalent desire to help those who already can help themselves. The continual expansions of the capital-gains exclusion along with the restoration of the financial "haircut" demonstrate this point. Less clear and more tentative has been the impulse to help those households with the greatest need. The restrictions placed on refunding both the Child and the Saver's Tax Credits offset the more generous benefits offered by the expanded EITC. This ambivalence aside, what is most striking about this recent legislative history is how relentless and targeted the policy changes have been.

Looking at the numbers

While the preceding discussion conveys a lucid pattern, it does not adequately communicate the extent or magnitude of these changes. Figure 8.2 illustrates how

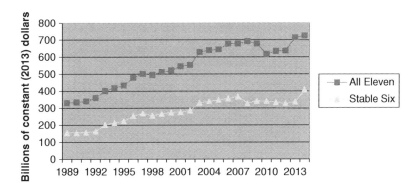

FIGURE 8.2 Estimated value of tax deductions
Source: Joint Committee on Taxation, 2013

extensively the 11 tax deductions have grown over the period. In just over two decades, the inflation-adjusted value of these 11 tax deductions has easily doubled, from $329 billion to over $700 billion in annual benefits.[22] Although the reintroduction of the capital-gains exclusion contributes mightily to this increase, the major cause is not due to program changes. Given the limitless generosity of these tax deductions, their value simply rises with household wealth. Examining the course of the "stable six," those deductions that went unchanged during the period make this point. Even they doubled in value during the period. Interestingly, the link between household wealth and value of these deductions holds even during the Great Recession. The fall in household wealth from 2007 to 2010 generates a parallel dip in these figures. As household wealth has reverted to its normal rising trend, the expansion of these tax deductions has resumed as well. In the absence of any limits, these deductions will continue to increase over time simply in response to rising household wealth, providing evidence for another self-reinforcing feedback loop.

The evidence shows a similar rise in the value of tax credits over this period, as depicted in Figure 8.3. The growth in tax credits is even more striking as they rise from about $10 billion to over $120 billion annually; yet, the underlying cause is very different. In this case, program expansion is driving the increased values as evidenced by the noticeable bumps in the early and late 1990s and again in 2011. Unlike the case of tax deductions, expanding household wealth has a minimal and likely negative impact on the growth of their costs. To the extent that rising net worth lifts the prospects of the least affluent, their rising fortunes will decrease their eligibility for these tax credits.

Turning to the estate and gift tax collections, Figure 8.4 illustrates a very different pattern. Over the first decade, tax collections rise rapidly, nearly tripling in value. This climb exceeds the rise in tax deductions, though the amounts are much, much smaller. In a world that favors the wealthy, there is more wealth to pass along to descendants. As wealth becomes more concentrated, more will be subject to taxation, boosting tax collections further. As such, these taxes were functioning just as

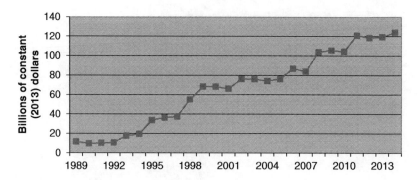

FIGURE 8.3 Estimated value of tax credits
Source: Joint Committee on Taxation, 2013

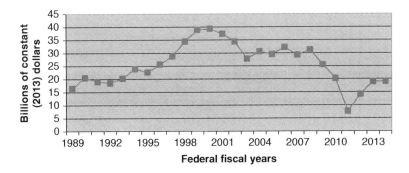

FIGURE 8.4 Estate and gift tax collections
Source: Adapted from Office of Management and Budget, 2015, table 2.5

ordered; they left the accumulation of earned wealth unhindered while limiting the unearned wealth passing from one generation to the next. As the absolute growth in tax collections was smaller than either the increases in tax deductions or credits, one can only fault these taxes for lacking a greater bite.

Even so, the tax reform initiated in 1997 and supplemented in 2001 sharply reversed this trend. Tax collections initially leveled out and then subsequently collapsed late in the decade as the estate tax experienced its one-year expiration.[23] Over this decade, the ever rising thresholds left increasing numbers of estates untouched. While the tax legislation in 2012 has stabilized tax revenues, it has done so at levels comparable to those a generation earlier, despite the substantial increase in wealth concentration. Without a robust estate tax or its alternative, our federal wealth policy will function to undermine the remaining vestiges of a meritocratic system as it fosters an enduring plutocracy. Insistent calls to eliminate permanently the estate or "death" tax will only expedite this transformation.

Our evolving federal wealth policy has affected the relative importance of its component parts and also its distributional impact on households across the wealth spectrum. Earlier in the chapter, I discussed four recent studies, all of which had shown that the most affluent households, by income, benefited disproportionately from selected tax expenditures. At this point, I intend to emulate their analysis using household wealth instead. To do this, I use some fairly simple, yet persuasive assumptions to generate illustrative estimates. For example, two of the largest tax deductions, the exclusion on capital gains and the home-mortgage deduction, respectively benefited households to the tune of $161 and $70 billion in 2013. According to the SCF, the wealthiest quintile of households realized 96 percent of the prior year's capital gains and paid 42 percent of the home-mortgage payments that year. As the bottom wealth quintile realized 0 percent of the capital gains and made but 7 percent of the mortgage payments, their share of these resources would be proportionately smaller. The figures in Figure 8.5 reflect such estimates.[24]

Clearly, other factors would affect the actual shares received. As more affluent mortgage holders pay lower interest rates, their actual share of the mortgage

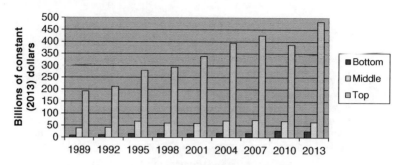

FIGURE 8.5 Tax deductions shares by selected wealth quintiles
Source: Joint Committee on Taxation, 2013 and author's calculations

deduction would likely be lower than their share of the total mortgage payment. Other complexities likely would influence these numbers around the margins as well. Yet, the figures in Figure 8.5 neglect two important issues already discussed. Most of these tax deductions require that households itemize their deductions rather than take the standard deduction on their taxes. Wealthy households do so in greater numbers. According to Glaeser and Shapiro (2002, table 1), not quite 4 percent of households in the lowest income quintile itemize while over two thirds of households in the top income quintile do so. More importantly, a given tax deduction is worth nearly double in value to an affluent household in the 28 percent tax bracket as compared to a household in the 15 percent bracket. As the figures in Figure 8.5 don't reflect these complexities, they offer a lower bound estimate of the true value of these tax deductions to wealthier households. As such, the estimates understate rather than exaggerate the disparate benefits provided by these generous tax deductions.

Figure 8.5 illustrates how the different wealth quintiles benefit from the rising value of the 11 tax deductions over the period. The spoils were shared unevenly. While the top wealth quintile held a $150 billion advantage over the middle wealth quintile in 1989, this ballooned to over $400 billion in 2013. The growing gap between the top and bottom shares was even wider. These widening disparities offer evidence of this self-reinforcing feedback loop. More wealth leads to larger deductions that fuel greater wealth. To be sure, these widening disparities reversed themselves during the Great Recession; yet, this looks to be a temporary anomaly as the rising trend appears to resume in 2013.

Measuring how different households benefit from the tax credits requires overcoming different hurdles, given that the three tax credits have income thresholds. For most of the period, over 90 percent of the EITC payments went to households earning under $30,000 (U.S. Congress Joint Committee on Taxation, n.d.). To estimate the relative shares received by each wealth quintile, I calculated the percentage of households earning less than this threshold in each group. I then allotted a share of the total tax credit proportional to their representation. Similarly, the Saver's Tax Credit benefits households whose income is sufficient to pay modest federal income taxes, but does not exceed the income cap. Hence, I estimated the relative share of households from each wealth and racialized group earning income between $40,000 and $55,000 annually.[25] Lastly, the Child Tax Credit has income restrictions at both the bottom and top income levels. With these limits in mind, I calculated the share of child dependents among each group to estimate the relative shares this credit distributes.

Figure 8.6 illustrates the likely distribution of these tax credits. As mentioned, their value rose over the period, mostly due to program expansions. Indeed, the creation and subsequent enhancement of the Child Tax Credit is the sole source of credits going to the top wealth quintile. The figure also demonstrates the inverted focus of these tax credits. They funnel their assistance to households at the bottom of the wealth pile. In this way, they offset the advantages that tax deductions give to the wealthy.

What happens when we combine the two figures and examine their cumulative impact? As shown in Figure 8.7, the magnitude of the tax deductions largely overwhelms the impact of the credits. The majority of government assistance devoted to wealth building went to those households already holding the wealth. While the inclusion of tax credits eliminated much of the advantage the middle

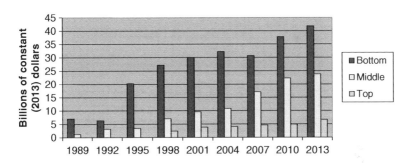

FIGURE 8.6 Tax credit shares by selected wealth quintiles
Source: Joint Committee on Taxation, 2013 and author's calculations

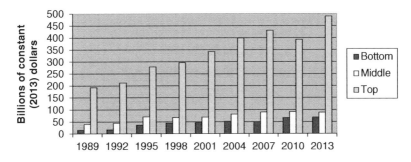

FIGURE 8.7 Shares of tax deductions and credits by selected wealth quintiles
Source: Joint Committee on Taxation, 2013 and author's calculations

quintile gains over the bottom quintile, the rising gap between these two groups and the wealthiest households is hardly affected. When we consider these two legs of the wealth policy stool, it is clear that the bulk of the federal largesse goes to the wealthiest households. Given the current design of these policies, there is no reason to expect this trend to change. Lastly, when we add the dismantling of our estate and gift tax system, the transformational role our federal wealth policy is playing is simply inescapable. Not only is the policy encouraging the concentration of wealth among the very wealthiest, but it also is permitting the transfer of this wealth to subsequent generations.

The transformational impact of our federal wealth policy is not simply widening the wealth gaps in our society. Given the substantial links between wealth status and racialized group, there are strong racialized consequences as well. Figure 8.8 depicts the relative shares directed toward each racialized group. As the figure illustrates, the bulk of wealth assistance provided by the selected tax expenditures benefits White households. Although the assistance received by each group is rising over the period, it is clear that White households receive the greatest share. In 1989, White households collected $250 billion more in tax exemptions than all other households combined; by 2013, the gap had more than doubled, even adjusted for inflation. As White households earn higher incomes and pay higher tax rates, the actual value of these tax exemptions are likely greater than the figure depicts. In any event, the current designs of these federal tax expenditures favor White households in ever increasing amounts.

Of course, one major reason why White households get such a preponderant portion of the tax benefits is their numbers in U.S. society. The distribution of these tax benefits is driven as much by demographics as by household income and wealth. To capture the influence of population, Figure 8.9 compares the estimated benefits collected by White households with a benchmark that assumes no racial disparities. In each year, the share of benefits received from the selected tax expenditures were greater than if the benefits were based simply on demographics. Further, the benefit gap is rising over time. While White households as a group typically gain about 20 percent more of the benefits than their numbers suggest,

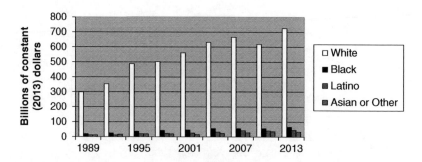

FIGURE 8.8 Tax expenditure shares by racialized group
Source: Joint Committee on Taxation, 2013 and author's calculations

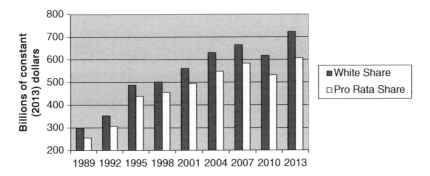

FIGURE 8.9 The benefits of being White
Source: Joint Committee on Taxation, 2013 and author's calculations

Black and Latino households get about 50 percent while Asian or Other households obtain about 90 percent. Not only does federal wealth policy funnel its help to our most affluent households, it functions equally to preserve wealth in White hands.

Conclusion

Of all of the sources of wealth privilege examined in this book, those raised in this chapter are among the most disturbing. In earlier chapters, many of the identified sources of privilege are endemic to our market economy, making their removal neither easy nor necessarily desirable. Though we might question the fairness of lenders offering wealthier borrowers lower interest rates because they constitute a lower risk of default, I doubt we want to encourage a system of lending that ignores credit risk. Similarly, we might lament that wealthier households can take increased risks with more diversified portfolios, offering them safety and reward simultaneously. In both cases, the cost of eliminating the sources of privilege is prohibitively high. With many privileges, the issue is not whether we can take them away from the few that have them, but rather how we might extend them to all who want them.

The sources of wealth privilege discussed in this chapter do not result naturally from a market economy. Special exemptions given to pension funds, mortgage credit, and capital gains do not naturally emerge from our economy; rather, they result from intentional choices in designing public policy. This does not suggest that amending or eliminating these exemptions would not generate adverse consequences. Any student in Economics 101 learns nearly all policy decisions incur opportunity costs. But the mere existence of these costs does not defend the status quo. Restricting or ending any of these tax deductions would reverberate throughout the economy, but none of these options would undermine it.

The substantial changes in our federal wealth policy over the past generation reveal shifts in the underlying impulses driving that policy. Most dramatically, the virtual dismantling of our estate and gift tax system exhibits an evaporation of our concern about concentrated wealth as it transfers from one generation to the next. The distinction between "earned" and "unearned" wealth is largely gone. Largely unchanged is the government's desire to help households accumulate wealth. Over this period, Congress has resurrected one major tax deduction, expanded several others, and adopted two smaller tax credits. Some of this federal largesse has targeted the struggling poor through the expansion of the EITC and the creation of the Saver's Tax Credit. However, particularly with the latter, its design hampers both its reach and effectiveness. The overwhelming impulse driving our policy today is to help those already wealthy. As the value of these tax exemptions drains the U.S. Treasury, the vast majority of this bounty benefits the affluent. All of this is occurring as the U.S. is experiencing an unprecedented rise in the concentration of household wealth. That so much help is going to the fortunate few offers irrefutable evidence that we are creating a plutocracy. There is no other reasonable conclusion.

Nor can we ignore the racialized consequences of our federal wealth policy: the overwhelming beneficiaries are White. Given our history of wealth and race in this country, we must take seriously the charge that they are explicitly and deliberately linked. As discussed earlier, our history is littered with examples of how policies and laws functioned to help White people advance at the expense of one group of color after another. We cannot ignore the similarities and links that connect the desire to ensure the future prospects of one's children through unhindered transfers of wealth to past willingness to steal the fertile land occupied by native peoples or the impulse to enslave others to build an estate. Though the methods are different, the underlying motivations as well as the consequences of a two-tiered system are similar.

The evidence raised in this chapter makes it clear that there exists a fundamental contradiction between the rhetoric of the American Dream and our federal wealth policies. While the former requires asset-building policies that are not only inclusive, but target families with minimal resources, our current policy is funneling its largesse on those already wealthy. The weakening of our estate and gift taxes means that more wealth will be transferred from one generation to the next, thereby reinforcing the transition from a system of merit to one of inherit. At the same time, these policies further expand the racial wealth gap that remains a persistent reminder of our racialized past. As such, these policies continue to promote a White plutocracy, even as overtly racialized policies are no longer tolerated.

Notes

1 They also examined several direct outlays that brought the total aid to $335 billion.
2 The Joint Committee on Taxation examines the impact of these tax exemptions only on individual income taxes. The CBO study adds the impact on payroll tax savings as well.
3 The calculation is simply 35 percent x $1,000 = $350.
4 The lone exception in Table 8.1 is the capital gains exclusion. TRA 1986 lowered and reduced marginal tax rates to two brackets, 15 and 28 percent. The law also directed capital gains to be treated like normal income, thereby eliminating the exclusion. Just four years later, the exclusion was restored, indicating its political support.
5 Other tax deductions benefited businesses and corporations. While these deductions benefit individual households indirectly, their benefits to individual households are too

difficult to track. Perhaps surprisingly, they represent a rather small portion of the total, only adding another \$27 billion to the figure given above.

6 The estimates assume a constant tax rate and therefore underestimate the value of these deductions to affluent households in higher tax brackets. A fuller explanation can be found in Appendix D.

7 As nearly all function in similar ways today, this discussion serves as more than a history lesson.

8 This represents an additional benefit to those discussed earlier. Recall that health insurance shields its recipients from a variety of out-of-pocket costs as well as catastrophic medical costs.

9 This includes six separate tax expenditures, including tax exemptions on defined benefit, defined contribution, and "Keogh" plans as well as traditional and Roth individual retirement accounts.

10 Early withdrawals were subject not only to the same tax, but also to a stiff penalty.

11 State and local government spending can improve the quality of living and even local property values.

12 There is a fourth that is recognized by the Office of Management and Budget (OMB), but not by the Joint Committee on Taxation. It is the net imputed rental value of owner-occupied homes. I have not included it in this analysis because it is extremely difficult to measure. OMB estimates of its benefit only go back to 2004.

13 The mortgage interest deduction encourages homebuyers to put down as little as possible and borrow as much as possible to benefit from the deduction. This pushes homebuyers to seek pricier homes that will augment their wealth more rapidly.

14 Homeowners could claim up to \$100,000 of interest costs on their home-equity loans.

15 Gervais and Pandey (2008) argue that the elimination of the mortgage-interest deduction would cause homeowners to rebalance their portfolio as they liquidated some of these assets to pay down their mortgage debt. As they liquidated these assets, they would pay less income tax, thereby reducing the actual savings of eliminating the mortgage-interest deduction.

16 However, the size of the credit increased along with one's earnings, up to annual earnings of \$6,500. Thus, not all households received the maximum credit.

17 The unchanged tax deductions are the exemptions for health coverage, home mortgage interest, tax-exempt bonds, charitable contributions, life insurance, and the estate step-up basis.

18 For assets held longer than five years, the rates were 8 and 18 percent.

19 In 2012 and 2014, both the pensions exemptions and the health insurance deduction are larger than the capital gains exclusion.

20 Persons over age 50 can contribute up to \$6,500 annually.

21 No other deduction experienced the same growth in benefits from 1989 to 2013, as did the exclusion on capital gains. Virtually all of these benefits went to the very wealthy.

22 Using current U.S. population estimates, eliminating these tax deductions would generate an annual tax refund of \$2,000 for each person. This likely gives us an upper bound estimate as household adjustments to their elimination would likely reduce the actual impact on the Treasury as Gervais and Pandey (2008) argue.

23 One might be surprised the collections were not zero in 2010. A number of technical issues—differences in fiscal versus tax calendar years, probate delays, and the continued existence of gift taxes—all explain this apparent discrepancy.

24 The interested reader can consult Appendix D to review the full range of assumptions used to generate these estimates.

25 I explain the methodology in greater depth in Appendix D.

Bibliography

CBO (2013). *The distribution of major tax expenditures in the individual income tax system.* Washington, DC: CBO.

Cho, S. W. S. and Francis, J. L. (2011). Tax treatment of owner occupied housing and wealth inequality. *Journal of Macroeconomics* 33 (1): 42–60.

Gale, W. G. (2004). *The Saver's Credit: Issues and options.* Washington, DC: Brookings.

Gervais, M. (2002). Housing taxation and capital accumulation. *Journal of Monetary Economics* 49 (7): 1461–89.

Gervais, M. and Pandey, M. (2008). Who cares about mortgage interest deductibility? *Canadian Public Policy* 34 (1): 1–23.

Glaeser, E. L. and Shapiro, J. M. (2002). *The benefits of the home mortgage interest deduction.* Washington, DC: National Bureau of Economic Research.

Howard, C. (1999). *The hidden welfare state: Tax expenditures and social policy in the United States.* Princeton, NJ: Princeton University Press.

Joint Committee on Taxation (2013). Estimates of federal tax expenditures for fiscal years 2012–2017. Washington, DC: Government Printing Office.

Looney, A. and Moore, K. B. (2015). *Changes in the distribution of after-tax wealth: Has income tax policy increased wealth inequality?* Washington, DC: Federal Reserve Board.

Office of Management and Budget (2015). *Historical Tables* (FY 2016). Retrieved from www.whitehouse.gov/sites/default/files/omb/budget/fy2016/assets/hist.pdf.

Tax Policy Center (2014). Tax subsidies for asset development. Retrieved from www.taxpolicycenter.org/publications/tax-subsidies-asset-development-overview-and-distributional-analysis.

U.S. Congress Joint Committee on Taxation (n.d.) *Estimates of federal tax expenditures.* Retrieved from www.jct.gov/publications.html.

Woo, B., Rademacher, I., and Meirer, J. (2011). *Upside down: The $400 billion federal asset-building budget.* Baltimore, MD: Annie E. Casey Foundation.

Woo, L., Schweke, W. and Buchholz, D. (2004). *Hidden in plain sight: A look at the $335 billion federal asset-building budget.* Washington, DC: Corporation for Enterprise Development.

9

THE WHITE PLUTOCRACY SYSTEM

Weaving the fabric

As we reconsider the U.S. economy over the past quarter century, two widely divergent periods become apparent. From 1989 to 2007, the U.S. experienced an era of substantial economic growth and relative prosperity. Over this period, the economy suffered two mild recessions, experienced modest inflation, and generated steady employment growth. Families were able to save some portion of their income, invest in new assets, and reap the benefits of rising asset values amidst this prosperity. Indeed, as Figure 9.1 shows, average real wealth nearly doubled, from $340,000 per household to over $620,000 in 2007. Even median household wealth grew substantially, from almost $85,000 to over $135,000. Then came the financial crisis and the onset of the Great Recession. Spiraling unemployment and plunging asset values ravaged whatever gains earned by households since 1989. Under financial duress, families liquidated their real assets, drained their bank and retirement accounts, and even sold their homes to mitigate the financial damage. From 2007 to 2010, average household wealth fell by 15 percent. Three years later, that figure remained largely unchanged, suggesting the financial carnage wreaked by the Great Recession had subsided. In 2013, median household wealth had returned to levels experienced a generation earlier. While this might suggest that the Great Recession simply wiped out the gains earned by the typical family over the prior generation, the situation is more complex.

Although these two periods affected household net worth in vastly different ways, they share one consequence. Throughout the last quarter century, there has been a relentless march toward increased wealth concentration. The growing gap between average and median household wealth as depicted in Figure 9.1 offers witness to this trend.

Figure 9.2 makes the point even more convincingly. Whether one examines the relative wealth shares of the top wealth quintile or subsets of that group, the

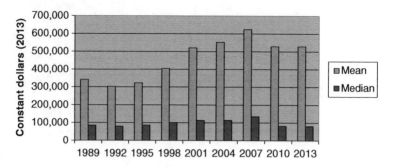

FIGURE 9.1 Household wealth over time
Source: SCF, 1989–2013

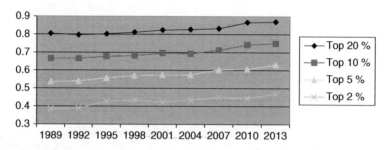

FIGURE 9.2 Shares of wealth among top wealthholders
Source: SCF, 1989–2013

wealthy have continued to capture rising shares of available household wealth. The share of total wealth earned by the wealthiest quintile rose from 80 percent to 87 percent while that of the wealthiest 2 percent rose from 39 to almost 50 percent. Although the trend is relentless, the underlying causes vary from period to period. In Chapter 5, I discuss the various facets of the Wealth Privilege model that benefit the wealthy during times of expanding economic growth and appreciating assets. In Chapter 7, I show how household wealth blunted the worst damage generated by the Great Recession and spared the wealthiest households from making detrimental decisions. While the wealthy suffered substantial injury, most of this was reversible paper losses. In contrast, many households suffered unemployment, home fore- closure, business failure, and personal bankruptcy among other maladies. As first the stock market and later the housing market rebounded, only the affluent were well positioned to benefit. Not only do we see this bump in the figures in Figure 9.2, but the 2013 values measure levels of wealth concentration that haven't been seen in 80 years (Piketty and Goldhammer, 2014; Shammas, 1993).

Of course, this trend toward increased wealth concentration has racial implica- tions. Throughout the period, White households have held over 90 percent of the household wealth, even as their share of the population has declined significantly.[1] As such, the share of wealth in White hands relative to their share of the population stands at its peak for the entire period. Since the share of wealth held by Asian or Other households is comparable to their proportion in the population, Black and Latino households are the primary casualties of the racial wealth divide. In earlier chapters, I have documented the particular liabilities and challenges that confront most Black and Latino families.

Another way of illustrating the racial wealth gap is by examining the differences in wealth held by typical families from each of the racialized groups. Figure 9.3 does this as it measures the differences in wealth between the median White and their Black, Latino, and Asian or Other counterparts. Consequently, it depicts the typical White advantage. For example, the typical White family in 1989 held about $120,000 advantage over both Black and Latino families. Their advantage was only about $60,000 when compared to the typical or median Asian or Other family. As Figure 9.3 shows, the experiences of Asian or Other households are clearly different from their Black and Latino neighbors. As discussed before, Asian or Other households typically started the period with much greater wealth resources than either Black or Latino families, enabling them to gain more from the benefits of wealth. In addition, their high rate of homeownership (as well as other forms of real estate) and their disproportionate concentration in states that experienced more fully the housing boom largely explains the results in both 2004 and 2007.[2] The resulting collapse in real-estate values yielded a return in the wealth gap by 2010. In contrast, Latino and Black households typically faced a rising wealth gap throughout the period leading up to the Great Recession. The onset of the recession and its depressing impact on wealth reduced the size of this gap to levels comparable to those found 20 years earlier. However, the damage discussed in Chapter 7 and the trend revealed from 2010 to 2013 raise the concern that rising wealth gaps will return with greater force.

It is astonishing that over the past quarter century the American economy has generated an increase in household wealth of over 50 percent while the net worth of typical American families, whether White, Black, or Latino is remarkably similar in 2013 to what it was in 1989. These facts give witness to the extraordinary capacity of the American economy to produce wealth, a

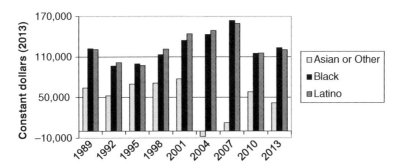

FIGURE 9.3 Typical White advantage
Source: SCF, 1989–2013

trait that is only surpassed by the narrowness of its generosity. In looking to the future, we should fully expect more of the same—both rising concentrations of wealth as well as expanding racial wealth divides—though with some disturbing differences.

The role that wealth privilege plays in contributing to these trends is quite clear. As I have discussed, the three pathways to wealth accumulation are self-reinforcing by nature. Once beyond a threshold of affluence, families find saving increasingly undemanding as past investments yield new income that supports additional saving. Increased net worth permits greater diversification and more tolerance for risky but higher-yielding investments. On average, such investments generate higher returns that in turn encourage further ventures. Sufficient net worth enables parents to share their fortune with their kids as they fund college educations, down payments on homes, and start-up capital for new businesses. With such help, their children can access each pathway well beyond any threshold and begin building their own net worth immediately. The three pathways complement each other and offer households limitless support in accumulating wealth.

The evidence documents other ways in which wealth privilege functions. Wealthier households experience fewer bouts of unemployment and enjoy greater protection from the financial ravages caused by disease or injury. Larger financial cushions insulate them from unexpected expenditures that might cause them to fall behind on bills or even into bankruptcy. An improved credit rating offers greater access to credit and lower interest rates, enabling them to reduce expenses and leverage more opportunity. With deeper pockets, affluent homebuyers can purchase homes in exclusive neighborhoods that appreciate more quickly. Their wealth allows them to diversify their assets and to take calculated risks that often lead to generous rewards. In times of need, their friends and family serve as a financial safety net. In these ways and more, affluent households can harness the advantages of wealth in their pursuit of greater financial security.

Wealth privilege not only helps wealthy households accumulate wealth, it protects them during times of calamity and recession. As mentioned above, they are better insulated against the rising unemployment that accompanies these periods. Though the wealthy are more vulnerable to tumbling asset values, they are shielded from the worst consequences, such as foreclosure, business failure, and bankruptcy. Frequently, they hold greater equity in their investments, allowing them to weather asset price declines more easily. If properly diversified, their portfolio suffers reduced losses. Most importantly, their deeper pockets offer protection and allow them to benefit as asset values resume their normal ascent.

For all of this talk about virtuous cycles, wealth privilege has its disturbing underside as we consider its impact on wealth-poor households. Struggling to make ends meet, these families face very different circumstances. Getting behind in their bills, they pay unavoidable fees and higher interest costs, making their struggle ever more difficult. Mounting debt reduces what income they can devote to meeting current needs, causing other bills to go unpaid and exacerbating the downward spiral. With limited assets, they lack any cushion to buffer unexpected misfortune. Often, they must sell or hock whatever assets they have at a deep discount, simply to keep afloat. Even in good times, they rarely have the means to take advantage of opportunities. They can expect little financial help from their families; indeed, they are often asked to assist other family members in need. Rather than accumulating wealth for the future, their primary aim is to avoid falling into a debt spiral that often results from job loss or illness. In any event, low-wealth households experience very different circumstances along each of the wealth pathways.

Given these varied circumstances, one would expect our federal wealth policy to favor households that are struggling financially. Yet, the evidence reveals a different reality. The mix of tax exemptions showers our wealthiest households with the greatest share of public largesse. Recall that the bulk of federal tax deductions that directly support wealth accumulation go to the richest households. Further, these policies are designed to offer limitless help to those on top. It is true that recent expansions in tax credits have targeted struggling households; but these efforts are modest and hesitant. In contrast, Congress has shown no such restraint in eliminating the estate tax. All but the largest estates now pass across the generations unhindered by any tax liability.

Taken together, the sources and benefits of wealth privilege explain why the concentration of household wealth is reaching unprecedented levels. Wealth's fecundity in producing more wealth in a prosperous economy cannot help but contribute toward, if not cause, our surge in wealth inequality. This is not to deny that affluent persons may have worked hard and intelligently for their reward. Rather, the circumstances of wealth privilege simply mean that the fruits of disciplined effort, astute decision making, and careful planning are simply greater the further one progresses along the wealth pathways. The systemic realities of wealth privilege mean that such efforts yield much greater rewards as one gains wealth. In looking forward to the future, there is little reason to expect that this system will not continue to generate results in which "the rich get richer and the poor fall further behind." Indeed, there are two reasons to think we can expect even more skewed results in the future.

First, there is cause to believe that the advantages of wealth privilege will become even more pronounced in the future. Over the past generation, stagnating wages and salaries have contributed to increasing income inequality among American families. Those households that are earning the lagging salaries will find it increasingly challenging to save some portion of their meager income as a means to building their wealth. High-income households typically earn comparatively more today than their counterparts a generation ago, easing their way to save and accumulate wealth. In many ways, the consequences of the Great Recession have left wealth-poor households today in worse shape than their counterparts a generation ago. While 7 percent of families in 1989 held zero or negative net worth, today the comparable figure is above 11 percent.[3] Regarding homeownership, the most important wealth-building asset for families, there are further reasons for concern. Currently, the racial homeownership gap is comparable today to what it was in

1989. Yet, among current homeowners, the incidence of "under-water" homes is
five times its normal rate and twice its normal size. Both fall most heavily on Black
and Latino homeowners as they struggle to overcome their financial challenges. It
is likely that homeownership rates among these groups will decline further. In
addition, the experiences of the past decade will add credit barriers to aspiring
homebuyers who have more ambition than actual financial means.

Wealth's unique quality—its transferability across generations—points toward
future trends that are even more alarming than what we have experienced. This feature of wealth generates two concerns, one promising an altered future and the other
cementing an undesirable legacy of our past. We can only anticipate a future in which
the rising disparities in (wealth) outcomes continue to undermine the equality of
opportunity, thereby diminishing the role of merit in our future. At the same time, the
prevailing forces of wealth privilege will maintain, if not exacerbate, the racial wealth
gap that is largely a legacy of our racist past. I turn now to each of these concerns.

Recall that simply the presence of highly unequal wealth distribution does not
preclude a functioning meritocracy. Unequal distribution of natural talents and
skills across a population can produce lopsided outcomes. However, the unhindered capacity to transfer wealth across generations threatens the long-term survival
of that meritocracy. Disparities in earned wealth from one generation can generate
unearned advantages for the next. Young adults fortunate to have affluent parents
can access immediately the self-reinforcing portions of the wealth pathways. The
opportunity to complete college debt free and purchase a home early in life gives
young householders substantial advantages over their peers. Of course, parents will
seek to use whatever means they have to ensure the well-being of their children.
Yet, to allow affluent parents to do this without limit will surely result in a future
plutocracy. Rather than starting on a level playing field, young persons will start
their lives along an increasingly disparate wealth continuum. With each generation,
this system of wealth privilege will lead to ever greater wealth disparities.

Evidence exists that this is already happening. In 1989, over 15 percent of
householders, 35 years or younger, reported receiving an inheritance. Among these
beneficiaries, the median gift was $28,476 while the average inheritance was over
$150,000.[4] Figure 9.4 examines how these giving patterns have shifted over time,

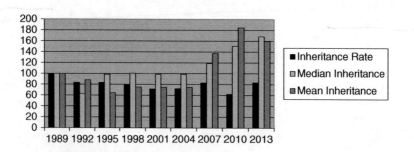

FIGURE 9.4 Inheritances among young households
Source: SCF, 1989–2013

by indexing subsequent years back to their 1989 levels. For example, inheritance rates after 1989 fall below 100, indicating they never exceeded the 15 percent threshold afterward. Even as household wealth has increased by nearly 50 percent, fewer young householders are getting family gifts. At the same time, median inheritances are following a different pattern. After dipping initially in 1992, the typical inheritance remained remarkably constant through 2004. Thereafter, it has increased by 50 percent. Average gifts to the wealthiest households followed a similar pattern. After declining through the first half of the period, average inheritances have increased substantially ever since. Both measures indicate that current recipients are receiving substantially larger gifts today, even adjusting for inflation. Although the flow of help from families to their children appears to be narrowing, the levels are clearly deepening.

Unsurprisingly, the inheritance patterns just discussed have racial consequences as well. In 1989, young Black- and Latino-headed households collectively received about 9 percent of the total inheritances reported. Given they comprised nearly one quarter of all such households, their disproportionately low share reflected the limited resources in their communities. Figure 9.5 tracks what has happened since. Their relative share of inheritances received by young householders has fluctuated, exceeding 15 percent only once. At the same time, the percentage of young householders that are Black or Latino has increased from a quarter to a third of the population. In contrast, young White as well as Asian or Other households comprise a decreasing portion of this group, yet their share of family transfers remains undiminished.

No doubt, the shifting patterns in family inheritances are having some impact on the distribution of wealth across families just starting out. By whatever measure is used, the disparities in household wealth among families headed by persons 35 or younger are slowly widening as well. Yet, the expanding gap is not solely the result of fewer households getting larger inheritances. Over the past quarter century, an increasing number of these young families simply had no net worth. As depicted in Figure 9.6, the percentage of young households with zero or negative net worth is rising throughout the period. Even worse, when depreciating assets like cars and trucks are subtracted, more than one third of these families have zero or negative

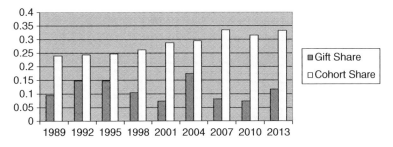

FIGURE 9.5 Young Black and Latino householder shares
Source: SCF, 1989–2013

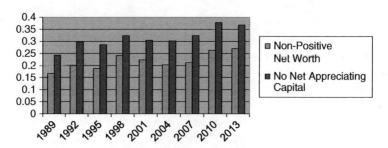

FIGURE 9.6 Young households without net assets
Source: SCF, 1989–2013

(appreciating) wealth.[5] For these households, the rewards of the Asset Appreciation pathway remain a distant possibility. While many of their peers have the means to buy homes and invest in other appreciating assets, their circumstances severely curtail these opportunities. In most cases, they come from families with limited resources. Devoid of family help and with negligible resources of their own, an increasing number of these households must rely solely on the Household Saving pathway to accumulate any family wealth. Eventually, many will acquire assets that reliably appreciate over time; nonetheless, they will have fewer years to build up a retirement nest egg.

In one important way, young householders today are better positioned than their peers were just a generation ago—they hold a college degree. As depicted in Figure 9.7, the percentage of households headed by persons age 35 or younger having a college diploma has risen from 30 percent in 1989 to over 40 percent in 2013. Acquiring a college education is crucial to gaining employment in occupations that pay well and provide important benefits. Unfortunately, the rising cost of college has caused these same households to incur increasing amounts of debt. The percentage of young households holding a college degree, but saddled with education loans, has nearly doubled from 29 percent to 55 percent today. Even worse, their debt burdens have skyrocketed. In 1989, the typical outstanding balance on educational loans was under $9,000 for young families with a college graduate.

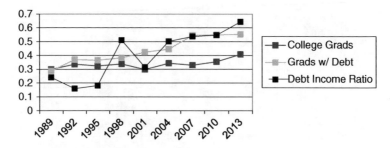

FIGURE 9.7 Tracking college debt among young households
Source: SCF, 1989–2013

Today, the figure has more than doubled to $22,000 for a typical family. More-over, the ratio of remaining education debt relative to household income typically has increased from 24 percent in 1989 to 64 percent in 2013. Largely due to this debt, fully one quarter of all such families with a college graduate have zero or negative net worth. Likely, the college degree will pay off in the future as it enables an income that permits regular saving and other benefits. However, it means that those able to gain a college degree, but without family or other sources of financial support, are saddled with debt loads that will delay significantly their ability to acquire appreciating assets. Over the past quarter century, the cost of acquiring a college education has risen much faster than inflation and certainly the financial means of most families. For too many families, acquiring more debt has been their only realistic alternative.

The rising challenges that many young persons face in acquiring a college degree along with the narrowing and deepening of inheritance gifts are affecting the "starting line" for each cohort of young households. Figure 9.8 illustrates the changing circumstances. It compares among each survey year the typical starting position for younger-headed households, regarding appreciating wealth only. Despite a period of massive wealth creation, young households today are starting typically with half of the resources that their predecessors did a generation ago. Starting with fewer assets they can use to leverage their future, younger householders today will have a longer wait until they can effectively access the Asset Appreciation pathway. As the typical household income for this group has remained unchanged since 1989, they will face similar challenges in accessing effectively the Household Saving pathway as well. While this figure shows that the "starting line" for most families today has been shifted back, it means that those fortunate to gain parental help with college tuition, down payments on homes, and starting capital for businesses will likely experience an ever greater lead over their peers.

It's now time to reprise one of the figures from Chapter 1, presented here as Figure 9.9. Whereas it appears that a generation ago the wealth inequality among young householders was similar to the distribution of wealth among all households, it now appears that there are substantial inequalities among those households just

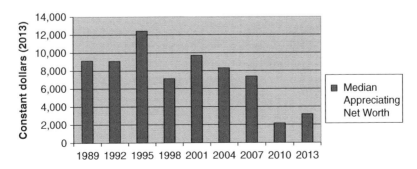

FIGURE 9.8 The Wealth Accumulation "starting line"
Source: SCF, 1989–2013

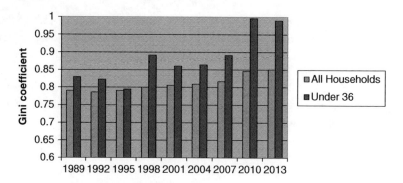

FIGURE 9.9 Trends in wealth disparity
Source: SCF, 1989–2013

starting out. Now that we have investigated the various facets of the Wealth Privilege model and examined key evidence, we can better understand the underlying
connections. Clearly, the rising concentration of wealth among the population at
large means that the fortunate few born in wealthy families are the recipients of
larger family gifts and inheritances. The trend toward fewer, but larger family
inheritances offers corroboration of this point. However, the causes of increasing
wealth inequality among the young are not simply operating at the upper end of
our cohort. At the same time, greater numbers of young householders are starting
out with no net appreciating capital, or even worse, zero or negative net worth.
Relative to the Asset Appreciation pathway, the typical young household is less able
to access this pathway than a generation ago. No doubt, the rising wealth inequality
among the general population is partially responsible here as well as parents are
decreasingly able to help with college or even avoid making financial demands on
their children. Also at fault is the rising cost of a college education and the growing
debt burden that confronts so many young households. Only after paying down
this looming debt can these households fully access both the Household Saving and
the Asset Appreciation pathways as they strive for financial security. Given this
corroborating evidence, the recent jump in the Gini coefficient among young
households seems more than simply some statistical anomaly, but rather evidence of
some structural changes. Our rising inequality of outcomes appears to be influencing
our equality of opportunity in harmful and disturbing ways.

All of this portends a disturbing future. While a select group of young adults can
expect more generous help in starting their lives, the vast majority will begin their
adult lives with diminishing resources. With stagnant incomes and reduced net
worth, most young households will experience reduced access to the virtuous
cycles afforded by the pathways in yielding substantial wealth accumulation.
Indeed, young households today are less likely to own their own home or have a
business than were their counterparts a generation ago. To be sure, their higher
college graduation rates offer some promise, once they are able to pay off their
substantial college loans. All of these factors suggest many will spend years making

limited headway. For increasing numbers, these challenges will limit their attainment of the American Dream.

The same structural changes that are limiting the opportunities of most young households will also function to expand the racial wealth gaps. Recall that households of color, particularly Black or Latino, still lag behind White households in their levels of wealth, income, homeownership, educational attainment, family support, and many other related measures. Due to our racial history, households of color occupy a disproportionate share of those young households who have not received a family inheritance. Their lower incomes and reduced net worth cause them to start even further behind on each wealth pathway. Each of these circumstances generates additional headwinds as they strive to find financial security.

At the same time, it is true that some households of color have earned substantial wealth. Some are included in the small elite of households able to shower their children with sizeable gifts. Yet, the vast majority of such households are White. As Figure 9.10 illustrates, White households continue to hold 90 percent of the ✓ wealth, even as their share of the population drops to 70 percent. The widening gap between the net worth and population lines on the figure offer a vivid depiction of the racial wealth gap. Moreover, the White share of gifts and inheritances exceeded its share of net worth in all but two of the survey years. This suggests that our current policies and inheritance laws are functioning effectively in keeping most of the country's wealth in White hands.

The White plutocracy system

The capacity to replicate wealth disparities from one generation to the next completes what I call the White plutocracy system. Under this system, household wealth should continue to concentrate within a relatively few, largely White set of hands. The intrinsic advantages that come with wealth should permit those born in affluent families to augment their wealth substantially. Generous tax deductions that offer boundless help to the fortunate will swell their rewards. Households unable to access the virtuous cycles of the wealth pathways will simply lag further behind. Each generation of parents will offer their children whatever support they

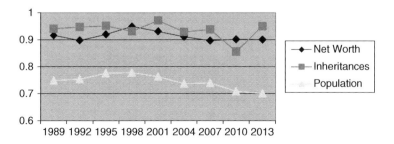

FIGURE 9.10 White shares in wealth, inheritances, and population
Source: SCF, 1989–2013

can to improve their prospects. Lax estate and gift laws will enable the rich to give generously to their kids. With each passing decade, the starting positions of young households will widen. Increasing numbers of households will fall short of full entry into the wealth pathways, causing the wealth gaps to expand. While periods of calamity and financial turbulence might slow this process, even they may sow the seeds of further disparities. Given our history, this economic caste system inevitably takes on racial hues as well. White households will continue to dominate household wealth even as their numbers decline proportionately.

Already, we can see clear evidence of this system at work. Figure 9.11 depicts the rising share of wealth held by the wealthiest Americans. As noted earlier, the rising prosperity of the past generation swelled the net worth of the rich while leaving largely untouched the next eggs of most American households. Despite the prodigious expansion of real wealth, only the upper two wealth quintiles exhibited any gain. Even between these two groups, the absolute difference in their median wealth nearly doubled while the rest of American households fell hopelessly behind.[6] Indeed, over this period, the top wealth quintile's share of total household wealth rose from almost 81 percent to nearly 87 percent, thereby squeezing the wealth shares of the remaining groups over the period.

The distribution of wealth across racialized groups offers a similar, though admittedly more complex, pattern as depicted in Figure 9.12. Over the past generation, average White household wealth increased substantially, almost 50 percent above inflation.[7] Among Asian or Other households, mean wealth nearly kept pace. In contrast, average wealth among Black and Latino households lagged far behind, causing the racial wealth gaps to widen substantially. The evidence clearly shows that White households retained predominant control over our nation's wealth. Yet, the different experiences among the communities of color (as reflected in Figure 9.12) can offer some additional insights. On the one hand, many might use this evidence to advance the "model minority" argument discussed in earlier chapters. The rising wealth experienced by Asian or Other households appears to corroborate this view. However, a closer look at the evidence suggests an alternative perspective. Even in 1989, average wealth in the Asian or Other community more closely resembled White wealth than either Black or Latino wealth. Most of

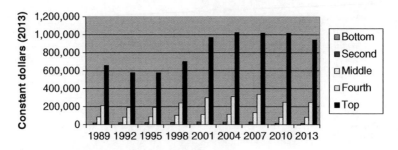

FIGURE 9.11 Median net worth by wealth quintiles
Source: SCF, 1989–2013

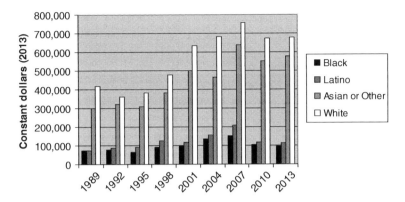

FIGURE 9.12 Mean wealth by racialized group
Source: SCF, 1989–2013

their relative success in building wealth came prior to this period. Since 1989, their share of wealth in comparison to White households has only modestly increased. Indeed, the evidence in Figure 9.12 largely corroborates the White plutocracy argument, given the largely static rankings of wealth across the racialized groups. As they started the period with greater affluence, White along with Asian or Other households have benefited disproportionately from the privileges of wealth. The growing wealth disparities simply confirm the selective treatment.

Moving beyond mere statistics, I argue that the White plutocracy system is cementing into place vastly different circumstances for American households based on their wealth. Those at the top, with a net worth that approaches $1 million, have achieved financial security as well as the means to support their children as needed. They own homes in desirable neighborhoods and send their kids to well-regarded schools, enhancing their prospects for college scholarships. Although these households may have worked hard and budgeted wisely, many of them received direct financial help from their own parents. Even more will assist their own kids with college tuition, a down payment on a home, or start-up funds for a business.

Perhaps unaware of their good fortune, the children of the wealthy will benefit from a generous head start in their lives. With a college diploma, they can earn premium salaries, enhanced benefits, and protection from unemployment. Minimal college debt enables them to save almost immediately for a home. Buying a home at a younger age means they can benefit more fully from rising home values. With parental help, they can buy in select neighborhoods that are likely to appreciate faster. Their generous salaries allow greater household saving, enabling them to build a diversified portfolio. Even as they are augmenting their wealth, they can take greater risks, knowing their parents can help them, if needed. As their net worth grows, they discover a variety of tax deductions that assist their efforts. With less need to support their own parents, they can offer their own children the same or greater advantages than they received. Of course, over 90 percent of this privileged group is White.

At the bottom of the wealth spectrum, American households experience very different conditions. Their total net worth remains below $20,000 while many among this group have negative net worth. Their modest means determines where they might live; usually, they cannot afford those areas with the best schools. By attending schools with fewer resources, their children may struggle academically and elicit fewer scholarship offers. Given the high tuition costs, their kids may defer a college education to help the family with an extra income. Alternatively, their children may complete college, though with substantial loans to repay. Although a bare majority of these households is White, almost 60 percent of all Black and Latino households find themselves within this group.

Without a college education, these children will face a challenging future. Most will find lower-paying jobs that offer limited opportunities for advancement. They will experience more frequent and longer periods of unemployment. Although the absence of health and retirement benefits may not matter much when they are young, these deficiencies will loom larger as they age. Some eventually will graduate from college and even purchase a home; but in completing these accomplishments at a later age, they will benefit less financially than their wealthier peers. With lower salaries, they will find it harder to save. Without the means to buy assets, they will miss the relative ease in which asset appreciation can generate wealth. Many tax deductions available to their wealthier peers will remain outside their grasp. As their parents outlive their limited resources, these children will likely receive calls for help. Whatever assistance they can offer will diminish what aid they can devote to their own children.

Not only do these vastly different circumstances produce dramatically dissimilar life experiences, they also exert centrifugal forces on American society. The sources of wealth privilege will ensure the affluent continue to prosper and augment their wealth. Those without means will continue to struggle against the obstacles they encounter; while some will make modest headway in accumulating wealth, others will succumb to the debt cycle. Of course, individual circumstances will matter. Some dissolute heirs of wealthy families will squander all of their gifts. Extraordinary individuals, born in modest households, will parlay drive, self-discipline, and luck into substantial affluence. However, the underlying forces of wealth privilege, whether supportive or obstructive, will influence most households' life trajectory. As the wealth gaps widen, so will the difficulties in moving from one group to the other. Increasingly, the two Americas will pull apart, reinforcing the divergent circumstances facing each.

As the White plutocracy system solidifies the economic castes, we cannot ignore its racialized consequences. As relative wealth mobility inevitably declines, the faces of those at the top will remain overwhelmingly White. Although some will view the comparison as provocative and exaggerated, this system does produce conditions that resemble both slavery and Jim Crow. Clearly, the White plutocracy system does not exclude all persons of color from enjoying the system's spoils. Even today, persons of color head 10 percent of the wealthiest households. Yet, neither slavery nor Jim Crow precluded all persons of color from gaining some measure of prosperity. Through a variety of means, some enslaved Africans gained their free-dom while a few even became slaveholders. As the Cherokee were forced to march west on the Trail of Tears, some wealthy members brought their enslaved Africans with them. Although the Jim Crow system severely limited the opportu-nities afforded the vast majority of persons of color, it did permit prescribed opportunities to an elite. Segregation created spaces for members of these com-munities to serve as ministers, small business owners, and professionals in areas ignored by Whites.

Others will argue that the White plutocracy system does not benefit all White households and therefore is not comparable to these past systems of racial oppression. About one quarter of White households own a car and little else, causing them to benefit little from the privileges of wealth. Yet, not all Whites benefited (fully) from slavery or segregation. Most White Southern households did not enslave Africans during the antebellum period, though many benefited even without becoming slaveholders. Similarly, the Jim Crow system largely enriched those who could hire the cheapened Black labor or were sheltered from competition for land, jobs, and businesses. While most Whites benefited in some degree, relatively few profited handsomely. Neither system functioned to enrich all Whites, but both certainly privileged those individuals capable of exploiting the opportunities created.

One important difference does distinguish the White plutocracy system from past systems of enslavement and segregation. While these latter systems were overtly racialized, the White plutocracy system is not. The sources of wealth privilege have little to do with race per se, although they generate racialized consequences.[8] This is what makes the system even more insidious than its antecedents. Today it is legal, and even acceptable, to advocate and implement explicitly wealth-based policies, even though they may produce results similar to past, overtly racialized policies.

There is one looming "threat" to the White plutocracy system. While Asian or Other households collectively still lag behind Whites on measures of household wealth, they have surged ahead on measures of education attainment, professional employment, and household income.[9] These accomplishments place them as a group far along on the Household Saving pathway. As such, they have greater capability of accessing the Asset Appreciation and eventually the Family Support pathways. As they do so, they will begin to threaten the current White domination of wealth. However, the resistance of wealth to shifting demographic and socio-economic changes will delay such a possibility.

First response

To design an effective response to the rising concentration of wealth and the expansion of the White plutocracy system, it makes sense to ascertain what is driving their growth today. To do so, we should consider a broader, historical perspective. In the U.S., rising wealth inequality has not always been the norm. During the twentieth century, the evidence, though admittedly sketchy, suggests that household wealth became less concentrated from early in the century into the post–World War II period.[10] After the 1970s, the available evidence suggests that the trend reversed itself as wealth became more concentrated. Certainly, deep structural changes in the U.S. economy contributed to this shifting trend. No doubt, the Great Depression and its dramatic impact on declining real-estate values, stock prices, and business net worth all contributed to the decline in wealth concentration. New Deal-era tax increases on both income and estates likely had some effect. Significant wealth-building policies like the previously discussed G.I. Bill brought untold opportunities to those veterans able to earn a college diploma and purchase a home. This law alone—despite its invidious implementation—enabled millions of Americans to benefit more fully from the possibilities offered by two wealth pathways. More recently, the consequences of globalization, the increasing returns to ever more costly higher education, and the creation of increasingly sophisticated financial investments have all led to the rising trend in wealth disparities. Economic forces beyond the Wealth Privilege model have clearly influenced the concentration of household wealth.

Yet, it is important to consider which facets of the Wealth Privilege model may be influential as well. Throughout this book, I have identified a variety of culprits. Yet, some can be eliminated as major causes. No doubt, the wealthy always have found it easier to save and augment their wealth. Similarly, the rich always have had opportunities to invest in high-risk and high-reward ventures, whether it was financing whalers in the eighteenth century or railroads in the nineteenth. Many of the privileges of wealth discussed throughout this book long have been available to the affluent. Rather than eliminate such advantages, it makes more sense to make them available to all households. Of course, this requires us to accept a system that always will favor the wealthy.

On the other hand, one can argue that changes in our federal wealth policies could account for some of this shift in wealth trends. Take our federal estate policy as a case in point. During the 1930s, Congress enacted major changes in the treatment of personal estates as they lowered the exemption from $100,000 to $40,000 while raising the minimum tax from 1 to 3 percent and the maximum from 20 to 70 percent. Through the mid-1970s, these historically high tax rates caused the estate tax to levy funds from an increasing number of estates. After this period, repeated efforts have raised the threshold and lowered the maximum tax rate to 40 percent today. Similar changes were made to the gift taxes. The same arguments used to lower these wealth taxes were also being used to lower income tax rates, particularly on higher incomes. When we add the rising generosity of the tax deductions discussed in Chapter 8, there can be little doubt that these changes in our tax laws have contributed to the rising concentration in wealth experienced over the past 40 years. Given the inevitable tilt of our economic system in favor of the wealthy, our federal wealth policy should compensate for, not simply favor, the interests of the wealthy.

In the remaining pages, I intend to offer a number of policy prescriptions that would begin to redress the current imbalances in our wealth policies. Frankly, little in the pages to come is surprising given the previous discussion or new to the public forum. The prescriptions offered follow directly from the analysis and evidence provided in prior chapters. Most of these recommendations stem from the efforts of numerous researchers and scholars who have been addressing these issues for years. Most prominently, Michael Sherraden and his colleagues at the Center for Social Development have been developing and analyzing wealth-building strategies among the wealth-poor for over a generation. Following their lead, countless other researchers at the Corporation for Economic Development, Brookings, Urban Institute, the New American Foundation, and various universities have expanded their work. As such, there exists considerable research on how we should redirect our wealth policies, if our priority is to support those with the greatest need to accumulate wealth.

A new inheritance tax

The first remedy should restore our traditional distinction between "earned" and "unearned" wealth. While we should welcome the ardor parents have for helping their children, our society has a common interest in mitigating not the passion itself, but its harmful consequences. If we want to encourage hard work and thrift, we cannot let unearned gifts pass unhindered across generations, even as we tax current wages in multiple ways. To their recipients, these gifts and inheritances resemble other sources of income. Rather than treat this source of "unearned" income more favorably than salary income, it should draw an even higher tax rate. To ensure this change, we should shift from our current estate-tax system to an inheritance tax system.

Under an estate tax, the giver or the estate is responsible for paying the tax. With an inheritance tax, the recipient pays the levy. This change does more than simply shift the tax burden from the person who "earned" the wealth to those who did not. It also means that gifts will receive treatment similar to other forms of income and reflect the recipient's circumstances. These gifts would be subject to federal, state, and local income taxes. Higher-income recipients would pay higher rates than the less fortunate. Shifting to an inheritance tax would offer another important benefit. The giver can effectively lower the tax liability by spreading their gifts more widely as well as providing more generously to those with lower incomes. Both encouragements would work to reduce the concentration of wealth, however slightly.

Another issue needs mentioning. To assure different treatment of unearned income, wealth transfers should be subject to a tax surcharge, say 25 percent. This would cause the tax system to reflect the preference of "earned" over "unearned" income. Under current income-tax rates, this proposal would produce a top inheritance rate of 64.6 percent, similar to rates prevalent as recently as the early 1980s. To offer some relief to tax authorities as well as recipients, smaller annual gifts under $10,000 would be exempt. Effectively, this tax would reunify the levies on estates, gifts, and GSTs since the source would matter little. Switching to an inheritance tax would encourage the creation of more trusts to limit tax liability.[11]

Nonetheless, withdrawals from these trusts would simply count as income to the recipient and be taxed accordingly. Enacting these changes would still permit households to help their kin, while reducing the intergenerational transfers that insulate some from the need to compete. Equally important, this revamped tax would raise revenues that might fund wealth-building programs to assist those born without a silver spoon.

Prune our tax deductions

Given the variety of tax deductions, addressing this leg of our policy stool requires a more nuanced set of solutions. In some cases, we should eliminate the tax deduction altogether. For those tax deductions that produce substantial social benefits, we might redesign the exemption as a credit instead. Finally, we should cap the remaining deductions to limit their help to any individual household. Collectively, these changes in policy will reduce their drain on the U.S. Treasury as well limit their partiality toward wealthy households. As they clearly favor the wealthy, their elimination should reduce some wealth inequality.[12]

Clearly, the exclusion of capital gains should be eliminated. Twenty-five years ago, tax reform ended this exclusion, for good reason, and we should reaffirm that choice. Today, it stands as the largest tax deduction, one that showers almost all of its benefits to the wealthiest quintile. Its demise would discernibly slow the widening wealth disparities. While its elimination would discourage some asset holders from taking their capital gains, this is a relatively modest price to pay.

The only other tax deduction that so clearly favors the wealthy is the deduction on tax-exempt bonds. Although this deduction generates fewer benefits, fully 99 percent of its fruits go to the wealthiest households. Losing tax-exempt status will cause many public agencies, including state and local governments, to pay more to borrow funds. Its elimination will surely mean an increase in state and local taxes. No matter how this is done, the resultant changes can only mean a more broadly shared burden than is currently the case.

Next up for the chopping block is the exclusion of capital gains at death and the carry-over basis of capital gains on gifts. Three quarters of this $30 billion tax deduction goes to the wealthiest quintile. Ending this deduction would simply mean that the donor must pay taxes on any unrealized gains before gifting these assets.[13] No longer could they avoid paying these taxes either by giving the assets away or holding them until death. Indeed, ending this exemption would discourage those who hold onto assets simply for their tax-avoidance value and thereby encourage system liquidity.[14] In the event that the earlier recommendation to substitute an inheritance tax for the estate and gift taxes is accepted, much of the advantage of this exclusion would be eliminated anyway.

Lastly, we should end the exclusion on state and local property taxes paid on owner-occupied houses. All residents, homeowners and renters alike, bear the burden of local property taxes. Homeowners pay the tax directly while renters do so indirectly by paying higher rents. As such, this exemption unfairly tilts its benefits to those affluent enough to own their own home. Although its elimination would remove one financial attraction of homeownership, its passing would have little effect on homeownership. Given its modest size and relative obscurity, most homeowners likely become aware of this deduction only after acquiring their home. Eliminating all four of these deductions could save the U.S. Treasury roughly $260 billion annually, over one fifth of the total awarded in 2013.

One tax deduction, the Home Sales Exclusion, should be capped. Recall that this exclusion exempts most gains (up to $500,000 for an individual and $1 million for married couples) in the value of one's home from taxation. Given the role that rising home values play in most household nest eggs, it makes sense to permit this exemption in some fashion. Restoring the caps to their pre-1997 levels could help many households leverage homeownership into some degree of financial security.[15] Lowering the cap back to $125,000 would simply limit the level of help offered to those households less in need of this assistance.[16] Even when reduced, this exemption would favor the affluent given their higher tax bracket.

Three more tax deductions should undergo a transformation into a tax credit, if not elimination. The three are the exemptions on mortgage interest, on state and local taxes, and on charitable donations. In each case, the tax credit should be fully refundable to ensure assistance to those in greatest need. A 20 percent tax credit offers a good balance between providing effective incentives and mitigating a drain on the federal treasury. It would give every taxpayer a credit of $20 for every $100 of qualified expenses. This design would target assistance to those in lower tax brackets while still offering a credible benefit to wealthier taxpayers.

To limit the drain on the U.S. Treasury as well as the share of benefits to affluent households, each of the newly created tax credits should have a cap. In the case of mortgage interest, a tax credit up to $1,000 would offer comparable help to most moderate-income homeowners. Given there were fewer than 50 million homeowners with mortgages in 2011,[17] placing this cap clearly would lower the size of this tax exemption. Similar limits on the other proposed tax credits could mitigate their cost to the U.S. taxpayer while targeting assistance to those households needing the most help.

Revamping the exemptions on our pension and retirement savings system requires more discussion. Currently, we have a multitude of retirement plans and programs that gain different forms of preferential tax treatment. Simplifying the options and targeting their benefits actually could increase household saving. For example, the adoption of a Universal Retirement Savings Credit could replace all of the contemporary options, including the exclusions on pensions and on life-insurance funds. To encourage saving among households earning modest incomes, a substantial tax credit, ranging from 20 to 50 percent, is needed to encourage retirement saving.[18] Like the current Saver's Tax Credit, the size of the credit would fall with increases in household taxable income.[19] Even with an annual deposit limit of $2,000 per individual, most households could save six-figure nest eggs by retirement age through regular saving. To encourage additional saving, further exemptions could allow annual deposits up to $5,000 into these tax-deferred accounts. Under these changes, wealthier households would lose some of their current benefits; however, the empirical evidence suggests that the wealthy merely replace tax-subsidized saving with other forms of saving (Benjamin, 2003).

I recommend leaving the remaining tax deduction, the exclusion on health-insurance coverage, unchanged at this time. My recommendation on health-insurance payments reflects the tremendous upheaval already occurring in this area due to the implementation of the Affordable Care Act. It is better to wait and see than to add to the turmoil and uncertainty.[20]

Expanding our current tax credits

Among our current tax credits, the EITC does the best job at targeting its assistance to those households with the greatest need. As a highly refundable tax credit that many argue is our most effective anti-poverty program, the EITC needs little reform. With a phase-in rate of 45 percent, it offers households a strong work incentive. On the other hand, the Child Tax Credit is much less refundable to those who pay no federal income taxes. The credit is limited to 15 percent of any earned income above a $3,000 threshold. A much higher phase-in rate with no income threshold would ensure that those parents with the most pressing needs would receive a larger share. Though both credits can provide households with invaluable assistance, neither really functions to build household wealth.

While the Universal Retirement Savings Credit previously discussed would help with certain savings needs, it is not fully inclusive. Given the escalating cost of college along with its growing importance, children from less affluent households need greater help. One proposal that could provide effective assistance is the creation of Lifetime Savings Accounts (LSAs) supported with targeted tax credits. According to the proposed Aspire Act, each child born in the U.S. would receive a one-time deposit of $500.[21] Those households whose income is below 75 percent of the median income would receive an additional one-time deposit of $500. Each year, the household could supplement the account and get a 100 percent tax credit, up to $500. The tax credit would be directly deposited into the LSA. Households with higher incomes would receive declining matches until their income exceeded the median household income. Upon reaching 18, the account holder could withdraw the funds to pay for college tuition or wait and use the funds for a down payment on a home or start a retirement account. Making the maximum deposits each year and gaining the full match, parents could provide their kids with a stake in life that would exceed $20,000.

While a 100 percent tax credit might appear extreme, we can readily grasp its importance. For low-income households, saving anything from year to year represents a significant achievement. Despite the best of intentions, financial reversals like medical emergencies and periods of unemployment can wreak havoc on household budgets. For these households, the generous tax credit offers a unique opportunity. The equal match of funds offers an effective incentive that is both immediate and visible. It offers these parents a real opportunity to supplement those other non-financial gifts they can offer their kids as they reach adulthood. In years where their household fortunes flourish, their match will decline with the expectation that they can come up with the difference out of their own, fuller pockets. Unlike traditional tax incentives, this match offers a credible means to help the less affluent save for their children's futures.

Other scholars have proposed an even more generous and bold savings plan. Based on the Child Trust Fund implemented in the United Kingdom, they propose "baby bonds" in which every child in the U.S. receives a trust fund at adulthood that could be used for such asset endeavors like buying a home or starting a new business (Aja et al., 2014; Darity and Hamilton, 2012). They argue that federal contributions to these accounts should reflect family net worth, not income. Children raised in households in the bottom wealth group could receive $60,000 under their proposal. Assuming an average contribution of $20,000 per child, they estimate that such a proposal would cost around $80 billion a year (Tippett et al., 2014). Such a proposal would do much to restore the current inequities and enable more young adults a real shot at achieving financial security.

Concluding remarks

Armed with this knowledge of the sources of wealth privilege, along with the evidence demonstrating its significance in our society, we can now return to the skyscraper metaphor discussed in Chapter 1 with a new perspective. Recall the American Wealth building in which we all reside on floors assigned on the basis of our net worth. Given the realities of wealth privilege, it is clear that conditions are quite different at various levels of the building. Residents of the upper floors operate along all three pathways where they receive the greatest assistance. Further, they benefit fully from the generosity provided by our federal wealth policies. They can take full advantage of a variety of tax exemptions whose largesse knows no bounds. Their movement among floors can be both effortless and rapid, as if they have ready access to express elevators.

Much lower in the building, households have the means to access the virtuous cycles of some, but perhaps not all three pathways. They may have the resources to benefit from some sources of wealth privilege, but not as fully as their upper-floor neighbors may. Their modest assets may discourage them from increased risk taking and higher-yielding investments. Their moderate incomes may allow some saving, but college loans and requests for help from family members may limit their efforts. For most households at this level, moving to the next floor may not be as rapid, suggesting that they may travel by escalator, not elevator.

As we descend toward the ground floor, we find circumstances changing again. Most households at this level can reasonably access only the benefits offered by the Household Saving pathway. Most have no expectation of gaining any inheritance from family members. At best, they can hope to avoid any pleas for assistance. As their meager household assets are largely tied up in a car or truck, they have little prospect of help from the Asset Appreciation pathway. Saving some portion of their current income offers them the only real hope of augmenting their wealth. Upward mobility in this part of the building more closely resembles a stairway, or even a ladder without some of its rungs. Moving up to the next floor requires effort and discipline. Further, the residents here must worry about holes in the floors. Unexpected health problems, emergencies, and job losses can all cause them to tumble down, perhaps more easily than moving up. Missed payments, escalating fees, and higher interest charges all exacerbate their difficulties. Unlike their neighbors in the floors above, they can anticipate little help from the federal wealth policies available to others.

Recognizing these realities only partially explains the decline in economic mobility. While rare individuals with extraordinary talents will find a way to accumulate substantial wealth no matter their parents' circumstances, most households will gain access only to the means available on their level of the building. Households will continue to climb using the available ladders, stairways, and escalators; however, as the wealth gaps continue to grow, gaining access into the higher wealth ranks, available through elevators, will become increasingly unattainable. As the distances between the ground floor and penthouse grow, making this climb will become increasingly rare.

Even worse, the evidence demonstrates that most young households are starting out at lower levels than in 1989, despite the relative prosperity of the period. While a few young adults are receiving larger inheritances, the vast majority are starting their climb from a lower floor. Compared with their peers in 1989, young households today have lower net worth, earn less real income, and anticipate less help from their family. In regards to all three wealth pathways, they are starting further behind than their counterparts of a generation ago. Their prospects for achieving the American Dream are certainly bleaker. For young Black and Latino households, their hopes are even less bright. In understanding and redressing these circumstances, we can reverse the current trends and restore the American Dream to an increasing number of households. Beginning this change simply requires the political will needed to reorder the priorities in our federal wealth policies.

Notes

1   Among the SCF survey population, the share of respondents who are White has declined from a high of 78 percent in the late 1990s to 70 percent in 2013.
2   Unlike earlier and later years, Asian or Other households held greater amounts of non-financial assets, primarily real estate, than even White households in both 2004 and 2007. In these two years, they held fewer financial assets as well as more debt than did White families. Both suggest less financial resilience, which Figure 9.3 depicts.
3   These figures come from the 1989 and 2013 SCF.
4   When possible, gifts are valued at a 3 percent real rate of return from their receipt until the survey year.
5   Not only vehicle assets, but any vehicle debt is subtracted as well.
6   Because the median net worth of the bottom wealth quintile hovers so closely to zero, it does not appear on the figure.

7 Throughout, I have studiously used median figures rather than mean figures when measuring wealth. I make an intentional exception here. Since I want to capture the impact of rising wealth concentration on racial wealth shares, I use mean figures in this case.

8 In addition, persistent race prejudice can complement wealth privilege, as we saw in Chapter 7.

9 See Appendix B for a more complete discussion.

10 Piketty and Goldhammer (2014) argue the decline in wealth concentration is from 1910 to 1950 with another 20 years of relative calm before the trend is reversed. Wolff (1995) argues that household wealth became less unequal after 1929 until the trend shifted again in the 1970s. Shammas (1993) appears to fall somewhat between these two positions.

11 Such trusts could dole out the gift in smaller increments and thereby minimize the tax penalty.

12 In a carefully conducted simulation, Cho and Francis (2011) demonstrate that the elimination of those tax deductions that give preferential treatment to homeowners would reduce wealth inequality.

13 Family-held businesses (and farms) that generate unrealized capital gains might require special treatment to avoid the need to liquidate the business to pay the outstanding tax liability. Tax liens may be placed on the business and only paid when the property is sold later.

14 Curiously, supporters of the capital-gains exclusion argue vehemently that it encourages system liquidity. Rarely does one hear of these individuals railing against this tax deduction; its elimination would have the same effect.

15 Efforts to make homeownership more widely available make this proposal even more attractive.

16 Such a cap would have applied to only 23 percent of all households in 2010. Almost two thirds of all homeowners in 2010 had less than $125,000 in home equity.

17 "American Housing Profile: United States," *American Housing Survey Factsheet*, AHS11-1. Retrieved from www.census.gov/prod/www/construction_housing.html.

18 I propose this as a complement to the amended Saver's Tax Credit discussed shortly. The two tax credits should complement each other and perhaps even be integrated into one saver's tax credit.

19 A four-tiered system is one possibility. The least affluent households would warrant the 50 percent tax credit, followed by a 35 percent tier, a 20 percent step, and then zero for more affluent households. Even the wealthiest still could take advantage of the tax-deferral treatment on the accumulated earnings.

20 I am writing this in May 2016 in just the third year of the implementation of the Affordable Care Act.

21 "The Aspire Act of 2013: The American Saving for Personal Investment, Retirement, and Education Act," retrieved from www.newamerica.org/ on December 26, 2013. These limits would be adjusted for inflation over time.

Bibliography

Aja, A., Bustillo, D., Darity, W., Jr., and Hamilton, D. (2014). From a tangle of pathology to a race-fair America. *Dissent* 61 (3): 39–43.

Alexander, M. (2012). *The new Jim Crow: Mass incarceration in the age of colorblindness*. New York: New Press.

Benjamin, D. J. (2003). Does 401(k) eligibility increase saving? Evidence from propensity score subclassification. *Journal of Public Economics* 87 (5): 1259–90.

Beverly, S., Sherraden, M., Cramer, R., Williams Shanks, T., Nam, Y., and Zhan, M. (2008). Determinants of asset holdings. In *Asset building and low-income households*, ed. S. M. McKernan and M. Sherraden. Washington, DC: Urban Institute, 89–151.

Bonilla-Silva, E. (2013). *Racism without racists: Color-blind racism and the persistence of racial inequality in America*. New York: Rowman and Littlefield.

Cho, S. W. S. and Francis, J. L. (2011). Tax treatment of owner occupied housing and wealth inequality. *Journal of Macroeconomics* 33 (1): 42–60.

Darity, W., Jr. and Hamilton, D. (2012). Bold policies for economic justice. *Review of Black Political Economy* 39 (1): 79–85.

Piketty, T. and Goldhammer, A. (2014). *Capital in the twenty-first century.* Cambridge, MA: Belknap Press.

Shammas, C. (1993). A new look at long-term trends in wealth inequality in the United States. *American Historical Review* 98 (2): 412–31.

Shapiro, T. M. and Wolff, E. N. (eds) (2001). *Assets for the poor: The benefits of spreading asset ownership.* New York: Russell Sage Foundation.

Sherraden, M. (1991). *Assets and the poor: A new American welfare policy.* Armonk, NY: M. E. Sharpe.

Stiglitz, J. (2012). *The price of inequality: How today's divided society endangers our future.* New York: W. W. Norton and Co.

Tippett, R., Jones-DeWeever, A., Rockeymoore, M., Hamilton, D., and Darity, W. (2014). Beyond broke: Why closing the racial wealth gap is a priority for national economic security. Report prepared by Center for Global Policy Solutions and Research Network on Ethnic and Racial Inequality at Duke University with funds provided by the Ford Foundation.

Weller, C. and Ungar, S. (2013). The Universal Savings Credit. Center for American Progress. Retrieved from www.americanprogress.org/issues/economy/report/2013/07/19/70058/the-universal-savings-credit/.

Wolff, E. N. (1995). *Top heavy: A study of the increasing inequality of wealth in America.* New York: Twentieth Century Fund Press.

APPENDIX A: THE GINI COEFFICIENT

Illustrating the distribution of wealth and assessing its shifts over time is challenging to say the least. Many researchers turn to the Gini coefficient as the measure of choice, largely for two reasons. First, the Gini coefficient includes all of the observations in its measure of inequality. Presumably, this makes it more sensitive to shifting values than other measures like the interquartile range that focuses on two observations. Second, the Gini coefficient is quite simple to understand, at least conceptually. Consider the hypothetical in which all households line up, from left to right, according to their net worth. As we move up the line in ascending order, we simply sum each household's net worth as a percentage of total wealth. See Figure A.1. If we had perfect wealth equality—if all households had the same amount of net worth—then the 45-degree line that bisects the square would illustrate our circumstances. The first 10 percent of households would hold 10 percent of total wealth, the bottom 50 percent of households would hold half the wealth, and so on. In a world of wealth inequalities, the curve line in the lower half of the box would serve as a more realistic representation. The Gini coefficient simply measures the space labeled as "A" as a proportion of spaces "A" and "B." As such, the Gini coefficient normally can range from 0 (perfect equality) to 1 (perfect inequality). Greater inequality would push the curve downward to the right while decreasing inequality would do the reverse.

Nonetheless, the Gini coefficient as a measure of wealth inequality masks some problems. First, it only measures relative changes in wealth while ignoring absolute increases. Doubling the wealth of every household would increase the wealth gaps among households, but would have no impact on the Gini coefficient. As it is normalized by the mean wealth, the Gini coefficient is largely insensitive to purely absolute changes. To some, this means that the Gini coefficient can underestimate wealth inequality since it ignores absolute differences. Second, very different wealth distributions will generate the same coefficient. For example, both of the wealth distributions given in Table A.1 generate an estimated coefficient of 0.5. Consequently,

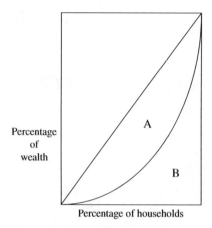

FIGURE A.1 The Lorenz curve

TABLE A.1 Wealth distributions

Household	Society A	Society B
1	0	500
2	0	500
3	0	500
4	2500	500
5	2500	500
6	2500	5000

household wealth may undergo substantial shifting without much recognition by the Gini coefficient. Lastly, as many households experience negative wealth, the actual wealth curve in the diagram will dip below the horizontal axis, causing computational problems in estimating the coefficient. Unlike income, a Gini measure of wealth can exceed 1, particularly as many households have negative net worth (Yitzhaki, 1998, p. 16). For these reasons, I use the Gini coefficient somewhat sparingly and in conjunction with other measures of inequality.

Bibliography

Yitzhaki, S. (1998). More than a dozen alternative ways of spelling Gini. *Research in Economic Inequality* 8: 13–30.

APPENDIX B: DISCUSSION OF ASIAN OR OTHER HOUSEHOLD EXPERIENCE AS SUGGESTED BY THE SCF EVIDENCE

In Chapter 5, certain evidence suggested that Asian or Other households as a group had largely erased the racial wealth gap. Table 5.2 illustrates how the median household wealth of this group grew from half of the typical White householder wealth in 1989 to nearly equal in 2007. In this same year, median income for Asian or Other households far exceeded the comparable measure for White households, offering further testimony to this point. Other evidence simply corroborated this conclusion. Asian or Other households enjoyed similar access to credit, paid similar borrowing costs, and gained comparable levels of health-insurance coverage as White families. Only when we examine the inheritance measures do we find differences. They are less likely to have inherited past gifts and have lower expectations regarding future gifts. Resembling the patterns of giving by Black and Latino households, they are much more likely to be giving distressed gifts to family members than bequest gifts. In all other ways, the evidence of Chapter 5 indicates that Asian and Other households have "made it" as a group.

All of this evidence offers support for what others have labeled the "model minority" phenomenon. This generally refers to the perception that Asian American households have overcome their historical disadvantages in American society and have recently achieved parity with White Americans. In the context of this book, their apparent overcoming of the racial wealth gap would mean they have both overcome the prejudicial policies discussed in Chapter 4 as well as wealth privileges afforded to White households who had their head start in wealth accumulation. These represent notable achievements.

Not all of the evidence supports the conclusion that Asians or Others as a group have erased the wealth gap with Whites. Although the gap did disappear in 2007, it reappeared in both the next two surveys. In 2013, White households typically had a wealth advantage of nearly $50,000 over Asian or Other households, a figure that is comparable to what it was a generation earlier. Geography explains much of this volatility.[1]

The majority of Asian Americans live in three states—California, New York, and Florida—and most live in urban areas (Lui et al., 2006, p. 210). Each of these areas experienced the recent housing bubble and burst in dramatic fashion. We can see the impact by comparing home equity of the typical White versus Asian or Other household in Figure B.1. After 2001, Asian or Other households witnessed dramatic gains in their home equity. Not only did they experience substantial appreciation, but also their homeownership rate jumped from 53 to 63 percent in this six-year period. Both explain the rapid rise in home equity among Asian or Other households. Collapsing prices after 2007 caused the homeowner gap to reappear.

To understand better what has happened, it is also worth noting the relative starting positions of all four racial groups on some key measures. Using White household levels as the benchmark, Figure B.2 compares the other three groups based on their college attainment, median income, homeownership rates, and

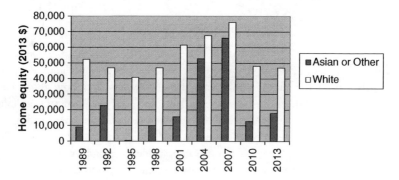

FIGURE B.1 Impact of the housing bubble
Source: SCF, 1989–2013

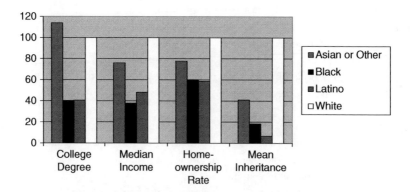

FIGURE B.2 Relative positions in 1989
Source: SCF, 1989

average inheritance. For example, the college attainment rates among Black and Latino households were about 40 percent of those among White households. One striking result of Figure B.2 is the recognition that Asian or Other households had a higher number of college graduates than did White households. Although there are varied reasons for this, one important one that often escapes attention is the consequence of immigration. With the passage of the Immigration Act of 1965, our immigration policy switched from targeting countries of origin to selecting immigrants based on their skills and professional expertise. This change permitted rising numbers of highly educated, middle-class immigrants from various Asian countries (Lui et al., 2006, p. 256). Even by 1989, this tide of immigrants meant that many within the Asian or Other community were able to take advantage of available opportunities, particularly as one compares their circumstances with those of Black and Latino households.

Given their favorable position in 1989, Asian or Other households were able to benefit more from the privileges of wealth than Black or Latino families. Figure B.3 permits us to compare the relative positions in 2013. During the intervening years, Asian or Other households earned bachelor's degrees at record levels. Their strong lead in educational attainment generated household income typically exceeding those in the White community. However, these gains have yet to erase the still considerable wealth gap. Asian or Other households still lag behind Whites in their homeownership rates and in their average level of inherited wealth. In both areas, they maintain a substantial advantage over levels experienced by Black or Latino households. Nonetheless, their "progress" reflects wealth's greater resistance to changing circumstances than income measures.

The unique position occupied by Asian or Other households in our society does suggest future shifts. Their high levels of educational attainment and income indicate their ability to access most of the benefits of the Household Saving pathway. A continuation of current immigration patterns in which so many talented and skilled individuals from Asia come to our shores will only add to this capacity. These

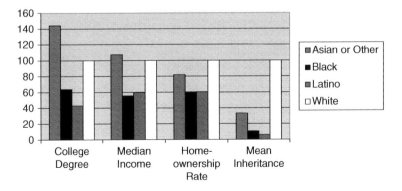

FIGURE B.3 Relative positions in 2013
Source: SCF, 2013

affluent households will gain ever increasing access to the Asset Appreciation pathway and subsequently to the Family Support pathway. As they do so, eventually they may erase their portion of the racial wealth gap and "threaten" White domination over available wealth. How that might play out is beyond the scope of this book.

Note

1 Some of this volatility is due to the small numbers of Asian or Other households in the SCFs.

Bibliography

Lui, M., Robles, B., Leondar-Wright, B., Brewer, R., and Adamson, R. (2006). *The color of wealth*. New York: United for a Fair Economy.

APPENDIX C: LOGIT REGRESSION: WHICH HOUSEHOLDS INCREASED NET WORTH BETWEEN 2007 AND 2009?

TABLE C.1 Logit regression that examines which households increased net worth between 2007 and 2009, weighted and unweighted samples

Variable	Weighted sample		Unweighted Sample	
Wealth and ownership	Coefficient	P-value	Coefficient	P-value
Middle wealth tercile	−.70 ★★★	.000	−.60 ★★★	.000
Top wealth tercile	−.44 ★	.031	−.25	.162
Homeowner	−.30 ★	.039	−.25	.062
Years owned home	.01	.129	.01	.355
Landlord	−.12	.370	−.27 ★	.045
Business owner	.07	.603	.06	.587
Shareholder	.03	.835	−.03	.753
Financial vulnerability				
Has health coverage	.15	.224	.23 ★	.041
Saved regularly	.26 ★	.011	.20 ★	.036
High payments	−.28	.096	−.22	.154
Unemployed	−.37 ★★	.001	−.39 ★★★	.000
Family background				
Gave distressed help	−.32	.075	−.12	.362
Expect inheritance	.13	.366	.12	.412
Attitudes				
Long-run horizon	.05	.667	.00	.988
Risk taker	−.05	.676	−.02	.822
Credit vacation Ok	.04	.778	−.08	.497
Other				
White	.26 ★	.033	.22 ★	.027
Constant	−.28 ★	.040	−.26 ★	.039
F-statistic	5.51	.000	6.11	.000

APPENDIX D: METHODOLOGY FOR ESTIMATING DISTRIBUTIONAL SHARES OF TAX EXPENDITURES

Estimating the distributional shares of each of the 11 tax deductions discussed in Chapter 8 follows a reasonably straightforward methodology. For the five tax deductions given below, I simply used the household share of the relevant assets:

- Pension assets
- Share of total pension assets
- Capital-gains exclusion
- Share of prior year's capital gains
- Charitable contributions
- Share of reported charitable contributions
- Life-insurance exclusion
- Share of cash value of life-insurance policies
- Tax-exempt bonds
- Share of tax-exempt bonds

As the estimates ignore differences in tax brackets and their impact on the actual value of these deductions, they underestimate the actual shares gained by affluent and White households. In the case of charitable contributions, whether households itemize their deductions or simply take the standard deduction would also affect the actual distributional shares.

The estimates for the remaining six deductions are based on less direct evidence. The home-mortgage deduction is based on the share of home-mortgage payments. As these payments include both principal and interest, they may overestimate modestly the distributional share of the wealthy households. Wealthy homeowners will likely incur lower interest rates and may pay off their mortgage more quickly. The next two tax deductions are based on the share, not of actual payments, but rather household income and primary residence property values. Both ignore any differences in local and state tax rates. Nonetheless, household income and property value offer reasonable estimates on which households will benefit from these deductions:

- Home-mortgage deduction
- Share of home-mortgage payments
- State and local tax exclusion
- Share of household income
- Home property tax deduction
- Share of value of primary residence
- Health-insurance deduction
- Rate of privately provided insurance
- Estate step-up exclusion
- Share of recent inheritances
- Home-sales exclusion
- Share of unrealized capital gains in home

The health-insurance deduction is based simply on what proportion of households in each group has household coverage by private insurance. This ignores any differences in the quality of such coverage. Lastly, the remaining two tax exclusions reflect not the past year's activity, but something different. While the exclusion on taxable estates would only reflect the past year's activity, I use the share of recent inheritances (five years or less) to provide a somewhat broader estimate and better comparability from survey to survey. In the case of the home-sales exclusion, I use the share of unrealized capital gains in one's home. This is not quite the same as those homeowners that experienced a gain in the past year.

As the estimates are based on less direct measures, they are likely to contain some errors. Yet, none of these estimates reflect the higher value of these deductions to households in higher tax brackets. In addition, the values of the first three deductions depend on whether households itemize their deductions or not.

As there are different income limits to each of the tax credits, estimating their distributional impacts follow slightly different calculations. According to Joint Tax Committee estimates, virtually all of the EITC during the early years are collected by households earning under $30,000 annually. More recently, households earning between $30,000 and $40,000 annually gain up to 15 percent of the tax credit. I determine what percentage of households from each wealth quintile and racialized group earns incomes below these two thresholds. I use the lower threshold for years 1989 to 2004 and the higher threshold for the subsequent years. I assume all households who are eligible for the tax credit collect it.

Joint Tax Committee estimates show that households earning less than $10,000 or more than $200,000 annually collect little of the Child Tax Credit. As such, I examine what proportion of households from each group earn incomes within these thresholds and have children or grandchildren under 18 living in the home. I allocated the tax credit on this basis.

Since the Saver's Tax Credit is non-refundable, one study estimated that few households eligible for the most generous portion of the tax credit could benefit from it since they paid no taxes (Gale 2004). According to Joint Tax Committee records, households earning less than $30,000 annually have a negative tax liability. As such, I calculated the share of households from each group that earned between $30,000 and $55,000, the upper limit. Even though households earning less income were eligible for a larger tax credit, I assumed that all of the households in this range benefited equally. Though households making incomes near the upper threshold collected a less generous credit, their income made increased saving somewhat easier.

Bibliography

Gale, W. G. (2004). *The Saver's Credit: Issues and options*. Washington, DC: Brookings.

INDEX

Taylor & Francis eBooks

Helping you to choose the right eBooks for your Library

Add Routledge titles to your library's digital collection today. Taylor and Francis ebooks contains over 50,000 titles in the Humanities, Social Sciences, Behavioural Sciences, Built Environment and Law.

Choose from a range of subject packages or create your own!

Benefits for you

» Free MARC records
» COUNTER-compliant usage statistics
» Flexible purchase and pricing options
» All titles DRM-free.

REQUEST YOUR FREE INSTITUTIONAL TRIAL TODAY

Free Trials Available
We offer free trials to qualifying academic, corporate and government customers.

Benefits for your user

» Off-site, anytime access via Athens or referring URL
» Print or copy pages or chapters
» Full content search
» Bookmark, highlight and annotate text
» Access to thousands of pages of quality research at the click of a button.

eCollections – Choose from over 30 subject eCollections, including:

Archaeology	Language Learning
Architecture	Law
Asian Studies	Literature
Business & Management	Media & Communication
Classical Studies	Middle East Studies
Construction	Music
Creative & Media Arts	Philosophy
Criminology & Criminal Justice	Planning
Economics	Politics
Education	Psychology & Mental Health
Energy	Religion
Engineering	Security
English Language & Linguistics	Social Work
Environment & Sustainability	Sociology
Geography	Sport
Health Studies	Theatre & Performance
History	Tourism, Hospitality & Events

For more information, pricing enquiries or to order a free trial, please contact your local sales team:
www.tandfebooks.com/page/sales